COMPLETE CONDITIONING FOR TENNIS

SECOND EDITION

Mark S. Kovacs

E. Paul Roetert

Todd S. Ellenbecker

Human Kinetics

Library of Congress Cataloging-in-Publication Data

Names: Kovacs, Mark, author. | Roetert, Paul, author. | Ellenbecker, Todd S.,
    1962- author. | Roetert, Paul. previous edition. Complete conditioning for
    tennis,
Title: Complete conditioning for tennis / Mark S. Kovacs, E. Paul Roetert,
    Todd S. Ellenbecker ; with the United States Tennis Association.
Description: Second edition | Champaign, IL : Human Kinetics, 2016. | Revised
    edition of: Complete conditioning for tennis / E. Paul Roetert, Todd S.
    Ellenbecker. 2007 | Includes index.
Identifiers: LCCN 2016014190 (print) | LCCN 2016014912 (ebook) | ISBN
    9781492519331 (print) | ISBN 9781492521259 (enhanced ebook)
Subjects: LCSH: Tennis--Training.
Classification: LCC GV1002.9.T7 C66 2016 (print) | LCC GV1002.9.T7 (ebook) |
    DDC 796.342--dc23
LC record available at http://lccn.loc.gov/2016014190

ISBN: 978-1-4925-1933-1 (print)

This publication is written and published to provide accurate and authoritative information relevant to the subject matter presented. It is published and sold with the understanding that the author and publisher are not engaged in rendering legal, medical, or other professional services by reason of their authorship or publication of this work. If medical or other expert assistance is required, the services of a competent professional person should be sought.

The web addresses cited in this text were current as of April 2016, unless otherwise noted.

Acquisitions Editor: Justin Klug; **Senior Developmental Editor:** Cynthia McEntire; **Senior Managing Editor:** Elizabeth Evans; **Copyeditor:** Joanna Hatzopoulos; **Indexer:** Laurel Plotzke; **Permissions Manager:** Martha Gullo; **Graphic Designer:** Julie L. Denzer; **Cover Designer:** Keith Blomberg; **Photograph (cover):** Lance Jeffrey; **Photographs (interior):** © Human Kinetics, unless otherwise noted; **Visual Production Assistant:** Joyce Brumfield; **Photo Production Manager:** Jason Allen; **Art Manager:** Kelly Hendren; **Illustrations:** © Human Kinetics, unless otherwise noted; **Printer:** Versa Press

Human Kinetics books are available at special discounts for bulk purchase. Special editions or book excerpts can also be created to specification. For details, contact the Special Sales Manager at Human Kinetics. The video contents of this product are licensed for private home use and traditional, face-to-face classroom instruction only. For public performance licensing, please contact a sales representative at www.HumanKinetics.com/SalesRepresentatives.

Printed in the United States of America   10 9 8 7 6 5 4 3 2 1

The paper in this book is certified under a sustainable forestry program.

Human Kinetics
Website: www.HumanKinetics.com

United States: Human Kinetics
P.O. Box 5076
Champaign, IL 61825-5076
800-747-4457
e-mail: info@hkusa.com

Canada: Human Kinetics
475 Devonshire Road Unit 100
Windsor, ON N8Y 2L5
800-465-7301 (in Canada only)
e-mail: info@hkcanada.com

Europe: Human Kinetics
107 Bradford Road
Stanningley
Leeds LS28 6AT, United Kingdom
+44 (0) 113 255 5665
e-mail: hk@hkeurope.com

Australia: Human Kinetics
57A Price Avenue
Lower Mitcham,
South Australia 5062
08 8372 0999
e-mail: info@hkaustralia.com

New Zealand: Human Kinetics
P.O. Box 80
Mitcham Shopping Centre,
South Australia 5062
0800 222 062
e-mail: info@hknewzealand.com

E6667

COMPLETE CONDITIONING FOR TENNIS

SECOND EDITION

Contents

Video Contents

High-Performance Fitness Testing

Medicine Ball Toss Test, Forehand and Backhand
Medicine Ball Toss Test, Overhead and Reverse Overhead
Hexagon Test
Spider Run Test
Sideways Shuffle
30-Second First Step Test

Dynamic Warm-Up and Flexibility

Jogging With Arm Circles
Side Step With Arm Crosses
Carioca Step
Frankenstein Walk
Butt Kick Warm-Up

Speed, Agility, and Footwork

Forward and Backward Cone Slalom
Service-Box Crossover
Forward and Backward
Horizontal Repeater
Vertical Repeater
Diagonal Repeater
Volley Drill
Forehand and Backhand Agility
Condensed Deuce Court
Mini Tennis Z-Ball
Medicine-Ball Tennis
Skip
Butt Kick
High-Knee Run, No Arms

Core Stability Training

Seated Ball Rotation
Sit-Up With Medicine Ball Rotation Catch

Accessing the Online Video

This book includes access to online video that includes 55 clips demonstrating many of the exercises found in the book. Throughout the book, exercises marked with this play button icon indicate where the content is enhanced by online video clips. ▶

Take the following steps to access the video. If you need help at any point in the process, you can contact us by clicking on the Technical Support link under Customer Service on the right side of the screen.

1. Visit www.HumanKinetics.com/CompleteConditioningforTennis.
2. Click on the **View online video** link next to the book cover.
3. You will be directed to the screen in figure 1. Click the **Sign In** link on the left or top of the page. If you do not have an account with Human Kinetics, you will be prompted to create one.

Figure 1

4. If the online video does not appear in the list on the left of the page, click the **Enter Pass Code** option in that list. Enter the pass code that is printed here, including all hyphens. Click the **Submit** button to unlock the online video. After you have entered this pass code the first time, you will never have to enter it again. For future visits, all you need to do is sign in to the book's website and follow the link that appears in the left menu.

Pass code for online video: KOVACS-2YM84-0LV

5. Once you have signed into the site and entered the pass code, select **Online Video** from the list on the left side of the screen. You'll then see an Online Video page with information about the video, as shown in figure 2. You can go straight to the accompanying videos for each topic by clicking on the blue links at the bottom of the page.

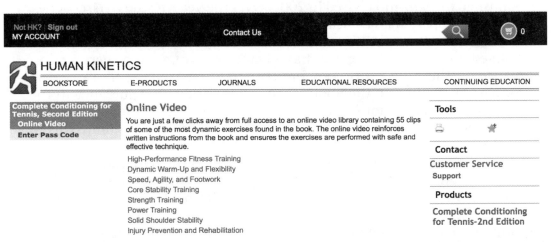

Figure 2

6. You are now able to view video for the topic you selected on the previous screen, as well as others that accompany this product. Across the top of the page, you will see a set of buttons that correspond to the topics in the text that have accompanying video:

High-Performance Fitness Testing

Dynamic Warm-Up and Flexibility

Speed, Agility, and Footwork

Core Stability Training

Strength Training

Power Training

Solid Shoulder Stability

Injury Prevention and Rehabilitation

Once you click on a topic, a player will appear. In the player, the clips for that topic will appear vertically along the right side. Select the video you would like to watch and view it in the main player window. You can use the buttons at the bottom of the main player window to view the video full screen, to turn captioning on and off, and to pause, fast-forward, or reverse the clip.

Preface

Welcome to *Complete Conditioning for Tennis, Second Edition.* This book is a culmination of many years of work by experts in tennis-specific sport science, medicine, performance, and conditioning. The sport of tennis has changed significantly since *Complete Conditioning for Tennis* was first published in 1998 and revised in 2007. Over the years researchers, coaches, players, and parents have learned more about strength and conditioning and about tennis-specific training. As the modern game of tennis has evolved, physical training also has advanced to improve players' performance on the court. This book presents training exercises in a practical format. In addition to the book's instructions and visual guidance in the form of tables and photos, the companion online video brings the book's instructions to life, showing you the execution of exercises and skills to reinforce learning.

The United States Tennis Association (USTA) is the national governing body for tennis in the United States. It promotes and develops the game and helps players move from one level to the next. The International Tennis Performance Association (iTPA) is the leader in tennis-specific performance education and certification. The exercises and programs in this book are based on information developed by the USTA and iTPA along with evidence-based research on training tennis players. The goal of the material is to help players improve performance and reduce the likelihood of injury.

Chapters 1 to 3 focus on the demands of tennis and how strokes and movements impact effective training for the tennis player. Without understanding the strengths and weakness of the athlete, designing the best program is unlikely. Therefore, chapter 4 focuses on testing and assessments designed specifically for tennis. Before training sessions, an athlete must perform a structured and appropriate dynamic warm-up, which is highlighted in chapter 5. Chapters 6 through 10 focus on training exercises for speed, agility, footwork, core stability, strength, power, and endurance. Chapter 11 covers how scheduling tournaments and fitting them in with your training schedule form the basis of effective periodization training. Periodization training allows you to schedule training to develop flexibility, strength, agility, speed, and other components of your conditioning program in the most effective manner.

Chapters 12 and 13 focus on exercises for improving shoulder stability and providing full-body injury prevention. Although performance enhancement is an important goal of training, stability and injury prevention are essential for long-term success on the court and quality of life off the court.

Chapters 14, 15, and 16 are new to this edition. Training for tennis cannot be fully optimized without appropriate nutrition. Chapter 14 highlights nutritional aspects of training and competing as a tennis player. Chapter 15 is completely focused on improving recovery. Without appropriate recovery, training effects are not as pronounced. In addition, training without proper recovery may result in poor performance and may increase the likelihood of injury or illness. Chapter 16 discusses age and gender considerations when planning and implementing training and competition. Not all tennis athletes can be trained the same way, and programs should be adjusted accordingly.

We (the authors of this book) have been fortunate to be directly involved in the game of tennis for decades; we have over 100 combined years of experience in tennis medicine, science, coaching, training, and administration. We have conducted numerous studies related to conditioning tennis athletes and have worked with thousands of athletes. All of this knowledge and experience allows us to provide you with the latest, state-of-the-art training techniques. The goal of this book and online video is to give you science-based information in an understandable and practical manner so that you can use it on the tennis court immediately.

We hope you enjoy using this book. See you on the courts!

Acknowledgments

The authors would like to thank those individuals at the United States Tennis Association who greatly assisted during the preparation of this book: Dr. Paul Lubbers, senior director of Coaching Education and Performance, provided great leadership during the process; Satoshi Ochi, head strength and conditioning coach, provided thoughtful input; and David Ramos, manager, Coaching Education and Performance, provided photos and technological advice during the entire process. We would also like to thank the entire USTA Player Development staff (coaches, trainers, and administrators) for their support.

We have a saying that it takes a village to develop a world class player. It certainly takes a village to develop a world class book.

Chapter 1

Meeting the Physical Demands of Tennis

In a professional tennis match the athleticism, fitness, and physical prowess of the players are impressive. Since the 1990s, the game of tennis has changed considerably. The physical nature of tennis has increased at every level. The following facts about a tennis match help to explain why strength and conditioning (physical training) are major factors in an athlete's ability to play tennis at a competitive level.

- A professional tennis match can last from 45 minutes to more than 5 hours. Although most players are not likely to ever play a 5-hour match, a long three-set match can certainly surpass the 2-hour mark. That time is equal to the time it takes a world-class runner to finish a marathon.
- Within that time period, a tennis player typically runs 3 to 5 miles (4.8-8 km) total.
- Most of those miles are spent moving in a variety of directions—side to side, forward and backward, and diagonally—interspersed with many short rest periods.
- A typical tennis point lasts only 3 to 10 seconds and requires a player to change direction several times.
- A tennis player performs 300 to 500 bursts of energy during a typical tennis match.
- The overall time of a match clearly shows that tennis has an aerobic component, and the characteristics of sprinting and changing direction also point to a significant anaerobic component.

> The longest match in professional tennis history so far was between John Isner (USA) and Nicolas Mahut (France) at the 2010 Wimbledon Championships. It lasted 11 hours and 5 minutes. Although this case was an anomaly, some professional matches between players on the men's professional tennis tour can last 4 or 5 hours.

Many players enjoy the fitness benefits of playing tennis. Some even play tennis in order to get fit. However, if your aim is to improve your game and reach the next level, you need to do more than simply play tennis to get fit; you must get fit to play tennis. Fitness is key for players at any level. To get to the next level in tennis, a middle school player, a collegiate player, an adult league player, a senior recreational player, and a professional tennis player all need to work on their overall fitness. The use of powerful strokes, the repetitive nature of the game, the various court surfaces, individual game styles, and the variety of movement and stroke patterns and stances in tennis call for a proper tennis-specific conditioning program. Such programs help players enhance their performance while staying injury free. Although the best conditioning programs are individualized to a player's personal body type, baseline fitness, and desire to improve, understanding the general concepts of conditioning can help players at all levels. This book outlines conditioning programs that help improve performance and prevent injury. This chapter explains the key components of a conditioning program, such as flexibility, strength, power, agility, and speed, and it includes specific recommendations on how to improve each of them in practical terms. The components described in this chapter are also expanded on throughout the book. When players improve each of these components, their overall game improves by leaps and bounds.

As stated by Mark Kovacs in a 2010 *ESPN The Magazine* feature article on Roger Federer, "If you put him [Roger Federer] in the 40-yard dash, he wouldn't be the fastest athlete; if you put him in the weight room, he wouldn't be the strongest; but the overall composition [of athleticism] takes him off the charts" ("One among many," *ESPN The Magazine,* May 3, 2010, p. 60).

FLEXIBILITY

Tennis requires a player to hit the ball from some difficult and sometimes awkward positions. If you watch any match with Gael Monfils or Novak Djokovic, you will likely see them run wide, extending the body in extreme positions to get to the ball. Many of these positions require a great deal of flexibility. Even if you don't foresee yourself needing to do a full split on

Courtesy of the USTA.

Moving from the split step is an important component of tennis movement and requires a lot of flexibility.

court, having a proper amount of flexibility is an essential part of a successful game. Consider some of the positions you might take on the court, such as extending the body to reach a wide ball, reaching to retrieve a lob, lunging forward to cover a drop shot, or stretching wide to return a serve. All of these body positions require a significant amount of flexibility. To perform at their best, your muscles must be strong throughout a full range of motion. Any deficits in flexibility will limit your movement efficiency and effectiveness, restricting how much force your muscles can generate. Good flexibility can help prevent injury, particularly considering that tennis is played on a variety of surfaces. In addition, keep in mind that your opponent's job is to move you around the court, try to get you out of position, and require you to make shots from various awkward positions. Therefore, you are not always able to make your shots from a perfectly balanced setup. The more flexible you are, the more options you have on the tennis court.

STRENGTH AND POWER

If you observe how hard today's players hit the ball, you can see that both strength and power are necessary for players to reach the top of their game. The top male servers can hit serves between 150 and 160 miles per hour

Madison Keys highlights the loading stage of the forehand.

Courtesy of the USTA.

(about 241-258 kph), and they consistently hit serves between 130 and 140 miles per hour (about 209-225 kph). The top female servers hit serves between 120 and 130 miles per hour (about 193-209 kph). Today's players use their strength and power to rip groundstroke winners from essentially anywhere on the court. Players are now able to produce offensive shots from positions on the court that used to be considered defensive. This shift occurred because of their physical development, specifically the strength and power that players can generate in these difficult positions on the court. You too can improve your game by becoming stronger and more powerful. Additional strength and power increase not only the speed of the ball through the air but also the amount of spin you can produce. Both recreational and competitive tennis players need to be able to handle the power produced by their opponents and generate power themselves.

Strength relates to how much force your muscles can generate, while power relates to explosiveness and how quickly you can generate those forces. Playing tennis requires that you have sufficient strength in the muscles of your body, particularly in the legs, core, upper back, and shoulders, to handle the forces of the game and minimize injury. Because tennis is a game in which you repeat the same movements over and over, it is easy to develop strength imbalances throughout the body that can lead to injury. Keep in mind that daily activities and overall lack of activity also can contribute to poor posture and muscle weaknesses. Therefore, developing a strong base off the court assists in injury prevention as well as improved movement and stroke performance. Once that base level of force is established, you can then work to develop greater power (moving those forces more quickly) to enhance performance on court.

Both upper-body and lower-body power are important in tennis. Having an explosive first step allows you to cover the court more efficiently, and being able to effectively flex and extend the legs allows you to maximize the power in your serve. Similarly, having power in the core and shoulders allows you to generate the pace behind virtually any stroke.

Developing strength and power requires that you apply appropriate resistance to allow for positive adaptations (the change, or the process of change, by which an organism or species becomes better suited to its environment). To truly maximize these aspects of your game you have to do more than just play tennis. Consequently, all tennis players should incorporate exercises that build strength, power, and endurance first to prevent injuries and also to enhance performance.

ENDURANCE

One of the ways to help prevent injuries is to develop muscular endurance. Tennis players need the strength to be able to use the same muscles and patterns of movement over and over again, ideally being able to hit the

Courtesy of the USTA.

Scoreboard highlighting a long five-set match between Roger Federer and Juan Martin Del Potro in a Grand Slam match. This type of match requires the player to have a significant amount of tennis-specific endurance to compete at a high level.

ball with the same amount of force at the end of the match as they did at the start of the match. When you consider that a five-set match can last more than 5 hours, and (what's more likely for most of us) a three-set match may last more than 3 hours, it is easy to see how important muscular endurance is in tennis. Many of the tennis-specific exercises in this book use a high range of repetitions. The purpose of this high range is to address the important component of muscular endurance based on the needs of the tennis player.

SPEED AND AGILITY

A typical 5-second point in tennis requires as much as four changes in direction, making agility (the ability to change direction) a critical component of the game. Being able to start and stop quickly provides you with more time to get into position, set up to hit the ball, and recover for the next shot. Good agility also relates to movement efficiency and therefore allows you to save energy throughout a match. Because hundreds of changes of direction are required in a match, becoming more efficient in these movement patterns allows for better overall on-court performance.

Speed is also important in tennis. Being fast allows you to get to more balls and set up the next shot with more time to prepare. To some degree speed is genetically determined. Players born with more fast-twitch muscle

Madison Keys sprinting for a short ball.

Courtesy of the USTA.

fibers are usually able to generate more force and are faster than those with fewer fast-twitch muscle fibers. However, all players can improve their speed by engaging in exercises and drills designed to build speed and power. These drills assist in training the muscles and the nervous system to react quickly by recruiting the right amount and type of muscle fibers in the most efficient manner possible for the best results. Remember, the faster you can get to the ball, the more time you will have to set up for the next shot. This results in more options for the types of shots you can hit and allows you to dictate the points, both of which directly impact your strategy.

OPTIMAL BODY COMPOSITION

Body composition refers to the makeup of your body (how much fat, muscle, bone, and water are in the body). The amount of bone and water in the body remain relatively constant, so to alter your body composition you need to think about the amount of muscle mass and fat you are carrying around. Obviously, you want to decrease unnecessary body fat and appropriately increase muscle mass. In fact, female tennis players should generally aim for a body fat percentage of 15 to 25 percent while men should strive to be within 8 to 18 percent. The higher the level of

Courtesy of the USTA.

Different body shapes and sizes can be successful playing tennis. Here is (a) Roger Federer and (b) Sloane Stephens waiting to move from the top of the split position.

competition, the more important this composition becomes. Each 5-percent increase in body fat negatively impacts speed of movement and endurance and also increases pressure on the joints. Strength training helps to add muscle mass, but in order to lose or maintain body fat you also need to eat healthful foods, hydrate properly, and engage in regular exercise. While tracking body weight can give you some indication how well you are doing to change your body composition, weight alone does not tell the whole story. It is possible to lose fat but still gain weight if you are also adding muscle to your frame.

It is also important for tennis players not to get caught up in many of the fad diets that are available. Most diets restrict a certain type of food or an entire food group. Eating a healthful, well-balanced diet is important for ensuring that all macro- and micronutrients are consumed and you do not become deficient in an area because of poor nutritional habits. Combining a proper diet with several days a week of aerobic exercise (such as tennis) and strength training can make these goals attainable.

DYNAMIC BALANCE

If you stand on one foot and don't fall over, you may think you have pretty good balance. However, try balancing on one foot and slowly lowering your body into a partial squat position. If you are like most people you will find that maintaining your balance during movement—even a slight movement such as squatting on one leg—is more difficult than staying balanced in a static position. Now think about how much more difficult it is to balance yourself when you are moving at a high speed and making frequent direction changes during a tennis match. Dynamic balance (balance with movement) is a much more difficult skill to master, yet it is this ability that allows you to maintain control of your body when hitting those difficult shots from extreme positions. Having good dynamic balance will allow you to play with control and be able to hit shots with power and accuracy even while on the run. Also, having appropriate stability, including the use of the smaller, supporting muscles in your body, aids in the development of good dynamic balance. A further challenge to dynamic stability is the presence of an injury or even a history of injury. Players who have suffered an ankle sprain or knee injury often have compromised dynamic balance. Working on this important component is even more important for these players to optimize performance and decrease risk of re-injury.

AEROBIC AND ANAEROBIC FITNESS

People often ask whether tennis is an aerobic (endurance) or anaerobic sport. One could argue the point for either choice. The body's aerobic energy system provides fuel to muscles for endurance events, which are

Courtesy of the USTA.

Tommy Paul demonstrates great dynamic balance during the follow-through of a forehand groundstroke.

activities lasting longer than several minutes. The anaerobic energy system provides energy to fuel short, high-intensity bursts of activity. Therefore, the proper response is that tennis is a sport requiring high levels of anaerobic fitness for energy during points and high levels of aerobic fitness to help with recovery between points and to last multiple hours during matches.

Even when played on clay, a typical point in tennis lasts less than 10 seconds, and most points actually last less than 5 seconds. As mentioned in the chapter introduction, during a match a player may have to generate 300 to 500 bursts of energy, tapping into the anaerobic energy system to fuel the muscles each time. Given these facts, it's clear that tennis is a sport that relies primarily on the anaerobic energy system, right? Well, that's not the whole picture. Think about the entire match. Nearly all competitive matches last an hour or more, which qualifies it as an endurance activity. In addition, while you may go all out for the 5 to 10 seconds while a point is being played, you have 20 to 25 seconds between points and 90 seconds during a changeover between games or sets. During this time the aerobic energy system plays a greater role to replenish the body's energy stores. Someone with poor aerobic fitness will find it difficult to recover between points and is likely to be tired at the end of the match. Armed with this evidence, it's clear that tennis is primarily an aerobic activity, right? In reality, both energy systems are important in tennis and should be trained appropriately. A properly designed tennis-specific training plan incorporates some aerobic training and some anaerobic training; your present level of fitness and your style of play determine the amount of each type of training.

> The term *tennis-specific endurance* refers to training specifically to improve both the anaerobic and aerobic capabilities needed to be a successful tennis player.

TESTING, TRAINING, AND TRACKING YOUR CONDITIONING PROGRAM

How do you know what aspects of your game you need to work on, and how do you know if you are making the necessary improvements that will take your game to the next level? The answer is to follow a three-part plan: testing, training, and tracking.

The first component is to undergo periodic testing that will identify your strengths and weaknesses. It is important to test as many of the physical components you need in tennis as possible, including flexibility, speed, power, agility, and endurance. Chapter 4 provides more specific information about which tests to use and how best to assess the tennis athlete.

Once you identify areas that need work, structure your training to focus on these areas. If you need to improve speed, plan to get more speed training under your belt. However, if power is lacking in your game, include some plyometric exercises that will help build explosiveness. The chapter that highlights power training in tennis (chapter 9) provides a series of key exercises to aid with this area. Each player will have a slightly different program to target specific needs.

Finally, track your progress. Are you noticing you have more energy at the end of a match after the last 2 months of increased aerobic training? Do you find you have a quicker first step and are getting to more balls? The subjective measures are important, but so is retesting yourself on your battery of fitness tests. Keep a record of how well you are doing, and use this information to adjust the focus of your training. A certified strength and conditioning specialist can help you in each of these components.

PLANNING YOUR PROGRAM: PUTTING IT ALL TOGETHER

Whether you're a professional player chasing a top 10 world ranking, an elite developing junior player, or a recreational player who plays doubles a few times a week, you can benefit by planning your tennis training and thinking about how everything fits together. Players who have been around the sport scene for a while may have heard the term *periodization training.* Periodization training describes how to set up a schedule that takes your goals, competition schedule, training, and—most important—rest into account. One of the best ways to approach designing a training plan is to work backward from your major competitions. Answer the question *When do you want to be at your best?* With that goal established, you need to identify a period of time, or several periods, that you can devote to putting in the work and building a base level for the physical, technical, tactical, and mental aspects of your development. Then as you get closer to your major competition, make your training more tennis specific, boosting the intensity while dropping the volume of physical work. Also realize you cannot go at 100 percent all the time, so schedule regular rest into your training plan. Chapter 11 discusses periodization training in greater detail. For now, keep in mind that you must have a clearly understood method to strength training and conditioning for tennis.

It is also important to consider your game style (how you play the game of tennis) when planning your training. Are you a serve-and-volley player who looks to end points quickly at the net? If so, you may want to focus on power development and anaerobic training. Are you a counterpuncher whose approach is to outlast your opponent and force him or her to make mistakes? If so, aerobic conditioning and muscular endurance may be more important to you than developing power. Put all this information together to help you design your own training plan.

SUMMARY

This chapter highlights the multifaceted demands that tennis imposes on the human body and the important areas of emphasis for training and conditioning. The rest of the book provides greater detail for players of all levels to prevent injury and enhance their performance.

Playing tennis at a competitive level requires training methods that are structured around the demands of a match. Structuring your training to incorporate all the various physical aspects of tennis is important for optimal success. To accelerate your improvement and help personalize your training, you should understand the demands of your tennis competitions and work toward designing a training program that focuses on improving your strengths as well as your weaknesses. This comprehensive approach to training ensures that you can compete at the highest level possible. The following chapter highlights how muscles work during different tennis strokes.

Chapter 2

Muscles and Tennis Strokes

The significant changes in how tennis is played since the turn of the century have resulted in technique changes, which consequently created changes in game styles. Racket and string technology has contributed to top-level players hitting the ball harder, with more spin, and with an increase in variable stances. Currently players are hitting serves at 130 mph (about 209 kph)—and sometimes even harder—and they are using both forehands and backhands as major weapons from almost anywhere on the court. To be able to handle these modern strokes, players need a solid base of muscle strength, flexibility, endurance, and power. To enhance performance and minimize injury, using proper technique is also a must. The field of biomechanics helps explain the science of tennis technique and also the muscles that are involved in effective and efficient technique. This chapter describes various game styles in tennis and the biomechanics involved in current tennis stroke technique.

GAME STYLES

A tennis player tries to coordinate the lower body, upper body, and arm swing all at the same time in order to produce the greatest outcome with the least amount of wasted energy. The human body has 600 muscles and 206 bones, which are held together by tendons and ligaments. All these components have to produce the correct joint positions and movements for each of the tennis strokes. Add to this task that tennis is played on a variety of court surfaces with different game styles, and it is clear that mastering proper technique can be a complex and difficult task. Understanding your game style is important for designing a proper training program. A player who runs around the court and retrieves balls all day long needs a lot of muscle endurance, whereas someone who always serves and volleys must focus a bit more on the power component of strengthening the muscles, yet both require excellent flexibility. Although many classifications of game styles exist, typically they fall into these four major categories:

- **Counterpunchers** usually have excellent movement skills and quickness as well as steady groundstrokes, accurate passing shots, and well-controlled lobs. Therefore, superb conditioning is a must.
- **Aggressive baseline players** need quickness, muscular strength and power, and endurance. Good footwork and steady balance are also key characteristics of this style of play.
- **All-court players** are typically athletic, quick, and have excellent movement skills enhanced by endurance and a high level of fitness.
- **Serve-and-volley players** are often most comfortable at the net, where they possess good reach, agility, a powerful overhead, and a soft touch.

Regardless of game style, all players require some flexibility, strength, power, endurance, and balance, but knowing your game style will still help you individualize a training program based on that style. At the highest levels of the game, most players fall into the category of aggressive baseline player or all-court player. Even players who are more defensive in nature usually can still be aggressive when needed.

MUSCLES USED IN CURRENT STROKE TECHNIQUES

Which muscles are most important for today's tennis players to train? As is apparent in many of the chapters in this book, dozens of exercises are provided for the various physical areas in need of training. Keep in mind that different exercises are used for different purposes. For example, you need to be sure that those muscle groups providing the power source for each shot are well prepared. In addition, those muscles need plenty of endurance. Finally, you must train those muscle groups that oppose the muscles that generate force. Certain muscles work eccentrically (they lengthen under stress), such as the muscles of the upper back and back of the shoulder when hitting a serve or forehand. In many cases, this eccentric action is crucial for providing joint stability and protection against injury. A properly designed training program also contains concentric exercises (exercises in which muscles shorten under tension) to help prepare these muscles for concentric action. Before you design a training program, you need to know which muscles are involved in various tennis strokes. They are described next.

The forehand groundstroke involves a preparation phase (sometimes referred to as the loading phase) of the stroke, which stores the athlete's energy, followed by an acceleration phase of the stroke, which releases the stored energy up through the body and into the ball. The stroke is then completed by a follow-through (deceleration) phase. The muscles involved in the forehand are highlighted in figure 2.1. They also recruit major muscles in the lower body and trunk region as well as many of the stabilizing muscles of the upper body.

Like the forehand, the backhand groundstroke involves a preparation phase (sometimes referred to as the loading phase) of the stroke, which stores the athlete's energy, and then an acceleration phase of the stroke, which releases the stored energy up through the body and into the ball. This stroke is then completed by a follow-through (deceleration) phase. The muscles involved in the one-handed backhand are highlighted in figure 2.2, and the muscles involved in the two-handed backhand are highlighted in figure 2.3. Although some differences do exist with muscle recruitment patterns between the one- and two-handed backhands, the overall energy transfer from the ground to the upper body and out to the ball are similar.

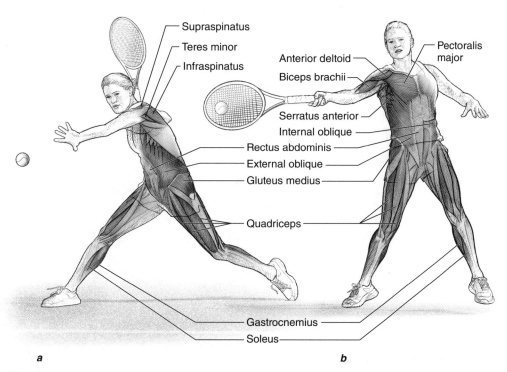

Figure 2.1   Muscles involved in an open-stance forehand: (*a*) backswing; (*b*) forward swing.

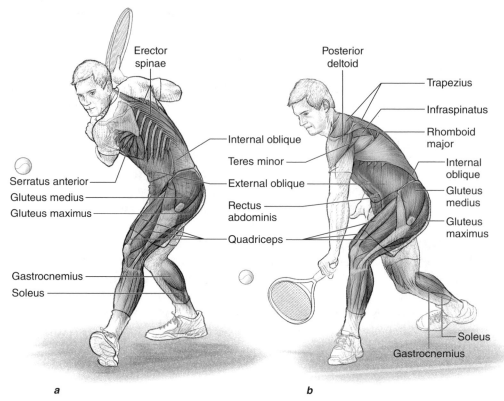

Figure 2.2 One-handed backhand: (a) backswing; (b) forward swing.

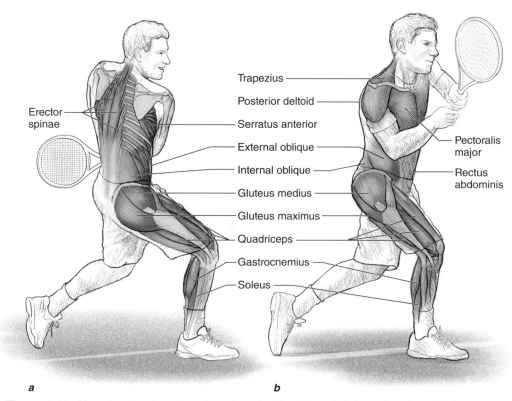

Figure 2.3 Muscles involved in a two-handed backhand: (a) backswing; (b) forward swing.

The differences are highlighted in the involvement of the dominant and nondominant arms during the stroke. The one-handed backhand has greater involvement of the dominant arm (right arm for a right-handed tennis player), whereas the nondominant arm (left arm for a right-handed tennis player) plays a more relevant role in the two-handed backhand.

The tennis serve is arguably the most important stroke in tennis. It is the only stroke that does not depend on your opponent, therefore you have complete control over your serve. As in the groundstrokes, the serve involves three phases (preparation/loading, acceleration, and follow-through). However, because of the complexity of the stroke, coaches and researchers describe eight stages to help better define the different aspects of the service motion. The eight stages are start, release, loading, cocking, acceleration, contact, deceleration, and finish. Most tennis players serve with one of two positions of the feet on the serve: a foot-up serve technique (figure 2.4) or a foot-back serve technique (figure 2.5). Both these serve techniques can be successful. The decision to use one over another is usually based on personal preference and comfort.

The overhead shot is one of the more unique shots in tennis. It has some similarities to the serve, but it also has some differences. The three phases (preparation, acceleration, and follow-through) are similar, but the lower-body mechanics due to positioning are different and the length of the stroke is often smaller (figure 2.6).

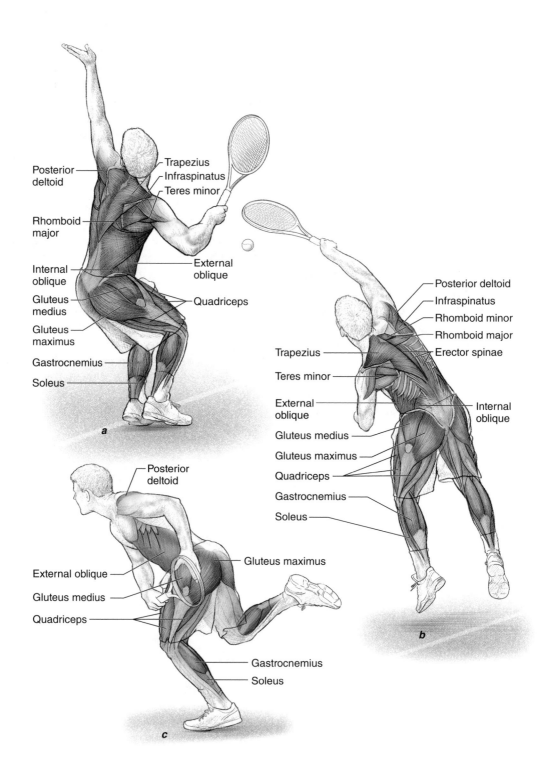

Figure 2.4   Muscles involved in a foot-up serve: (*a*) loading; (*b*) acceleration; (*c*) follow-through.

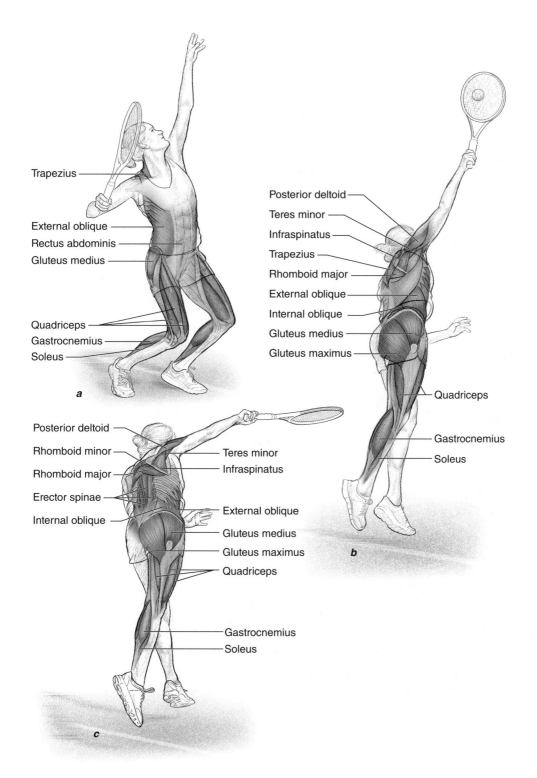

Figure 2.5 Muscles involved in a foot-back serve: (*a*) loading; (*b*) acceleration; (*c*) follow-through.

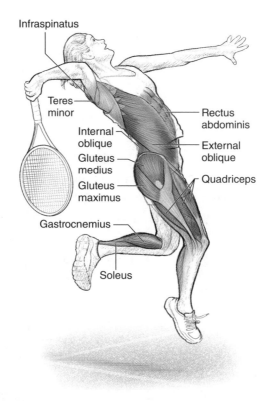

Figure 2.6   Muscles involved in a backswing
before hitting a scissor-kick overhead shot.

SUMMARY

It is clear that proper technique can help players hit the ball more efficiently and effectively. Training all the correct muscle groups in the right way is the basis of a well-designed training program. Getting in position for the ball (you can't hit it if you can't get there) allows for proper balance in setting up for each shot, and sequencing the correct body parts in each of the strokes allows for the efficient transfer of forces. Although a single correct form to hit the ball may not exist, several key positions and movements are common to all efficient stroke patterns. These fundamentals form the basis of proper technique. This chapter introduced the game styles and the muscles and strokes used in modern tennis. Chapter 3 discusses the muscles and movements in tennis.

Muscles and Movements

Tennis requires you to move quickly in all directions, change directions often, and stop and start, while maintaining balance and control to hit the ball effectively. Developing tennis-specific movement requires more than just running some sprints. Working on appropriate footwork patterns that link with the movements to the forehand, backhand, volley, and overhead is key to optimizing performance by using the ground in the most effective and efficient manner possible. The sprinting, stopping, starting, and bending nature of tennis puts repetitive demands on the bones, ligaments, and muscles to absorb force. Therefore, properly designed training that includes strength, balance, stability, and flexibility exercises is critical for injury prevention. The more you practice tennis strokes correctly, the better these strokes become. Equally important is the ability to get to the ball using correct technique. In addition, practicing correct tennis movements on and off the court is just as valuable to the overall development of the tennis player as practicing the correct technique for forehands, backhands, serves, returns, and volleys.

MUSCLE ACTIONS AND MOVEMENTS

Players and coaches must understand the muscle actions used for the large variety of movement patterns used in a tennis match or training session. Tennis players can usually cover 10 to 20 inches (0.25 to 0.5 m) more on the forehand side than on the backhand side, which results in slightly different requirements on the leg closest to the ball (i.e., left leg for the left-handed tennis player), and the training must be adapted accordingly. Also, tennis movement distances are typically shorter than for many

---

CONDITIONING TIP

Of the many physical components necessary to be a good tennis player, agility and speed are the best predictors of success in young tennis players. Therefore, training the legs is important from the perspective of speed, agility, strength, and flexibility. In fact, this training serves as the foundation for most young tennis players to develop into world-class players and is a major training focus of most tennis federations and academies around the world. Many of the top young U.S. players have started focusing on this type of program as well. Just as it is important for young elite players, this type of training can be beneficial for collegiate and adult players who are looking to improve on-court performance. Speed, agility, and quickness are essential to your ability to arrive at each shot in a balanced position. This balanced position, in turn, allows you to use proper technique on each and every shot and to prepare quickly for the next shot.

---

other sports, so it is beneficial to tailor training to be more specific to the distances seen on a tennis court.

Tennis is played in a multidirectional way, and lateral (side-to-side) movements make up a large percentage of all tennis movements. Therefore, if your goal is to improve tennis-specific movements, you must train lateral and multidirectional movements. Linear acceleration (accelerating in a straight line), linear maximum velocity (running at maximum rate of change in a straight line within given time), and agility (start, decelerate, change direction, and accelerate again quickly while maintaining body control) are separate and distinct biomotor skills that need to be trained separately. Training one will not directly impact the improvement of the other. The International Tennis Performance Association (iTPA) has published preferred training recommendations for tennis that suggest focused training between 60 to 80 percent of the time on lateral and multidirectional movements, 10 to 30 percent of the time on linear forward movements, and only about 10 percent of the time on linear backward movements (figure 3.1).

INFLUENCE OF TENNIS COURT SURFACES ON MOVEMENT

Tennis is played on a variety of playing surfaces, even at the professional level. Although dozens of playing surfaces exist, hard court, clay court, grass court, and indoor carpet are the major surfaces typically used. Each surface demands unique movement requirements due to the speed, cush-

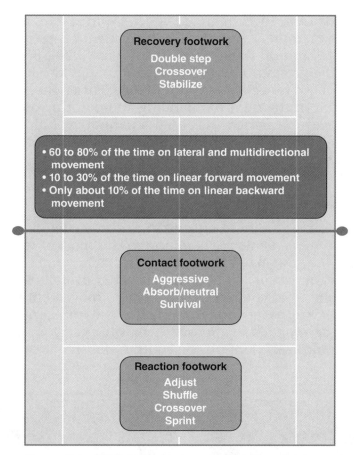

Figure 3.1   iTPA training recommendations for tennis-specific movement training.

ioning, and friction of the court. For example, depending on the surface, as much as a 15 percent difference in ball speed can occur after the bounce. Typically, a clay court is slower than a hard court. This reduction in ball speed allows athletes more time to reach the ball, therefore lengthening the duration of points played on clay courts. The clay court also allows for more sliding into strokes, which requires certain types of training to ensure that the athlete has appropriate technique and is highly efficient, knowing when and how to best slide into and out of different strokes.

SPLIT STEP

Early descriptions of the split step reported both feet landing on the court simultaneously after the athlete made a small jump and then reacted left, right, forward, or backward, depending on where the ball was hit. Now it is known that good athletes react in the air during the split and land on the foot farthest from their intended target a split second ahead of their other foot. For example, a right-handed player who is preparing to hit a forehand would land on the left foot first (figure 3.2*a*). Before the right foot touches the ground, the athlete subtly rotates the foot externally toward the intended movement toward the ball. For a right-handed player, this would result in the right foot landing and pointing outward (figure 3.2*b*). This movement pattern has been a natural evolution to improve the athletes' ability to react to the incoming ball and maximize their ratio of movement to time.

MAJOR MOVEMENTS

Although thousands of movements occur in a single tennis match, a certain number of movements are common to the sport of tennis. Becoming proficient in these major movements will help you become a better mover on the tennis court and therefore a better overall player. Training for tennis requires that you repeat good quality movement patterns on a regular basis. Having a clear understanding of the correct movement patterns and how best to train to improve them will speed your improvement and make you more efficient on the court. Over time it can also reduce

Figure 3.2   Split step landing: (*a*) loading on left foot; (*b*) right hip rotation.

the chance of injury resulting from inefficient movements, poor loading patterns, and overuse as a result of inappropriate mechanics.

The *jab step* is defined as stepping first with the lead foot in the direction of the oncoming ball (figure 3.3).

The *pivot step* involves pivoting on the lead foot while turning the hip toward the ball and making the first step toward the ball with the opposite leg (figure 3.4).

The *drop step* (i.e., run-around forehand) involves explosively turning the hips and dropping the outside leg behind the body to instigate the first movement when working on setting up for a run-around forehand stroke (figure 3.5).

Figure 3.3 Jab step.

Figure 3.4   Pivot step.

Figure 3.5   Drop step.

MAJOR RECOVERY MOVEMENTS

Most movements in tennis require three phases: starting, stopping, and starting again. The stopping and starting again phases are usually described as recovery movements. All great tennis players have the ability to stop quickly and then accelerate again, nearly always in a different direction. This ability to recover quickly and effectively is a major differentiator in many tennis players. All the top tennis athletes at each level of the game hit good forehands and backhands, but when observing different levels of the game, one of the major differences seen is how well they move, specifically how well they recover from different positions on the court. Training appropriately to improve recovery movements for tennis is one of the best ways to improve your on-court movement.

The *lateral crossover* is a movement in which the outside leg crosses over the front of the body to help move the body back from where it came. The lateral crossover is more appropriate for movements that require quicker responses and when greater distances will be covered (figure 3.6).

The *lateral shuffle* is when the outside leg comes back to the center of the body without crossing over the opposing leg. This movement saves energy, but it is slightly slower that the lateral crossover movement. The lateral shuffle is more common when the athlete has a little extra time to get back in position before having to explosively move to the next shot (figure 3.7).

TRANSFER OF FORCE

Storing elastic energy in the legs through a coordinated effort of eccentric (lengthening under tension) muscle actions and concentric (shortening under tension) muscle contractions assists in the transfer of forces from one body part to the next. In fact, transferring forces from the ground up all the way to the racket is one of the most important concepts to understand in analyzing good tennis movement. It is called the kinetic link principle, kinetic chain, or linked system of transferring forces. The demands of tennis movement are vastly different from those of other sports, and appropriate

---

CONDITIONING TIP

Unlike the muscle strength of the upper body, the muscle strength of the legs is relatively equal in tennis players.

Figure 3.6 Lateral crossover.

Figure 3.7 Lateral shuffle.

training programs should address the ratios of work-to-rest ratios, distance, number of directional changes, and types of movement inherent in the sport. When structuring tennis movement sessions, incorporating all these actions is essential.

SUMMARY

Tennis movement is unique in many respects. To succeed at a high level, you must use specific footwork and movement patterns. This chapter highlighted the major movement patterns that are used most consistently on the tennis court. Learning how to improve your movements in these specific areas will translate into getting to the ball faster and being more balanced during many aspects of your strokes. Equally important is the focus on your recovery. Recovery movement is one of the largest limiting factors in many tennis players at all levels of the game. So far the chapters in this book have explained the demands of the game and also how the muscles influence strokes and movements. Next you will learn about the best ways to test and assess your strengths and weaknesses from a physical perspective. Testing and assessment are vital to your understanding of where you are as a tennis athlete, how you compare to your peers, and what you can do to improve.

Chapter 4

High-Performance Fitness Testing

What makes the great tennis players so good? Their skill level is obviously outstanding. They hit great serves, groundstrokes, and volleys. They have amazing power, too, but they also have the ability to maintain their power throughout long matches, demonstrating remarkable endurance as well. In addition to hitting the ball well and having sound mental skills, they work very hard on their physical fitness. Over the past decade the physicality of tennis has increased. This increase is a direct result of extra fitness training.

No matter what your ability, you can't play your best tennis if you're not physically fit. Being physically fit means that your heart, blood vessels, lungs, and muscles can function at maximum efficiency. When you are fit, your body adjusts more easily to increased physical demands. Another important component of proper fitness is injury prevention. If a player is injured, it is impossible to develop his or her game and hone on-court skills.

This chapter outlines certain tests you can use to evaluate and monitor your fitness and also test key parts of your musculoskeletal system to aid in the prevention of injury and enhance your performance.

FITNESS AND PERFORMANCE TESTING PROTOCOL

The United States Tennis Association (USTA) and the International Tennis Performance Association (iTPA) identify essential components of fitness and injury prevention. These components include flexibility, strength and power, muscular endurance, agility and speed, body composition, stability, dynamic balance, and aerobic and anaerobic fitness. Keeping track of your testing results will help you pinpoint strengths and weaknesses, design or refine your training program, and monitor your progress. Based on the test results of many junior tennis players, the USTA established percentiles* for different age groups and genders for some tests; in other tests, key ranges are provided to give you a place to start when setting goals and interpreting your test results. From your test results you can determine which fitness area needs improvement for the purposes of injury prevention and performance enhancement.

Testing sessions should follow a standardized protocol that you can repeat to ensure as much reliable information as possible. This protocol also allows for valid comparison of different test occasions. Where practically possible, the testing protocol should be done in the following order, as outlined by the iTPA:

1. Anthropometry (body composition, height, weight)
2. Injury prevention and flexibility screening (flexibility, stability)
3. Power tests (vertical jump, medicine ball throws)
4. Agility and speed (e.g., 20-yard dash, spider run)
5. Strength and muscular endurance tests (e.g., 1RM = one repetition maximum testing, or modified version of 1RM testing; this type of testing determine an athlete's strength level, and programs can be built based on this information)
6. Repeated sprint tests
7. Aerobic endurance

You can do these fitness tests with a coach, trainer, or partner. Some tests may need a qualified physical therapist, athletic trainer, strength and conditioning professional, or tennis performance specialist who has a background in testing and assessing tennis athletes.

When selecting tennis-specific tests, take into account these factors:

• Training age (years of competitive training)
• Biological age
• Chronological age
• Level of competition
• Gender
• Time available for testing and training
• Space and equipment available
• Purpose of specific tests

---

*A percentile is defined as the point on the distribution below which a given percentage of the scores is found.

ANTHROPOMETRIC ASSESSMENT

Anthropometric testing includes evaluating body composition and measuring height and weight. Consistently measuring height in young athletes helps to monitor changes in growth and speed of growth and determine when an athlete may be going through a major growth spurt. It is useful to periodically measure body weight, but more important than body weight is body composition. Body composition is the end result of measuring, through various methods, the approximate percentages of fat, muscle, bone, and water that make up your body. Percent body fat gives a good indication of your physical condition.

The amount of bone and water that makes up your body remains constant, so when attempting to alter body composition, pay attention to muscle and fat. Proper strength training can increase the amount of muscle in the body. However, it is not enough to just increase muscle mass; you must also work to maintain an appropriate level of body fat.

Body fat percentages to shoot for are approximately 8 to 18 percent for men and 15 to 25 percent for women. If you follow a balanced diet and include appropriate exercise (e.g., a few sets of tennis) in your training regimen, these percentages are attainable.

Many methods now exist to estimate body composition. Some require large or expensive equipment, and some are more affordable or portable.

Skinfold Test

Skinfold measurements provide a relatively simple and non-invasive method of estimating general fatness. The sum of three sites is taken and entered into an equation for the prediction of body composition.

Caution

To ensure accuracy, a trained professional should administer this test.

Procedure

1. The sites measured on men are the chest, abdomen, and thigh. The sites measured on women are the triceps, suprailium, and thigh.

2. Have a qualified professional measure the skinfolds at three sites on your body.

3. Add the sum of the three skinfold measurements.

INJURY PREVENTION AND FLEXIBILITY SCREENING

Flexibility is the motion available (how far you can move around) at a joint such as the shoulder, elbow, wrist, hip, knee, or ankle. For a complete discussion of flexibility and how to improve it, see chapter 5.

Few people are as flexible around all of their joints as they need to be. Every player would like to have the flexibility of Novak Djokovic or Serena Williams, but both these athletes have worked for many years to increase and optimize their flexibility. Tennis places tremendous demands on various body parts in their extremes of motion, such as when your arm is fully extended over your head as you reach for an overhead shot. Throughout a match you are called on to generate great force from a variety of body positions, such as changing direction, reaching for a shot, stopping quickly, and serving. Strength throughout a flexible, unrestricted range of motion will help prevent injury and enhance performance.

Sit-and-Reach Test

Are you able to touch your toes while keeping your knees straight? If not, you are like many tennis players who have poor low-back flexibility. Research has shown that on the men's professional tennis tour, 38 percent of players have missed at least one tournament because of low-back problems. Hitting tennis balls involves not only a lot of body extension but also a lot of twisting. The key to having good flexibility is to stretch your muscles on a regular basis (see chapter 5). A stretching routine will help you prevent injuries and reach the really wide shots that you could never get to before. How do you know if you are flexible enough? Take a sit-and-reach test, and see if you can reach past your toes. This test measures the flexibility of the lower back and hamstrings.

Procedure

1. Sit with your knees extended and legs flat on the floor, feet up against a box. Have a partner hold your knees so they do not come off the floor.

2. Lean forward with your arms extended, and have your partner measure the distance from your fingertips to your toes. Your hands should be placed next to each other with your index fingers touching (figure 4.1).

3. Record your score. If you reach your toes, record a zero. If you do not reach your toes, record the number of inches between your fingertips and toes in negative inches. If you do reach past your toes, record the number of inches between your fingertips and toes in positive inches.

4. Compare your scores with the percentiles in table 4.1.

Figure 4.1   Sit-and-reach test.

Table 4.1   Sit-and-Reach Test Percentiles (in inches*)

	Female		Male	
	Adult	Junior	Adult	Junior
Excellent	>6	>8	>3	>4
Good	4 to 6	7 to 8	1 to 3	2 to 4
Average	2 to 4	5 to 7	0 to 1	1 to 2
Needs improvement	<2	<5	<0	<1

* 1 inch = 2.5 centimeters

Hip Flexor Flexibility Test

The hip flexors are important muscles that originate on the spine and cross the front of your hip joint. Due to the postures maintained and positions used during tennis play (such as being slightly bent forward in an athletic posture, also called ready position), hip flexor tightness is common among many players. In addition, tightness of the hip flexors and quadriceps can cause low-back dysfunction and decrease a player's lower-body power and movement capability.

Procedure

1. Lie supine (on your back) on a treatment table so that both your legs hang over the edge of the table and the edge of the table is at the level of the middle of your femurs (thigh bones).
2. Bring both knees up toward your chest.

3. Hold one leg toward your chest, and let the other leg drop over the edge of the table (figure 4.2).

4. Achieving neutral hip extension (thigh touching table) is normal length. Inability to achieve neutral hip extension indicates a positive test, and a goniometer can be used to measure the angle of resultant hip flexion from horizontal. Additional testing to assess muscle length of the rectus femoris can be performed using the same procedure and ensuring that the leg being lowered can assume a position of 90 degrees of knee flexion (knee bent to 90 degrees) without creating a flexion response at the hip. The leg not being tested remains against your chest throughout these maneuvers.

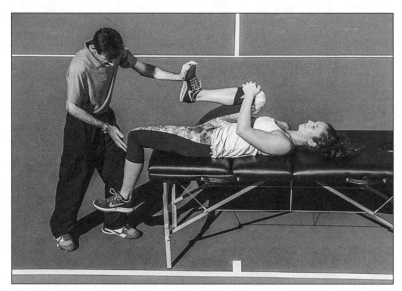

Figure 4.2   Hip flexor flexibility test.

Hamstring Flexibility Test

A hamstring flexibility test measures the amount of stretch in the muscles in the back of the thigh. Tennis players use the muscles of the hamstrings to help them stop, start, run, and jump. During your next tennis practice, after warming up, try a lunge (reach forward with one leg while keeping the back leg stationary) as if you were reaching for a wide volley. If you feel tightness in the lower back or the back of the thigh, your flexibility is probably not good enough to effectively make this shot without potential injury. If not properly stretched, the hamstrings can be easily strained or injured by the fast movements in tennis.

Caution

This test should be administered by a trained professional such as a physical therapist or athletic trainer.

Procedure

1. Lie supine on a table with a partner stabilizing your pelvis (holding down your hip bone).
2. Raise one leg straight (no bend in the knee) until you feel tightness in the back of the leg (figure 4.3).
3. Your partner measures the angle at your hip with a goniometer.
4. Repeat the test with the other leg.
5. Compare your scores with the scores given in table 4.2.

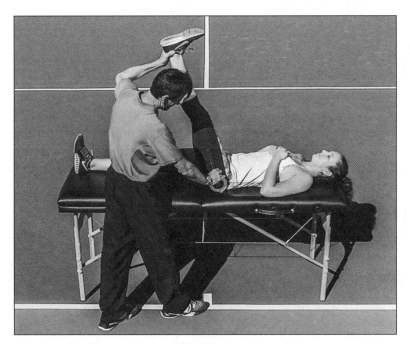

Figure 4.3   Hamstring flexibility test.

Table 4.2   Hamstring Flexibility Scores (in degrees)

	Female	Male
Excellent	>85	>80
Good	75 to 85	70 to 80
Needs improvement	<75	<70

Prone Hip Rotation Test

A lack of hip rotation decreases the ability of a player to generate maximal force from the lower extremities and transfer that force to provide power during tennis strokes. The hip rotator muscles are important stabilizers of the hip joint and can become very tight with all the multidirectional movements and stopping and starting inherent in tennis play. Measuring the tightness of these muscles helps to prevent hip and low-back injury and improve overall hip motion on court.

Caution

This test should be administered by a trained professional such as a physical therapist or athletic trainer.

Procedure

1. Lie prone (facedown) on a treatment table.

2. The tester will place your hips in neutral abduction and adduction positioning (hips are not rotating inward toward the midline of the body but outward away from the midline of the body) with the knees flexed 90 degrees so that the heels are pointing directly toward the ceiling. This is the starting position.

3. From this position, the tester will internally rotate your hips (heel and foot moved outward) simultaneously (figure 4.4a). You then will be asked to hold or maintain the position at the end range of motion while the tester places a goniometer with the moveable arm along the anterior aspect of the tibia and the stable arm in a vertical position relative to the supportive surface. The axis of the goniometer is in line with the long axis of the femur. Placing both extremities simultaneously in this position minimizes compensatory trunk rotation.

4. To measure external hip rotation, straighten one extremity, keeping it in neutral abduction and adduction against the treatment table. Keeping the other limb in 90 degrees of knee flexion, externally rotate the limb, moving the foot inward (figure 4.4b). The tester stabilizes the proximal hip and pelvis during the unilateral movement into hip external rotation to limit compensation through the use of downward pressure. When a stable endpoint is obtained, the goniometer is used with identical landmarks and placement. Both extremities are measured and recorded.

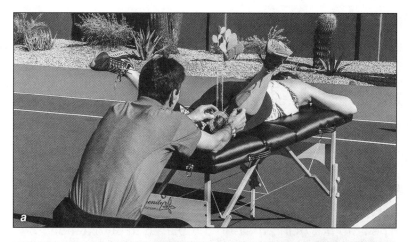

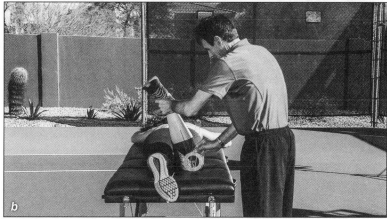

Figure 4.4   Prone hip rotation test: (*a*) internal; (*b*) external.

Note

To best interpret the findings, the hip values for hip internal and external rotation are added together, forming a measurement called hip total rotation range of motion. Recent research has shown that tennis players should possess equal hip total rotation range of motion (flexibility) in both legs. Players should strive to have equal range of motion in both hips to maximize their performance and minimize injury risk.

Quadriceps Flexibility Test

The quadriceps is the large muscle in the front of the thigh. It is responsible for straightening your knee and flexing your hip. Quadriceps flexibility is important to decrease the risk of knee injury and improve range of motion in the lower body.

Caution

This test should be administered by a trained professional such as a physical therapist or athletic trainer.

Procedure

1. Lie prone (facedown) on a treatment table with both legs straight. The limb not being measured is placed in an extended position.
2. A qualified examiner bends the knee of the testing leg to bring the heel toward the buttocks. Adequate flexibility requires the heel to touch the buttocks. If the examiner cannot touch the heel to the buttocks, he or she uses a goniometer to measure the knee angle achieved during the test (figure 4.5). Record this number to track progress, and compare one leg to the other.
3. Perform the test on both legs. Both sides should be equal.

Figure 4.5   Quadriceps flexibility test.

Shoulder Flexibility Test

Shoulder flexibility describes how far you can move your arm around your shoulder joint. Adequate range of motion, both internally and externally, is essential to injury prevention and good technique during strokes. With your upper arm at a 90-degree angle to your upper body (abduction), internal rotation is when your fingers point toward your toes. External rotation is when your fingers point above your head. If the internal or external rotator muscles are tighter than they should be, imbalances and shoulder injuries are more likely to occur. Many tennis players have poor internal rotation flexibility.

Caution

This test should be administered by a trained professional such as a physical therapist or athletic trainer.

Procedure

1. Lie supine on a treatment table. A qualified examiner will stabilize your scapula (shoulder blade) during testing to ensure an accurate measurement.

2. The upper arm is positioned at a 90-degree angle to the upper body (abduction) and remains in this position during the test. The elbow should be bent at a 90-degree angle so that the fingers point toward the ceiling. This is the neutral starting position.

3. The examiner will ask you to rotate your shoulder internally (figure 4.6a) and externally (figure 4.6b) while the scapula remains stabilized by the examiner's hand. The maximum angle of movement is recorded using a goniometer. The examiner does not exert overpressure to influence movement.

4. Repeat the test with the other arm.

Note

To interpret your scores, simply add the internal and external rotation values together to form a measurement called total shoulder rotation range of motion. Research has consistently shown that for healthy tennis players the dominant arm should be within 5 to 10 degrees of the nondominant arm in total shoulder rotation range of motion. Elite players often lose internal rotation and hence have a total rotation deficit in range of motion of more than 10 degrees. If this finding is encountered, stretching the shoulder into internal rotation (chapter 12) is needed.

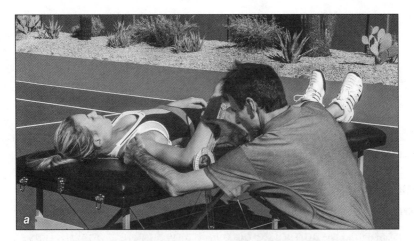

Figure 4.6 Shoulder flexibility test: (a) internal rotation; (b) external rotation.

Internal Shoulder Flexibility Test

This test is sometimes called the shoulder mobility test. It is another quick assessment of internal shoulder range motion. It needs minimal equipment and can be performed regularly to monitor improvement.

Procedure

1. Raise your right arm, bend your elbow (shoulder is in internal rotation), and reach down by your hip and behind your low back; the top of the hand is facing your back.

2. Reach your left arm up, bend your elbow (shoulder is in external rotation) so that your fingers move behind the head to the upper back and reach down; the palm is facing your back.

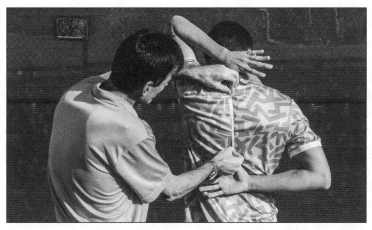

Figure 4.7   Internal shoulder flexibility test.

3. In one movement, place the hands on your back as close as possible to one another (figure 4.7).

4. Have another person measure the distance between the hands.

5. Repeat the test with the arms in opposite positions.

6. When the right arm is the lower arm, this is measuring the internal rotation and mobility of the right shoulder. When the left arm is lower, this is measuring the internal rotation and mobility of the left shoulder.

7. Compare the scores in centimeters. As a guide, results should be within 10 centimeters of each side. Most tennis players have more tightness on the dominant arm. Tightness identified on this test should be confirmed by a qualified health professional using the shoulder internal and external rotation flexibility measurement test.

POWER

Power is the amount of work you can perform in a given period. From a practical perspective, an athlete who has a high power output can generate high forces in a short amount of time. Power is required during activities requiring both strength and speed.

Tennis requires explosive movements. Greater power allows you to respond more quickly and produce more forceful movements with less effort. Players with explosive first steps get into position quicker, set up well, and hit more effective shots. In addition, an explosive first step will give you the speed to get to balls hit farther away. Both upper- and lower-body power are necessary in tennis. In order to maximize your power, your lower-body power must be transferred to the upper body.

Vertical Jump Test

Everybody is born with a certain amount of athletic ability. However, you can improve your vertical jump and lower-body power. Power is a combination of muscular strength and movement speed. Research shows that during an average 5-second point in a tennis match, you can experience as many as four direction changes. These quick changes require powerful legs. The vertical jump is a measure of lower-body power. It is the height you can jump from a standing position minus the height you can reach when standing.

Procedure

You can measure vertical jump using one of several pieces of equipment designed for this purpose.

1. After adjusting the height of the device, reach up with both hands, keeping your heels on the ground, to establish your reach height.
2. Jump as high as you can, hitting the vanes (slats) of the measuring device with your hand.
3. Perform at least two jumps, but continue until you do not hit any additional vanes (slats).

You can also measure your vertical jump without any special equipment.

1. Stand with your side to a wall. With your arm extended, touch the wall as high as you can.
2. Have a partner mark the spot where you touch the wall.
3. Extend and attach a measuring stick up the wall from the highest reach of your fingertips.
4. Put chalk on your fingers.
5. Jump with your side to the wall (do not take a step), reaching as high as you can on the measuring stick (figure 4.8).
6. The difference between your standing reach and the highest point of your jump is your score.
7. Compare your scores with the ranges in table 4.3.

Figure 4.8 Vertical jump test: measured against a wall.

Table 4.3 Vertical Jump Scores (in inches*)

	Female		Male	
	Adult	Junior	Adult	Junior
Excellent	>21	>22	>27	>28
Good	16 to 21	17 to 22	22 to 27	26 to 28
Average	12 to 16	13 to 17	17 to 22	21 to 26
Needs improvement	<12	<13	<17	<21

* 1 inch = 2.5 centimeters

Note

In addition to the vertical jump to estimate lower-body power, a physical therapist or athletic trainer can perform an isokinetic test to measure the strength of your thigh muscles (quadriceps and hamstrings). In addition to comparing your left and right legs and determining if any strength deficiencies are present, the machine allows for comparison between muscle groups to gauge whether you have proper muscle balance (hamstrings and quadriceps ratios).

Medicine Ball Toss Test, Forehand and Backhand

Training with a medicine ball can be practical because you can mimic tennis strokes and movement mechanics. Tossing the medicine ball involves the whole body (also called your kinetic chain). These tests relate specifically to the forehand and backhand groundstrokes in tennis. Pay particular attention to the technique of the tosses. Proper technique will involve knee flexion and extension and a significant amount of trunk rotation, not just a toss with the arms. The medicine ball forehand and backhand toss requires lower-body and trunk involvement to effectively use ground reaction forces and transfer energy from the ground, up through the legs and trunk, and out into the arms to release the ball.

Procedure

1. Stand at a designated spot facing forward, and hold a 6-pound (2.7-kg) medicine ball.
2. Take one step and toss the ball, simulating a forehand stroke, while staying behind the starting line.
3. Measure the distance from the line to the point where the ball landed.
4. Repeat this test for the backhand side.
5. Compare your scores with the percentiles in tables 4.4 and 4.5.

Table 4.4 Medicine Ball Toss, Forehand Scores (in feet*)

	Female		Male	
	Adult	**Junior**	**Adult**	**Junior**
Excellent	>30.5	>32	>39	>42
Good	25 to 30.5	26 to 32	32 to 39	35 to 42
Average	19.5 to 25	20 to 26	25 to 32	28 to 35
Needs improvement	<19.5	<20	<25	<28

* 1 foot = 30.5 centimeters

Table 4.5 Medicine Ball Toss, Backhand Scores (in feet*)

	Female		Male	
	Adult	**Junior**	**Adult**	**Junior**
Excellent	>30	>31	>37.5	>42
Good	24 to 30	25 to 31	30.5 to 37.5	34 to 42
Average	17.5 to 24	18 to 25	23.5 to 30.5	26 to 34
Needs improvement	<17.5	<18	<23.5	<26

* 1 foot = 30.5 centimeters

▶ Medicine Ball Toss Test, Overhead and Reverse Overhead

The overhead and reverse overhead tosses use the same muscle groups as those used in the serve and overhead. You will be most successful if you use ground reaction forces properly. Remember the principle of physics: *For every action there is an equal and opposite reaction.* Releasing the medicine ball at approximately a 45-degree angle will give you the best results.

Procedure

1. Stand facing forward behind a line, and hold a 6-pound (2.7-kg) medicine ball.
2. Toss the ball from an overhead position as far as possible using only one step. Do not cross the line.
3. Measure the distance from the line to the point where the ball landed.

4. Repeat the procedure for a reverse overhead toss. No step is taken on this toss.
5. Compare your scores with the ranges in tables 4.6 and 4.7.

Table 4.6 Medicine Ball Toss, Overhead Scores (in feet*)

	Female		Male	
	Adult	Junior	Adult	Junior
Excellent	>22.5	>23	>30.5	>34
Good	18.5 to 22.5	19 to 23	25.5 to 30.5	29 to 34
Average	14.5 to 18.5	15 to 19	20 to 25.5	23 to 29
Needs improvement	<14.5	<15	<20	<23

* 1 foot = 30.5 centimeters

Table 4.7 Medicine Ball Toss, Reverse Overhead Scores (in feet*)

	Female		Male	
	Adult	Junior	Adult	Junior
Excellent	>32.5	>34	>43.5	>46
Good	26.5 to 32.5	27 to 34	35 to 43.5	38 to 46
Average	20.5 to 26.5	20 to 27	27 to 35	31 to 38
Needs improvement	<20.5	<20	<27	<31

* 1 foot = 30.5 centimeters

AGILITY AND SPEED

Agility and speed describe the ability to move around the court quickly and smoothly to position yourself for a shot.

Agility is crucial to good court movement. It allows you to be in the correct position and provides a solid platform from which to hit the ball. Speed is important for getting to the ball. Although some people have more natural speed, all athletes can improve speed by training their muscles and nervous systems to produce more efficient movements. The faster you can get to a ball, the more time you have to prepare for your shot.

▶ Hexagon Test

The hexagon test measures foot quickness when changing direction backward, forward, and sideways while facing one direction. Facing the same direction during the test simulates facing your opponent during a match. The hexagon test also tests your ability to stabilize the body quickly between those changes of direction, because the body needs to be stable before the next jump can be performed. If the body is not stable, you will lose your balance.

Procedure

1. Use masking tape to create a hexagon (six sides with angles of 120 degrees) on the ground. Make sure each side is 24 inches (61 cm) long (figure 4.9).

2. Stand in the middle of the hexagon, and remain facing in the same direction throughout the test.

3. When your partner gives you the command "Ready, go," begin jumping forward over the tape and immediately back into the hexagon. Your partner will time you with a stopwatch.

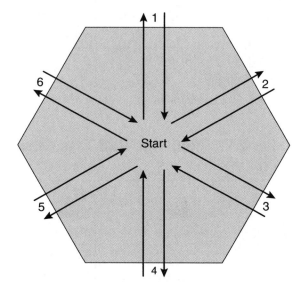

Figure 4.9   Hexagon test.

4. Continuing to face forward, jump over the next side and back to the middle. Repeat for each side.

5. Continue this pattern by jumping over all six sides and back to the middle each time for three full revolutions of the hexagon.

6. When the feet enter the hexagon after three full revolutions, your partner should stop the stopwatch and record your time.

7. Give yourself one practice trial. Test yourself twice, recording both times with the stopwatch, then make a note of your best time.

8. Compare your scores with the ranges in table 4.8.

Table 4.8   Hexagon Scores (in seconds)

	Female		Male	
	Adult	**Junior**	**Adult**	**Junior**
Excellent	<12.00	<10.48	<11.80	<11.10
Good	12.00 to 12.10	10.48 to 11.70	11.80 to 13.00	11.10 to 11.80
Average	12.10 to 12.40	11.70 to 12.30	13.00 to 13.50	11.80 to 12.70
Needs improvement	>12.40	>12.30	>13.50	>12.70

20-Yard Dash Test

At the time this book is being written, Kei Nishikori and Sloane Stephens are two of the fastest players in professional tennis. To achieve a high ranking, you need to be fast and be a great mover. You can't hit a good shot if you don't have enough time to get in position. Because points in tennis are rather short, explosive speed is very important. One of the best tests of speed is a straight-ahead sprint.

Procedure

1. Mark off 20 yards (18.2 m) on a tennis court with masking tape. The distance from the baseline to the opposite side service line is exactly 20 yards.
2. Have a partner stand at the finish line with an arm in the air and stopwatch in hand.
3. At the drop of the arm and the command "Ready, go," sprint toward the finish line.
4. Complete three trials. Record the best of the three scores.
5. Compare your score with the ranges in table 4.9.

Table 4.9   20-Yard* Dash Scores (in seconds)

	Female		Male	
	Adult	**Junior**	**Adult**	**Junior**
Excellent	<3.30	<3.20	<3.20	<2.90
Good	3.30 to 3.40	3.20 to 3.36	3.20 to 3.30	2.90 to 3.00
Average	3.40 to 3.60	3.36 to 3.54	3.30 to 3.50	3.00 to 3.30
Needs improvement	>3.60	>3.54	>3.50	>3.30

* 20 yards = 18.2 meters

Spider Run Test

The spider run is tennis' version of the shuttle run. Of all the physical fitness tests administered to players, the movement patterns in this test most closely simulate the actual movements during a tennis match. The stopping and starting actions of this activity make it an excellent test as well as a great training drill.

Procedure

1. Using masking tape, mark off a 12- by 18-inch (30- by 46-cm) rectangle behind the center of the baseline, using the baseline as one of the sides.

2. Position five tennis balls on the court—one on each corner where the baseline and singles sideline meet, one on each side where the singles sideline (S-line) and service line meet, and one ball on the center T (figure 4.10).

3. Start with one foot in the rectangle. Retrieve each ball and place it in the rectangle, one at a time, moving in a counterclockwise direction.

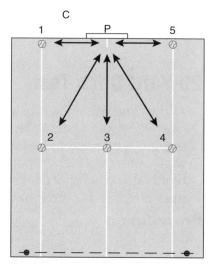

Figure 4.10 Spider run test.

4. Have a partner record your time with a stopwatch. As soon as the last ball is placed in the rectangle, the stopwatch is stopped.

5. Compare your score with the scores in table 4.10.

Table 4.10   Spider Run Scores (in seconds)

	Female		Male	
	Adult	**Junior**	**Adult**	**Junior**
Excellent	<17.30	<17.10	<15.00	<14.60
Good	17.30 to 18.00	17.10 to 17.16	15.00 to 15.30	14.60 to 15.00
Average	18.00 to 18.30	17.16 to 17.34	15.30 to 16.00	15.00 to 15.40
Needs improvement	>18.30	>17.34	>16.00	>15.40

Sideways Shuffle

The sideways shuffle is a speed and agility test that focuses on lateral movement. Many speed and agility tests measure forward speed; however, lateral speed is just as important in tennis. The majority of tennis movements are lateral. Moving quickly while staying balanced (keeping your center of gravity over your base of support) is critical in this test.

Procedure

1. Start on the center service line at the T with one foot on either side of the line, facing the net.
2. While facing the net, shuffle along the service line and touch the doubles sideline with your foot. Then shuffle to the opposite doubles sideline, and continue back to the center. 3. Crossover steps are not allowed.
3. Have a partner record your time with a stopwatch. After touching both doubles sidelines and returning to the center, the stopwatch is stopped.
4. Compare your score with the ranges in table 4.11.

Table 4.11 Sideways Shuffle Scores (in seconds)

	Female		Male	
	Adult	Junior	Adult	Junior
Excellent	<6.0	<7.0	<6.4	<5.5
Good	6.0 to 7.0	7.0 to 7.1	6.4 to 6.7	5.5 to 5.6
Average	7.0 to 7.3	7.1 to 7.4	6.7 to 7.0	5.6 to 5.7
Needs improvement	>7.3	>7.4	>7.0	>5.7

STRENGTH AND MUSCULAR ENDURANCE

Strength is defined as the amount of weight you can lift or handle at any one time. Muscular endurance is the number of times your muscles can lift a weight or the length of time your muscles can hold an amount of weight. Tennis players should be tested for muscular strength. In addition, because tennis matches and training sessions are often long, they also should be tested for muscle endurance, which is especially important at elite levels of performance.

Have you ever played in a long match that made your muscles sore the next day? That's because tennis requires you to have not only good strokes but also strength and muscular endurance. The soreness you may experience is usually a result of unaccustomed eccentric exercise. Eccentric exercise is when the muscle lengthens under tension. Throughout a match, you may have to hit hundreds of balls while running from side to side. Good muscular endurance, which means that you can apply force and sustain it over a period of time, can help you hit the ball just as hard at the end of a match as in the beginning. Not only that, it can also help prevent injuries.

1-Minute Sit-Up Test

In tennis, it is common knowledge that you need strong legs help you get around the court as quickly as possible and you need a strong arm to provide a forceful swing. Perhaps less obvious but equally important is that you need strong abdominal and low-back muscles. These muscles serve as a link between the lower and upper body as force is transferred from the ground all the way up to the racket. The muscles of the core region are heavily involved during nearly all tennis strokes. For training purposes, you may want to perform crunches to reduce the strain on your hip flexors and low back. However, for testing purposes, someone should hold your feet while you perform a complete sit-up. During testing, a sit-up performed through full range of motion provides an easier way to measure or score the sit-ups performed in certain time intervals. Bending the trunk beyond 45 to 60 degrees during the sit-up causes a significant amount of hip flexor activity and relies less on the abdominal muscles for movement. The exercises described in chapter 7 are recommended for training, but the full sit-up is used as an indicator of abdominal power and endurance during testing.

Procedure

1. This exercise is timed. Have a partner time you.
2. Lie on your back with your knees bent approximately 90 degrees and your feet flat on the floor.
3. You can have a partner hold your feet so that they don't move while you perform the exercise.
4. Cross your arms over your chest, and place your hands on the opposite shoulders.
5. Perform as many sit-ups as possible in a 60-second period. Have your partner count and keep an eye on the clock.

6. To count as a complete sit-up, the elbows must touch the knees in the up position (while keeping the arms against the body), and the shoulder blades must touch the mat in the down position (hips must stay in contact with the mat). (See figure 4.11.)

7. Compare your scores with the ranges in table 4.12.

Figure 4.11   1-minute sit-up test.

Table 4.12   1-Minute Sit-Up Scores

	Female		Male	
	Adult	**Junior**	**Adult**	**Junior**
Excellent	>53	>54	>58	>63
Good	46 to 53	46 to 54	51 to 58	56 to 63
Average	42 to 46	35 to 46	47 to 51	50 to 56
Needs improvement	<42	<35	<47	<50

Note

Players with a history of low-back pain may need to refrain from performing this test.

Prone Plank Test

One of the most important areas for all tennis players to train is the core of the body. This core is generally described as the abdominals, low back, and pelvis. It consists of many muscle groups that are responsible for stabilizing the spine and transferring forces from the lower body to the upper body during virtually all sport activities and movement patterns. Chapter 7 covers the core extensively with exercises to improve core stability for tennis players.

Procedure

1. This exercise is timed. Once in position, set a timer or have a partner set one for you.

2. Assume a prone (facedown) position on your forearms and toes (figure 4.12).

3. Maintain straight alignment from the head to the heels. Don't let your butt sag or stick up in the air, and align your neck so that your eyes are focused down toward the floor at a point approximately 12 inches (about 30 cm) in front of your hands.

4. Minimize wavering or other movement compensation during the period of static hold.

5. Hold this position for as long as possible without moving or wavering. When you can no longer hold the position, mark the time.

6. Compare your scores with those listed in table 4.13.

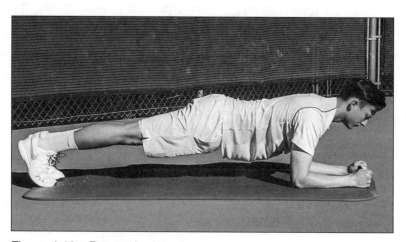

Figure 4.12   Prone plank test.

Table 4.13 Prone Plank Scores (in seconds)

	Adult	Junior
Excellent	>120	>90
Good	60 to 120	60 to 90
Average	30 to 60	30 to 60
Needs improvement	<30	<30

Side Plank Test (Right and Left Sides)

The side plank test is another important core assessment that can also function as a beneficial training exercise. As a test it looks at the muscular strength and endurance in the core muscles with an emphasis on the oblique abdominal muscles. Chapter 7 focuses on the exercises to help the core region.

Procedure

1. This exercise is timed. Once in position, set a timer or have a partner set one for you.
2. Lie on your left side on your forearm (with your elbow under your shoulder) and the left side of your left foot (figure 4.13).

Figure 4.13   Side plank test.

3. Maintain a straight alignment from the head to the heels, avoiding any upward positioning of the buttocks and extension of the neck. Also, minimize wavering or other movement compensation during the period of static hold.

4. Hold this position for as long as possible without moving or wavering. When you can no longer hold the position, mark the time.

5. Compare your scores with those listed in table 4.14.

6. Repeat this procedure on your right side, and compare your score with those listed in table 4.14.

Table 4.14 Side Plank Scores (in seconds)

	Adult	Junior
Excellent	>90	>60
Good	60 to 90	45 to 60
Average	30 to 60	30 to 45
Needs Improvement	<30	<30

1-Minute Push-Up Test

Do you want to hit your serve as hard as John Isner or Madison Keys? Performing push-ups may not guarantee that you'll be able to serve at top speeds, but having strong shoulders and arms can certainly help you hit the ball harder and also reduce your risk of injury. Doing push-ups is not necessarily a sport-specific movement for tennis unless you fall down a lot and find yourself having to push yourself up off the ground. However, the push-up does provide a good estimate of gross upper-body strength and muscle endurance, so it has been used in many testing protocols for years. If doing a full push-up is too hard for you, start by doing wall push-ups, then progress to supported push-ups from your knees.

Procedure

1. This exercise is timed. Have a partner keep time you.

2. Lie prone (facedown) with your hands shoulder-width apart and your toes curled under so that your lower body will rest on the balls of your feet.

3. Extend your arms, but keep your head, shoulders, back, hips, knees, and feet in a straight line.

4. Have your partner record the number of push-ups you complete in a 60-second period or to muscle failure.

5. To count as a complete push-up, the upper arms must reach parallel to the floor or below in the down position (figure 4.14), the arms must be completely extended in the up position, and you must maintain straight body alignment.

6. Compare your scores with the ranges in table 4.15.

Figure 4.14   1-minute push-up test.

Table 4.15   1-Minute Push-Up Scores

	Female		Male	
	Adult	**Junior**	**Adult**	**Junior**
Excellent	>44	>42	>49	>52
Good	36 to 44	34 to 42	40 to 49	49 to 52
Average	24 to 36	20 to 34	30 to 40	35 to 49
Needs improvement	<24	<20	<30	<35

External Rotation Manual Muscle Test

The rotator cuff is responsible for stabilizing the shoulder during virtually all arm movements. Strength and muscular endurance in the external rotator muscles (back part of the rotator cuff) are essential for the prevention of shoulder injury. This test manually evaluates the strength of the rotator cuff.

Caution

This test should be administered by a trained professional such as a physical therapist or athletic trainer.

Procedure

1. You may sit or stand. A qualified examiner places your shoulder in 90 degrees of abduction and 90 degrees of external rotation in the coronal plane (90/90 position). The elbow is bent to 90 degrees.

2. While using one arm to stabilize your elbow, the examiner exerts a force into internal rotation (figure 4.15). You should hold the initial 90/90 position.

3. The examiner grades and records the performance of both arms based on the following scale:

   5 (normal): ability to maintain 90/90 position without pain against maximal resistance exhibited by the examiner. The arm does not break from the 90/90 position with testing.

   4 (good): ability to maintain 90/90 position without pain against moderate resistance exhibited by the examiner. The hand and forearm move slightly into internal rotation with heavier amounts of resistance applied by the examiner.

Figure 4.15   External rotation manual muscle test.

3 (fair): inability to withstand any resistance applied by the examiner.

2 (poor): inability to place the arm in the 90/90 position.

4. The score is recorded as a ratio based on 5/5 as normal. Any score less than 5/5 would indicate the need for rotator cuff and scapular strengthening.

Note

A qualified health professional may also be able to use a handheld dynamometer, which measures more accurately the force the shoulder external rotators can produce. This tool is valuable, because a number is generated for side-to-side comparison of your strength as well as for gauging progress between testing sessions. In addition, an isokinetic test can be performed to measure shoulder rotation strength and muscular balance (i.e., external and internal rotation ratio).

Scapular Stabilization (Scapular Dyskinesia) Test

The scapula (shoulder blade) is the base for arm movement and an anchor for muscular attachment. The scapula must be lined up and move with the arm like a ball on a seal's nose. While tennis players have extraordinary strength in some areas, they often lack proper strength and development of the muscles in the upper back. This test checks for scapular motion and control of that motion.

Caution

This test should be administered by a trained professional such as a physical therapist or athletic trainer.

Procedure

1. Stand upright, holding a 1-pound (0.45-kg) weight in each hand.

2. Begin with your arms at your sides. When directed by a qualified instructor or medical professional, raise your straight arms to 180 degrees in the scapular plane for multiple repetitions (figure 4.16).

3. A qualified examiner observes the movement of the scapulae and notes any winging (protrusion of the scapulae away from the

Figure 4.16 Scapular stabilization test.

thorax) or overuse of the neck and upper trapezius muscles during both the ascent and descent phases of elevation.

4. The examiner watches scapular motion and notes any asymmetry, which is especially important as the descend.

Single-Leg Stability Test

This test indicates a player's ability to control the body over a planted leg. This stability decreases loads on the knee and leg (injury risk) and allows for explosive starts and stops (performance enhancement). This test is excellent for identifying weaknesses of the core, hip, and knee. In addition, it is an important screening tool for determining a player's ability to balance. Careful observation of a player's movement strategies can provide important information for training and injury prevention.

Procedure

1. Stand upright with your arms at your sides, and lift one foot off the ground. Bend the non-weight-bearing knee (knee of the lifted leg) to as much as 90 degrees.

2. Look forward, and bend the weight-bearing (standing) knee to approximately 30 degrees (partial squat; figure 4.17).

3. Repeat the movement several times on each leg.

4. A qualified examiner looks for several compensations during the single-leg stability test, including an inability to control the pelvis (Trendelenburg sign), corkscrewing (dynamic knee valgus), or the use of excessive trunk flexion during the descent. An inability to maintain proper balance throughout the testing process is also noted.

Figure 4.17 Single-leg stability test.

Drop Jump Test

The ability to maintain controlled leg alignment helps to protect the knee and ensure optimal balance and positioning on the court. For tennis this control is highlighted during change-of-direction movements and landing mechanics after the serve and overhead. This test measures the ability of the player to maintain proper leg positioning when landing from a vertical jump and then performing an explosive movement after landing.

Procedure

1. Start on top of a box 12 inches (31 cm) in height with your feet positioned 14 inches (35 cm) apart for consistency (figure 4.18a).

2. From this starting position, drop directly down from the box (figure 4.18b) and immediately perform a maximum vertical jump, raising both arms as high as possible (figure 4.18c). Do not jump up off the box; instead, drop down off the box and then perform a vertical jump with maximum effort.

3. A qualified examiner looks for abnormal movement patterns such as corkscrewing (dynamic knee valgus) as well as increased forward lean and asymmetrical limb loading. In addition, when viewed from the side, excessive movement of the knees forward over the toes would also be an abnormal finding.

Figure 4.18   Drop jump test: (a) starting position; (b) drop; (c) maximum-effort vertical jump.

Grip Strength Test

Good grip strength can help prevent wrist and elbow injuries. In addition, it can help you hold on to your racket better on those off-center hits. Although your dominant arm will be stronger than your nondominant arm, professionals recommend that the difference between the two should not be greater than about 25 percent. Grip strength measures the strength of the finger flexors and forearm muscles.

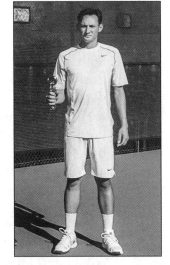

Procedure

1. With your arm against your side, squeeze a grip strength dynamometer (figure 4.19).
2. Record the result in kilograms (1 kg = 2.2 lb).
3. Repeat on the other side.
4. Compare your scores with the scores in table 4.16.

Figure 4.19 Grip strength test.

Table 4.16 Grip Strength Scores (in kilograms)

	Female		Male	
	Adult	**Junior**	**Adult**	**Junior**
Excellent				
Dominant	>39	>37	>60	>52
Nondominant	>27	>33	>36	>42
Good				
Dominant	34 to 39	34 to 37	51 to 60	48 to 52
Nondominant	24 to 27	27 to 33	31 to 36	34 to 42
Average				
Dominant	28 to 34	31 to 34	42 to 51	39 to 48
Nondominant	22 to 24	25 to 27	26 to 31	31 to 34
Needs improvement				
Dominant	<28	<31	<42	<39
Nondominant	<22	<25	<26	<31

REPEATED SPRINT TESTS

As tennis is a sport that involves fast, quick movements that need to be repeated many times throughout a match, it is important to include testing that can evaluate performance in this specific area. These repeated sprint tests are a great way to determine the physical levels for one of the most important aspects of success on the tennis court.

30-Second First Step Test

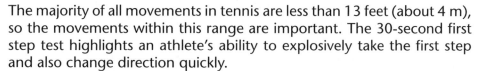

The majority of all movements in tennis are less than 13 feet (about 4 m), so the movements within this range are important. The 30-second first step test highlights an athlete's ability to explosively take the first step and also change direction quickly.

Procedure

1. Start in the center of the tennis court between the center line (T-line) and the singles sideline (S-line) with a tennis racket in your dominant hand. If testing is not taking place on a tennis court, set up two markers 13 feet, 6 inches (4.1 m) apart.

2. On the command of your tester (coach, trainer, or partner), run between the center line (T-line) and singles sideline (S-line) as fast as possible, making sure to touch each line with your racket every time for 30 seconds.

3. Record how many times you can touch the center line (T-line) and the singles sideline (S-line) in 30 seconds.

4. After each attempt, rest for 30 seconds. Repeat this trial three times. If your number changes between the first and third trial, you need to work on tennis-specific endurance. Table 4.17 has suggested numbers for competitive-level tennis players.

Table 4.17   30-Second First Step Scores (number of touches)

	Female		Male	
	Adult	**Junior**	**Adult**	**Junior**
Excellent	>31	>29	>35	>33
Good	27 to 31	28 or 29	31 to 35	32 or 33
Average	24 to 26	26 or 27	27 to 30	30 to 32
Needs improvement	<24	<26	<27	<30

MK Drill Test

Tennis-specific endurance requires a combination of anaerobic and aerobic energy. Developing this kind of endurance involves fast movements performed over time periods similar to tennis points and then quick recovery to be ready for the next point. The MK drill is designed for tennis and to assess tennis-specific endurance and repeated sprint ability.

Procedure

1. Start behind one doubles line (D-line) on the tennis court facing the other doubles line (D-line) on the same half of the court. If a tennis court is unavailable, measure a distance of 36 feet (10.97 m) to simulate the distance between the two doubles lines. If measuring heart rate (optional), you may either wear the heart rate monitoring strap and the watch to monitor heart rate readings or have a trainer hold the watch.

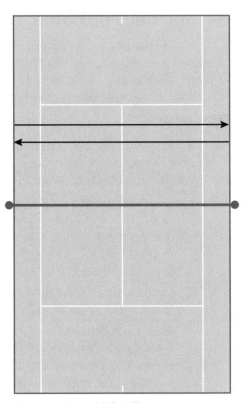

Figure 4.20   MK drill test.

2. On the signal, sprint to the other doubles sideline and back (figure 4.20). This distance is considered 1 repetition.

3. The number of repetitions and rest periods are determined by table 4.18. At the end of each series of repetitions, rest for the allotted time.

4. Using a timer, the tester records the time of each repetition on table 4.18 and, if available, your heart 5 seconds after each repetition.

5. Compare scores to tables 4.19 and 4.20.

Table 4.18 MK Drill Repetitions and Recovery

Repetitions	Recovery (sec.)	Date: Time (sec.)	Heart rate
1	15		
2	30		
3	45		
4	60		
5	90		
6	120		
6	120		
5	90		
4	60		
3	45		
2	30		
1	NA		

Adapted, by permission, from International Tennis Performance Association, 2015, *Certified Tennis Performance Specialist (CTPS) workbook and study guide* (Marietta, GA: ITPA).

Table 4.19 MK Drill Normative Data for Elite Players (in seconds)

Repetitions	Rest time	Female			Male		
		Excellent	Good	Average or needs improvement	Excellent	Good	Average or needs improvement
1	15	<5.5	<6.5	<7.5	<5.10	<6	<7
2	30	<11	<12.5	<13.5	<10.6	<12	<13
3	45	<17	<18.5	<20	<16.5	<18	<19
4	60	<22	<23.5	<25	<21.5	<23	<24
5	90	<29	<30.5	<32	<28.75	<30	<31
6	120	<36	<38.5	<40	<35.7	<38	<39
6	120	<36	<38.5	<40	<35.7	<38	<39
5	90	< 29	<30.5	<32	<28.5	<30	<31
4	60	<23	<23.5	<26	<23	<23	<25
3	45	<16	<19.5	<22	<16	<19	<21
2	30	<11	<12.5	<14	<11	<12	<13.5
1	~	<5.5	<6.5	<8	<5.2	<6	<7.5

Adapted, by permission, from International Tennis Performance Association, 2015, *Certified Tennis Performance Specialist (CTPS) workbook and study guide* (Marietta, GA: ITPA).

Table 4.20 MK Drill Normative Data for Recreational Adult and League Players

Repetitions	Rest time	Competitive tournament female player	Competitive tournament male player
1	15	<7.5	<7
2	30	<13.5	<13
3	45	<20	<19
4	60	<25	<24
5	90	<32	<31
6	120	<40	<39
6	120	<40	<39
5	90	<32	<31
4	60	<26	<25
3	45	<22	<21
2	30	<14	<13.5
1	~	<8	<7.5

Adapted, by permission, from International Tennis Performance Association, 2015, *Certified Tennis Performance Specialist (CTPS) workbook and study guide* (Marietta, GA: ITPA).

AEROBIC ENDURANCE

Aerobic endurance is the ability to take in, transport, and use oxygen. Aerobic energy is used during prolonged, steady-paced activities that mainly use the large muscle groups. Examples include jogging, cycling, and swimming.

Aerobic endurance is important in tennis. When you are aerobically fit, you can recover faster between points and perform longer before getting tired. A strong aerobic base allows you to recover efficiently between points even during long, close matches. As your endurance improves, your ligaments and tendons become tougher, reducing the risk of injury and laying the foundation for more intense training.

1.5-Mile Run Test

Although tennis involves many short sprints on the court, it also involves an aerobic endurance component. Matches can last 3 hours or longer, taxing the aerobic system. Although most of the training will involve repeated short-duration sprints over an extended period, having overall aerobic capacity is valuable. When completing the 1.5-mile (2.4-km) distance, you should focus on running at a consistent pace throughout the run. You should train for longer distances in the off-season and preseason.

Procedure

1. Stand at the start/finish line on a track.
2. A partner gives the command "Ready, go" and starts a stopwatch.
3. Complete 1.5 miles (2.4 km), which is six laps on a 440-yard track (slightly more than six laps on a 400-m track), and record your time.
4. Compare your score with the times in table 4.21.

Table 4.21   1.5-Mile Run Scores (in minutes:seconds)

	Female		Male	
	Adult	Junior	Adult	Junior
Excellent	<11:49	<10:30	<8:44	<9:45
Good	11:49 to 13:43	10:30 to 11:00	8:44 to 10:47	9:45 to 10:15
Average	13:43 to 15:08	11:00 to 11:30	10:47 to 12:20	10:15 to 11:00
Needs improvement	>15:08	>11:30	>12:20	>11:00

Note

Another test that an exercise physiologist or exercise laboratory can perform is a $\dot{V}O_2$max test. Using a progressive series of exercise stages on a treadmill or cycle ergometer, this test measures the maximum amount of oxygen that a player can use over time. This test can provide an excellent measure of aerobic fitness to identify players with either exceptional aerobic capacity or players who may need to further emphasize aerobic exercise in their off-court training programs.

SUMMARY

The tests described in this chapter can provide tennis players with critical indicators of athletic performance as well as specific measures of flexibility, strength and power, muscular endurance, agility and speed, body composition, stability, dynamic balance, and aerobic and anaerobic fitness. It is best to perform these tests before developing a tennis-specific complete conditioning program so that you can identify strengths and weaknesses and design an individual program to maximize effectiveness. In most cases, repeating the tests more frequently than 6 to 8 weeks will not show significant changes, because the human performance variables measured in these tests take time to develop. However, testing should occur at regular intervals to gauge improvement and allow for adjustments to the training regimen. You can apply more frequent testing following injury to more closely monitor progress and development. Use of the normative data provided in this chapter can quickly determine how one player stacks up to the large groups of players who were tested. However, the most valuable testing comparisons are between testing sessions, comparing players to themselves and monitoring each player's improvement.

Once testing has been established, the training aspect can move forward. The next chapter focuses on how best to warm up for tennis and for tennis-specific training, and it discusses the best methods for improving tennis-specific flexibility.

Chapter 5

Dynamic Warm-Up and Flexibility

To optimize performance and minimize risk of injury on the tennis court, players must perform proper warm-up and dynamic stretching exercises before playing tennis or doing other high-level physical activities. To create an effective warm-up and stretching program, understanding the essential components of a warm-up and knowing the differences between static and dynamic stretching are key. This chapter provides the information you need to create a sound tennis-specific warm-up and flexibility program.

The physical demands of playing tennis stress all regions of the body, so warm-up and flexibility training must include all areas of the body. Injuries to the upper and lower extremities as well as the spine and torso have been reported in elite and recreational players. These injuries are discussed in chapter 13.

WARM-UP

The warm-up plays an important part in the tennis player's conditioning program. Warm-up exercises should be considered a major aspect of training and competition, not an afterthought. The purpose of the warm-up is to prepare the body tissues to optimally respond to exercise, whether it occurs during a workout or as preparation for tennis practice or competition. An appropriate warm-up can also help reduce the likelihood of injury.

Athletes typically use two types of warm-ups. A passive warm-up involves the application of an external type of heat to the body, such as applying moist heat packs, using heating pads, or entering a warm whirlpool. These techniques do increase tissue temperature but are not always practical for most athletes.

A second type of warm-up is the active warm-up. An active warm-up involves low-intensity exercise that elevates tissue temperature, increases heart rate, and actively prepares the athlete for exercise. Examples of recommended active warm-up activities include jumping jacks, calisthenics, slow jogging or jogging in place, lightly jumping rope, low-intensity stationary cycling, and large arm circles (clockwise and counterclockwise).

A good indicator of the duration and intensity of a proper warm-up is the presence of a light sweat. Using the recommended active warm-up exercises, you would typically begin to sweat in 3 to 5 minutes. Additional benefits of a proper warm-up are improved tissue elasticity and a reduced risk of muscle and tendon injury.

FLEXIBILITY TRAINING

Flexibility training is often the most overlooked component of a quality conditioning program. Some of the reasons people do not adhere to flexibility programs include the following:

- Stretching may not feel particularly good.
- The on-court benefits are not obvious to the player.
- Most players have been given no specific individualized guidelines as to how, why, what, and when to stretch.
- Many coaches emphasize stretching less than the other components of conditioning

The term *flexibility* can be defined as the degree of extensibility of the soft tissue structures surrounding the joint, such as muscles, tendons, and connective tissue. Two main types of flexibility exist. *Static flexibility* describes the measured range of motion about a joint or series of joints, and *dynamic flexibility* refers to the active motion about a joint or series of joints. Dynamic flexibility is limited by the resistance to motion of the joint structures, the ability of the soft connective tissues to deform, and neuromuscular components.

Factors influencing flexibility include heredity, neuromuscular components, and tissue temperature. In regard to heredity, body design determines overall flexibility potential. While most people tend to be relatively inflexible, a small few are hyperflexible. Aspects of heredity and body design that affect flexibility potential include the shape and orientation of joint surfaces, as well as the physiological characteristics of the joint capsule, muscles, tendons, and ligaments. In addition, because of the nature of the movements performed while playing tennis and from the repetitive nature of these stresses, some areas of the tennis player's body can be very tight and inflexible. These areas include the hamstrings, low back, and muscles in the back of the shoulder. At the same time, other areas in the tennis player's body may be overly flexible, such as the front of the shoulder (external rotation). These adaptations are the result of many years of playing tennis.

Few people are as flexible around their joints as they need to be, and tennis places tremendous demands on various body parts in their extremes of motion. For example, the range of motion required of the shoulder in the position of external rotation during the serve places tremendous stress on the front of the shoulder. Tennis players generally are very flexible in external rotation of the shoulder but exhibit limited internal rotation on their dominant (tennis-playing) side. To demonstrate this concept, try this simple test: Place the back surface of both hands with the thumbs pointing up on the low back, reaching up toward the shoulder blades as high as possible (figure 5.1). Notice that your dominant arm is not likely to reach as high as the nondominant arm. This shows the loss of internal shoulder rotation that is common in elite tennis players and also in other types of throwing athletes. The stretches outlined for the posterior part of the shoulder later in this chapter should be able to enhance this joint range of motion and decrease the difference between the two extremities. To address this flexibility imbalance, specific stretches for the back of the shoulder are recommended, while exercises that stress the front of the shoulder by placing the arms behind the body in an extreme position (such as in a doorway) are not recommended for tennis players and other throwing athletes.

Additional examples of extreme ranges of motion incurred during tennis play include the following:

- Lateral movement patterns that stress the hip and groin
- Stabilizing muscle actions of the abdominal muscles during the tennis serve
- Explosive movement patterns by the calf muscles and Achilles tendon.

Throughout a match, players have to generate great force and speed many times while in an outstretched position. A conditioning program that includes flexibility exercises ensures that the range of motion necessary for optimal performance will be available. Note that flexibility, combined with

Figure 5.1　Internal shoulder rotation on right and left sides for a right-handed player.

the ability to produce power in these extremes of motion, is essential in tennis. Stretching alone will not prevent injury or enhance performance. However, balanced strength throughout a flexible, less-restricted range of motion will. This goal can only be attained using a complete conditioning program for tennis.

Flexibility offers many benefits, including the following:

- It allows the framework for sport-specific strengthening in motion extremes.
- It helps tissues distribute impact shock and force loads more effectively, thus allowing tissues to accommodate the stresses imposed on them.
- It lessens the work of opposing muscle groups by providing more unrestricted motion.
- It enhances blood supply and tissue nourishment.
- It allows for good form without compensation from other body segments.
- It overcomes imbalances created by the sport itself and by daily activities.

WARM-UP AND FLEXIBILITY ROUTINE

Major changes have occurred in the way athletes warm up and stretch before performing. The biggest change has been in the shift away from doing static stretches before playing or practicing and performing a more complete dynamic stretching (warm-up) routine to optimally prepare the body's muscles, tendons, and joints for the stresses of physical activity.

Historically, sport scientists and sports medicine professionals recommended static stretching before and after tennis play or any other type of vigorous exercise. The slow movements and periods of holding at or near the end of the range of motion characteristic of static stretching programs were found in several studies to provide success in increasing the length of the muscle tissues. Dynamic stretching and warm-up were mentioned but not necessarily emphasized in most workout routines.

However, research over the past decade has identified temporary decreases in skeletal muscle performance immediately after static stretching. This decrease in muscle performance includes decreases in both muscular strength and power and can last for up to 1 hour after a static stretching program. Applying this research to athletes has led sport scientists and medical professionals to now recommend static stretching before an activity such as tennis or physical training at least 30 to 60 minutes before that activity starts and to emphasize the importance of a dynamic warm-up immediately preceding tennis play, practice sessions, and vigorous training sessions. Specifically, the use of a generous warm-up (jogging in place or riding a stationary bicycle for 3 to 5 minutes to break a light sweat) is now highly recommended along with dynamic stretches immediately before the activity is performed. Static stretching, while still important and still used, is now applied primarily after training and will be covered in greater detail later in this chapter. Static stretching after the workout is thought to speed recovery and decrease soreness in addition to increase muscle length. Table 5.1 summarizes the recommended sequence for the incorporation of stretching for tennis play or practice sessions and includes the integration of static stretching into the overall program for the tennis player.

An important influence on flexibility involves the neuromuscular components. The muscle spindle is a watchdog mechanism, located between the muscle fibers. When a stretch that is too quick is imposed on it, the muscle spindle sends a message to the central nervous system to contract the muscle. With this stretch reflex, the muscle shortens, thus hindering the stretching process. Therefore, when stretching, a slow, gradual movement is recommended to minimize the reflex action of the muscle spindle mechanism and enhance the stretching process.

Table 5.1 Steps to Incorporate Stretching Into Tennis Practice or Play

Step	Purpose	Exercise examples
Step 1	General warm-up (3 to 5 minutes) to increase core and muscle temperature	Light jogging, light cycling, jumping rope, jumping jacks, light calisthenics
Step 2	Dynamic stretching sequence, progressively increasing range of motion, velocity, and tennis specificity	Side step with arm crosses, knee-hug lunge, side lunge, Frankenstein walk, torso rotation, arm hugs
Step 3	Tennis practice, competition, or physical training session	
Step 4	General cool-down (3-10 min) to slowly decrease heart rate and aid in recovery	Light jogging, light cycling
Step 5	Static stretching-based flexibility program focused on areas of the body that are tight or were used extensively during tennis play	Posterior shoulder stretch (cross-arm stretch), sleeper stretch, hamstring stretch, seated groin stretch, hip twist, calf stretch

Another factor that influences flexibility and is important during all stretching exercise applications is tissue temperature. Heat increases the extensibility of soft tissue. Warming up before stretching by raising the body's core temperature or by breaking a light sweat results in greater gains in flexibility, with less microtrauma to the tissues being stretched. Another benefit to the stretching sequence in this chapter is the emphasis on static stretching after exercise or tennis play. At this time, the body is maximally warmed up and very accepting to a static stretching program. Static stretching is one part of the flexibility training program that is most often overlooked or underutilized. In this flexibility sequence, static stretching after exercise holds an important spot in the sequence, and it gives the player an ideal time to improve muscle length for injury prevention and performance enhancement.

The best recommendation for integrating a series of dynamic stretches into a training program is to always perform a proper warm-up first. The warm-up is one of the most important aspects of all types of stretching programs. Recommended warm-up activities include slow jogging around the court while making progressively larger arm circles, riding a bike, using a slide board, or performing any other rhythmic aerobic type activity at a low intensity. The warm-up should be 3 to 5 minutes, occasionally more.

Once the player has performed the warm-up to the level where a light sweat has occurred, several repetitions of dynamic stretch sequences can be done with progressively increasing intensity. Table 5.2 contains a sample on-court dynamic stretching sequence. This program is typically performed with players moving across the width of the tennis court, which is 36 feet (10.9 m). One complete progression across and back the width of the tennis court is recommended for most players.

Recommended dynamic stretches include butt kicks, front and side lunges, jogging with arm circles, jumping jacks, and some tennis-specific stretches. Little guidance from the literature exists on how many repetitions of each stretch are optimal, but most likely it depends on individual needs. Performing multiple repetitions of each movement is recommended; more movements are recommended in cooler temperatures and during tournaments when frequent matches and overtraining may increase stiffness between sessions.

Table 5.2   Dynamic Stretching Sequence for Tennis Players

Step	Instruction
1	Walk or jog back and forth across the court while making progressively larger arm circles.
2	Cross the court by performing the knee-to-chest tuck with one leg and rising up on the toes with the other leg. Alternate legs as you proceed across the court.
3	Perform the figure-4 tuck.
4	Perform the side lunge across the court. As you move across the court, step farther to stretch the muscles on the inside of the upper thigh (groin).
5	Perform the Frankenstein walk.
6	Perform the high-step trunk rotation. Increase the amount of trunk rotation and the height of your knee as you cross the court.
7	Perform the front lunge. Be sure to keep your torso upright as you move forward, and don't let the knee extend past the toes.
8	Perform the torso rotation, progressing to torso rotation into lunge; you can do them in place.
9	Perform the backward lunge with trunk rotation. Reach with your arm to your opposite leg (e.g., right leg back, rotate to the left, and reach with your left hand to your right ankle).
10	Perform the butt-kick warm-up.
11	Perform arm hugs.

DYNAMIC STRETCHES

Jogging With Arm Circles

Focus

Improve flexibility in the shoulders, chest, and upper back.

Procedure

1. Start at the doubles sideline facing across the court.
2. Swing the arms forward in large circles as you jog at a moderate pace from doubles sideline to doubles sideline.
3. Change directions, swinging the arms in backward circles as you jog back to the start position.
4. Repeat one or two times across the court.

Side Step With Arm Crosses

Focus

Improve the flexibility in the shoulders, chest, and upper back.

Procedure

1. Start at the doubles sideline facing the net.
2. Lift the arms out to the sides to shoulder height while assuming an athletic stance (knees and hips slightly flexed with the torso relatively upright and facing forward).
3. While shuffling across the court using sideways shuffle steps, swing your arms across your body like you are hugging yourself, and then swing the arms backward until you feel a slight stretch in the front of your shoulders and chest.
4. Perform this exercise as you shuffle from doubles sideline to doubles sideline, once moving to your left and then returning to your right.

Carioca Step

Focus

Prepare the lower legs and trunk by improving flexibility.

Procedure

1. Assume an athletic position while facing the net on the doubles sideline.
2. Begin by pushing off the right foot and stepping outward with the left foot toward the middle of the court. Upon landing on the left foot, cross the right foot in front of the left foot.
3. Again push off the right foot, landing on the left foot. This time upon landing, cross the right foot behind the left foot.
4. Repeat this cycle until you arrive at the doubles sideline.
5. Perform a repeating cycle of crosses with the right foot crossing in front of and then behind the left foot as you proceed across the court. Reverse directions while still facing the net; this time the left foot crosses in front of and behind the right foot as you return to the baseline from which you started.

Knee-to-Chest Tuck

Focus

Improve flexibility in the hips, trunk, and lower extremities.

Procedure

1. Stand on the baseline facing the net.
2. Bring one knee toward the chest. Hug the knee up tight toward you as you straighten your other knee and rise up on your toes (figure 5.2).
3. Take a small hop forward, landing on the same leg while returning the other leg from the chest down toward the ground.
4. Repeat the action, alternating each leg up the court, and return to the starting position. Repeat once or twice up the court.

Figure 5.2   Knee-to-chest tuck.

Knee-Hug Lunge

Focus

Improve flexibility in the hips, trunk, and lower extremities; added benefit for hip flexors and quadriceps.

Procedure

1. Stand on the baseline facing the net.
2. Bring one knee up toward the chest. Hug the knee tightly toward you as you straighten your other knee and rise up onto your toes (figure 5.3a).
3. Take a small hop forward, landing on the same leg while returning the other leg from the chest down toward the ground.

Figure 5.3 Knee-hug lunge: (*a*) knee hug; (*b*) lunge.

4. Immediately take a large step forward directly into a lunge (figure 5.3*b*). Hold this position for 1 or 2 seconds.
5. Stand up after holding the lunge, driving upward with the front leg.
6. Repeat the cycle as you proceed up the court.

Inverted Hamstring Stretch

Focus

Improve flexibility and balance of the hamstrings and gluteal muscles along with a secondary benefit for the calf muscles.

Procedure

1. Start at the doubles sideline, facing across the court.
2. Stand up straight, and shift your weight to one leg (standing leg).
3. Keeping your back as straight as possible and the standing leg slightly bent, bend the torso forward, hinging at the hip joints.
4. Keep bending forward until you feel a stretch in the hamstrings of the standing leg.
5. Keep the back flat, and avoid twisting.

Figure 5.4   Inverted hamstring stretch.

6. Elevate the raised leg behind you, holding it in line with your body (figure 5.4), with your arms extended out to the side at shoulder height. Hold this position for 2 or 3 seconds.

7. To return to the starting position, slowly lower the elevated leg and step forward; this leg is the new standing leg.

8. Repeat the movement, alternating standing legs and making your way across the court to the other doubles sideline.

Figure-4 Tuck

Focus

Improve flexibility of the groin and hips.

Procedure

1. Start at the baseline, facing the net.

2. Standing on one leg, lift the other leg and, using both hands, cradle the leg around the shin area.

3. Turn the knee outward while lifting upward on the ankle (figure 5.5), result-ing in external rotation and a stretch in the deep rotators of the hip. Avoid grab-bing for the foot. Instead, keep a hand at the ankle to prevent twisting the foot and ankle.

Figure 5.5   Figure-4 tuck.

4. As you are cradling one leg, rise up onto the toes of the other, contracting the muscles and coming slightly up off the ground and hold the top of the movement for two seconds. Release the leg.

5. Repeat the exercise, alternating between the right and left legs are you proceed up the court.

Side Lunge

Focus

Improve flexibility in the hip and groin.

Procedure

1. Start at the doubles sideline facing the net. Assume an athletic stance.

2. Take a large step sideways into the court, keeping the stationary leg straight (figure 5.6). Bend your stepping leg until you feel a stretch in the groin. Hold this position for 2 or 3 seconds.

3. Resume the athletic stance by bringing the straight leg back under your body. Repeat until you reach the doubles sideline.

Figure 5.6 Side lunge.

4. Reverse directions to work the other leg as you return to the original doubles sideline.

▶ Frankenstein Walk

Focus

Improve flexibility in the hamstrings, gluteal muscles, and low back.

Procedure

1. Start on the doubles sideline, facing across the court. Hold your arms up in front of you.

2. Swing one leg upward and forward, keeping the knee as straight as possible as you try to touch your toes with the opposite hand.

3. As soon as you feel a stretch, pull the leg down using your hip and gluteal muscles. Forcefully strike the ground with the front part of your foot.

4. Repeat the action with the opposite leg, making your way across the court, alternating between the left and right legs while keeping your arms at the 90-degree angle the entire time.

High-Step Trunk Rotation

Focus

Improve flexibility of the hips and trunk.

Procedure

1. Stand on the doubles sideline facing across the net. Raise the arms to the sides to shoulder level.

2. Begin by bringing the right knee toward the chest while rotating your trunk to the right such that the right knee nearly touches the left elbow (figure 5.7).

3. Bring the leg down to the staring position, and step that foot forward.

4. Repeat the movement with the opposite leg while rotating to the left so that the left knee-to-chest pattern nearly brings into contact the left knee and right elbow.

Figure 5.7   High-step trunk rotation.

5. Continue alternating left and right across the court, and return to the starting sideline.

Front Lunge

Focus

Improve flexibility of the gluteal muscles, hamstrings, and quadriceps.

Procedure

1. Stand at the doubles side-line facing across the court.
2. Take a large step forward with one leg while maintaining an upright posture and looking straight ahead (figure 5.8). Ensure that the knee is properly aligned and moving directly in line with the second toe.
3. Alternate steps with the right and left legs until you have crossed the court one time and returned to the opposite sideline.

Figure 5.8   Front lunge.

Torso Rotation

Focus

Improve flexibility of the trunk, hips, and shoulders.

Procedure

1. Stand anywhere on the court where you have enough room to move freely. Establish a strong base of support.
2. Elevate the arms to shoulder height, and gently rotate the arms from one side to the other by twisting (rotating) the trunk (figure 5.9).
3. Perform twists to both sides, alternating left and right for approximately 30 seconds.

Figure 5.9   Torso rotation.

Torso Rotation Into Lunge

Focus

Improve flexibility of the trunk, hips, and shoulders.

Procedure

1. Stand anywhere on the court where you have enough room to move freely. Establish a strong base of support.

2. Elevate the arms to shoulder height, and gently rotate the arms from one side to the other by twisting (rotating) the trunk.

3. As you move from one side to another, gradually lower the body by bending the knees and pivoting on the balls of the feet (figure 5.10).

Figure 5.10   Torso rotation into lunge.

4. Perform twists to both sides, alternating left and right for approximately 30 seconds.

Butt Kick Warm-Up

Focus

Improve flexibility of the quadriceps.

Procedure

1. Stand on the doubles sideline, facing across the court.

2. Begin jogging across the court, exaggerating the heel-to-buttock (knee-bend) motion.

3. While the heels may not physically touch the buttocks, the exaggerated bend of the knee motion gradually increases in intensity as you proceed across the court.

4. As you reach the first doubles sideline, turn and return to the starting position, continuing the kicks.

Backward Lunge With Trunk Rotation

Focus

Improve flexibility of the hip flexors.

Procedure

1. Start at the doubles sideline with your back facing across the court.

2. With the right foot, step back into a lunge position. Gently rotate the torso to the right (figure 5.11).

3. Return the torso to a good resting posture after reaching while in the squat position. Stand up by driving up on the front leg to the starting position.

4. With the left foot, step back into a lunge position. Gently rotate the torso to the left.

Figure 5.11 Backward lunge with trunk rotation.

5. Repeat the sequence until you reach the opposite doubles sideline.

Backward Stepover

Focus

Improve flexibility of the groin and hip.

Procedure

1. Start at the doubles sideline with your back turned to the court or at the net with your back to the baseline.

2. Lift one knee to hip height. Rotate the hip out so that the knee points out toward the side.

3. Step back as if you were trying to step over a hurdle (figure 5.12). You should feel the stretch in the groin and hip region.

4. Perform this exercise, alternating sides, from doubles sideline to doubles sideline.

Figure 5.12 Backward stepover.

Arm Hugs

Focus

Improve flexibility of the upper back, chest, and shoulders.

Procedure

1. Stand anywhere on the court with your feet shoulder-width apart.
2. Raise the arms to shoulder level and hug yourself, holding this position briefly (figure 5.13*a*).
3. Then open the arms as wide as possible, as if you were hugging the world (figure 5.13*b*).
4. Repeat this sequence 10 to 15 times, increasing the stretch and intensity of the exercise as you proceed.

Figure 5.13   Arm hugs: (*a*) hug yourself; (*b*) hug the world.

Static Stretching

Static stretching still has a place in the tennis player's training program. Certain areas in the athlete's body become characteristically tight from tennis play. Performing static stretching after tennis play and training sessions with particular emphasis on problem areas is still highly recommended. Table 5.3 outlines the general procedure for static stretching.

Table 5.3 Static Stretching Procedure

Step	Instructions
1	If stretching 60 minutes before exercise, do a dynamic warm-up for 3 to 5 minutes. Otherwise, perform static stretches immediately after exercise as part of the cool-down.
2	Emphasize slow, smooth movements and coordinated deep breathing. Inhale deeply. Exhale as you stretch to the point just short of pain, then ease back slightly. Hold this static stretch position for 15 to 30 seconds as you breathe normally. Repeat two or three times.
3	You should feel no pain. If it hurts, or if you feel a burning, you are stretching too far.
4	Stretch your tighter side first. Sometimes you may want to stretch the tighter side for a longer period of time.
5	Stretch only within your limits.
6	Do not lock your joints.
7	Do not bounce.
8	Stretch larger muscle groups first, and repeat the same routine each day.
9	If you have areas of extreme tightness, ask a physical therapist or trainer to check your range of motion to gauge your improvement and guide your flexibility training program.

Although recommendations for the timing of static stretching have changed, the relative importance and effectiveness has not changed. Stretching the posterior shoulder (cross-arm stretch, racket arm across body at chest level) is still a very important stretch for tennis players due to the specific adaptations in range of motion that occur from repeated high-intensity serving, powerful forehand groundstrokes, and general tennis play. In addition to the cross-arm stretch, players can also perform several repetitions of the sleeper stretch. This stretch has gained popularity recently among overhead athletes who lack internal rotation range of motion. The exercise description shows specifically how to perform this stretch in the sidelying (sleeping) position, which gives the stretch its name.

Additional stretches for the upper body that are important for the tennis player include wrist and forearm stretches. Repetitive overuse by the forearm and wrist muscles can lead to tightness from the gripping inherent in tennis play.

Recognizing the critical role of flexibility in peak performance and injury prevention, some of the tests provided in chapter 4 are specifically focused on a tennis player's flexibility. Flexibility needs are specific to each person and each joint. Tests to measure flexibility can help to both identify areas of inflexibility as well as to demonstrate progress with a specific personalized flexibility program.

In many instances more than one static stretch is included for a body part. Some of these exercises are more basic than others. Some areas, such as the shoulder and hip, require greater emphasis in the tennis player's body. If one area of the body has particularly limited range of motion, you may want to perform more than one stretching exercise for that body segment. Once you are able to perform one of the stretches, you may want to progress to a more advanced stretch (other positions that place a greater stretch on a particular muscle group) for that area. You should focus on areas of the body identified as the most inflexible. Resist the urge to stretch only the areas that are perceived as the most flexible or easiest to stretch; it will take time from other areas that need special attention and may be counterproductive by decreasing joint stability or promoting imbalances. Flexibility imbalance is one predictor of potential injury, and it is important to limit the occurrence of major flexibility imbalances between sides of the body and also between the front and back of the body.

STATIC STRETCHES
FOR THE SHOULDER AND ARM

Posterior Shoulder Stretch (Cross-Arm Stretch)

Focus

Improve flexibility of the shoulder rotators and upper-back (scapular) muscles.

Procedure

1. Standing up, hold your right arm straight out in front of you. Place your left hand behind your right elbow.

2. Pull your right arm across your body with your left hand (figure 5.14). Do not allow your trunk to rotate. By placing the outside of your right shoulder and scapula (shoulder blade) against a fence post or door jam, you stabilize the scapula, which greatly enhances the effectiveness of this important stretch.

3. Hold the position, then switch sides.

Figure 5.14   Posterior shoulder stretch (cross-arm stretch).

Sleeper Stretch

Focus

Improve flexibility of the shoulder rotators and upper-back (scapular) muscles.

Procedure

1. Lie on your dominant shoulder as you would when sleeping on your side.
2. Place your dominant arm directly in front of you at a 90-degree angle, keeping the elbow bent 90 degrees as well.
3. Using your other arm, push your hand down toward your feet, internally rotating your shoulder (figure 5.15).
4. Hold the position for 15 to 30 seconds, then repeat the stretch on the other side.

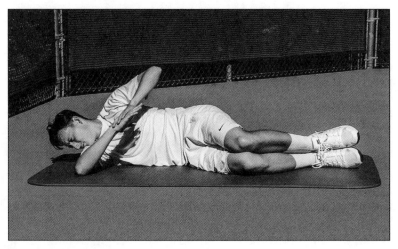

Figure 5.15　Sleeper stretch.

Note

You can make this stretch even more intense by placing your chin against the front of the shoulder you are lying on, pressing it down even more to provide greater stabilization to increase the stretch.

Forearm Flexor Stretch

Focus

Improve flexibility of the flexors and pronators of the forearm muscles.

Procedure

1. You can stand or sit for this stretch. Hold your dominant arm out in front of you with the elbow straight and your forearm supinated (palm up).
2. Use the opposite hand to stretch the wrist back (extension), keeping the elbow straight (figure 5.16).
3. Hold the position for 15 to 30 seconds, then repeat the stretch on the other side.

Figure 5.16   Forearm flexor stretch.

Forearm Extensor Stretch

Focus

Improve flexibility of the forearm extensors and supinators.

Procedure

1. You can stand or sit for this stretch. Hold your dominant arm out in front of you with the elbow straight and your forearm pronated (palm down).

2. Use the opposite hand to stretch the wrist downward (flexion), keeping the elbow straight (figure 5.17).

3. Hold the position for 15 to 30 seconds, then repeat the stretch on the other side.

Figure 5.17   Forearm extensor stretch.

STATIC STRETCHES FOR THE HIP AND LEG

Hamstring Stretch

Focus

Improve flexibility of the hamstrings and gluteal muscles.

Procedure

1. Lie on your back. Raise the leg to be stretched to a 90-degree angle at the hip.

2. Support the leg by grasping both hands behind the knee. Keep the opposite leg straight.
3. Straighten the leg, and pull it toward your torso (figure 5.18a). Use your hands to gently increase the stretch. Flexing your foot to pull your toes toward your face increases the stretch.

Variation

A method to help increase the range of motion through the hamstrings is to use a flexible stretching strap (figure 5.18b), which can help you increase the comfortable range of motion you can achieve above and beyond what may be achieved with your hands alone.

Figure 5.18   Hamstring stretch: (a) with hands; (b) with strap.

Quadriceps Stretch

Focus

Improve flexibility of the quadriceps and hip flexors.

Procedure

1. Stand on one leg. Bend the other knee, and reach behind you to grasp your foot or ankle on the outside (figure 5.19).

2. Keeping the back flat and the buttocks tucked under, pull your heel toward the buttocks and point your knee straight down toward the ground. Do not twist the knee.

3. Hold the position for 15 to 30 seconds, then repeat the stretch on the other side.

Figure 5.19   Quadriceps stretch.

Seated Groin Stretch

Focus

Improve flexibility of the groin and inner thighs.

Procedure

1. Sit with the bottoms of your feet together, knees out, holding onto your toes (figure 5.20).

2. Gently pull forward, bending from the hips to bring the chest toward the feet. Do not round your upper back. Use your elbows to gently push your knees toward the ground.

3. Hold the position for 15 to 30 seconds.

Figure 5.20   Seated groin stretch.

Hip Twist

Focus

Improve flexibility of the lateral hip muscles and lower back.

Procedure

1. Lie on your back with your knees bent and feet flat on the ground. Place your arms out to the sides on the ground with your hands at shoulder height as in a letter T to stabilize the upper back. Place your left ankle outside the right knee.

2. Use the left leg to pull the right knee across the midline of your body toward the floor until you feel a stretch along the outside of your hip or low back (figure 5.21). Keep the upper back and shoulders flat against the ground. The idea is not to touch the floor with the right knee but to stretch within your limits.

3. Hold the position for 15 to 30 seconds, then repeat the stretch on the other side.

Figure 5.21   Hip twist.

Figure-4 Stretch

Focus

Improve flexibility of the piriformis muscle.

Procedure

1. Lie on your back with the left knee bent. Place the right ankle just above the left knee.
2. Slowly bring the left knee toward the chest (figure 5.22). You will feel the stretch in the right buttock.
3. Hold the position for 15 to 30 seconds, then repeat the stretch on the other side.

Figure 5.22   Figure-4 stretch.

Hip Rotator Stretch

Focus

Improve flexibility of the hip rotators and lateral hip and thigh muscles.

Procedure

1. Lie on your back with your arms out to the sides with your palms facing up and legs straight.
2. Lift the exercising leg to 90 degrees, then allow it to lower across the other leg (figure 5.23). Keep the trunk and both shoulders on the ground throughout the stretch.
3. Hold the position for 15 to 30 seconds, then repeat the stretch on the other side.

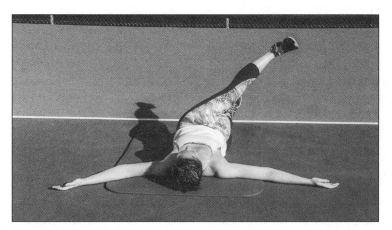

Figure 5.23   Hip rotator stretch.

Iliotibial (IT) Band Stretch

Focus

Improve flexibility of the iliotibial band.

Procedure

1. Stand with your right hand on a wall, your right leg approximately 3 feet (0.9 m) from the wall, and the left leg crossed over the right.

2. Gently push the right hip toward the wall (figure 5.24). Increase the stretch by standing farther from the wall.

3. Hold the position for 15 to 30 seconds, then repeat the stretch on the other side.

Figure 5.24   Iliotibial band stretch.

Calf Stretch

Focus

Improve flexibility of the calf muscles (gastrocnemius and soleus). Also may assist in range of motion around the Achilles tendon.

Procedure

1. Stand in front of a wall or fence with one leg approximately 2 to 3 feet (0.6-0.9 m) behind the other with the toes pointing straight forward.
2. Keeping the back knee straight and the heel on the floor, bend the front knee, and lean the trunk forward (figure 5.25*a*). Do not arch the back.
3. Repeat with the back knee slightly bent, keeping the heel on the ground (figure 5.25*b*).
4. Hold the position for 15 to 30 seconds, then repeat the stretch on the other side.

Figure 5.25 Calf stretch: (*a*) back knee straight; (*b*) back knee slightly bent.

STATIC STRETCHES FOR THE TRUNK

Knees-to-Chest Stretch

Focus

Improve flexibility of the low back and gluteal muscles.

Procedure

1. Lie on your back with your knees bent.
2. Bring your knees toward your chest by grasping the lower legs just below the knees (figure 5.26).
3. Hold the stretch for 15 to 30 seconds, then stretch each leg individually. Pull the right knee to the chest while keeping the left leg straight on the ground.
4. Repeat the stretch, pulling the left knee to the chest and keeping the right leg straight.

Figure 5.26   Knees-to-chest stretch.

Seated Spinal Twist

Focus

Improve flexibility of the lower back and hip rotators.

Procedure

1. In a seated position with the left leg extended forward, bend the right knee and place the right ankle outside of the left knee.
2. Bring the left arm around the right knee while keeping the right arm relaxed by your side. Slowly turn the shoulders and trunk to the right while looking over the right shoulder (figure 5.27).
3. Hold the position for 15 to 30 seconds, then repeat the stretch on the other side.

Figure 5.27   Seated spinal twist.

Additional Methods of Enhancing Flexibility

In addition to static and dynamic flexibility exercises, several other types of flexibility exercises exist. Ballistic stretching involves quick bounces at the motion extremes and has been recommended in some athletic populations. Because it is potentially harmful if performed incorrectly, it is not recommended for tennis players. Ballistic stretching often elicits the stretch reflex, so it can actually hinder flexibility by setting off a self-protective mechanism in a muscle, causing it to shorten. Ballistic stretching is potentially injurious; it is possible to exceed the extensibility limits of the tissue being stretched, which is harmful to the tissue.

Contract-relax stretching (sometimes called proprioceptive neuromuscular facilitation, or PNF stretching) is a technique that requires the use of an educated and skilled partner to assist with the stretching process. A brief contraction of the muscle being stretched is initially performed, immediately followed by a static stretch of that muscle or muscle group. The theory is that immediately after the contraction of the muscle is an enhanced relaxation of the muscle, making the stretching process easier. Physical therapists, athletic trainers, and certified tennis performance specialists often use this technique when working with injured athletes, and some research has supported this technique's use. If you are using this technique in your training program, be sure the person assisting you has experience with the technique and is qualified to perform it with you.

SUMMARY

Warming up and stretching help tennis players properly prepare their bodies for tennis play and training activities. The shift in focus to dynamic warm-up and dynamic movements preceding tennis play and high-intensity workouts requires players to strategically place static stretching after tennis play and workouts to target key areas of need and maintain proper flexibility to prevent injury and enhance performance. The tennis-specific stretching sequences in this chapter are suitable for tennis players at any level.

Speed, Agility, and Footwork

To be able to play tennis at a high level, you must develop the ability to move quickly in all directions, change directions often, stop, and start, all while maintaining balance and control to hit the ball effectively. Tennis truly is a sport of continual emergencies; with every shot your opponent hits, the ball can travel at a different velocity with a different type or amount of spin and can land in a different part of the court. Therefore, speed, agility, and quickness (i.e., proper footwork) are crucial to good movement and positioning on the court.

Although you should always work on grooving your strokes, don't overlook the importance of working on your movement on the court. Your footwork and movement, just like your tennis strokes, can be improved—if you work at it.

IMPORTANCE OF SPEED WHEN MOVING

Speed is the time it takes to get from point A to point B, and it is an important attribute in tennis. Speed development depends on muscular strength, power, and technique. Training that develops these attributes leads to improved movement and performance on the court. Tennis players can use exercises such as plyometrics to improve speed. Several key ideas about plyometrics are discussed next.

Plyometric exercises can place a great deal of stress on muscles and joints. Start with low-level plyometric exercises such as jumping rope or alley drills before progressing to more advanced drills such as box jumps. Establish a suitable strength base before you begin plyometric exercises.

Although adolescent players can use low-level plyometrics, more advanced exercises should be integrated into a training program only after puberty. Senior players, especially those with lower-limb injuries, should also take care when engaging in plyometrics because of the stress they place on the body.

Although speed is deemed important in tennis, players rarely attain top running speed during match play. In approximately 80 percent of points, the player does not move more than 30 feet (9 meters) from the position where he or she started. Yet within that distance, a player can only attain 75 percent of his or her peak running speed. So, although this chapter presents drills to improve running speed, two even more important concepts are quickness and acceleration.

QUICKNESS

In tennis a quick first step gives a player a distinct advantage. Being able to instantly recognize and react to the shot the opposing player is using can be the difference between getting to a ball or not, or attacking a ball to a winner as opposed to pushing back a defensive shot. Quickness is the ability to read, react, and explode—read and process cues as to what is happening, react with the appropriate response, and explode with quickness and power to maximize the time you have to set up for your shot.

All of these factors can be grouped into the term *response time,* which is the time it takes for a player faced with a decision or cue to make the appropriate movement. Response time takes into account both the time it takes to process the information and choose a response and the time it takes for the muscles to contract and the movement to occur. Accordingly, total response time depends on a player's reaction time (which deals with anticipation and the speed at which information is processed by the brain) and movement time (which concerns how quickly the muscles are activated and the movement is executed).

Response time = reaction time + movement time

By performing tennis-specific movement and agility drills, players can improve both reaction time and movement time, resulting in improvements in on-court movement. These improvements are exhibited by better agility and quickness.

REACTION TIME

Much of quickness depends on anticipation (reaction time). A player who is able to predict what is going to happen has an advantage over an opponent. Even if the player is not able to predict exactly what is going to happen, if he or she can at least narrow the options to a manageable number, the player has gained an advantage.

The first key to developing good anticipation skills is developing the ability to read cues from the opposing player. Where do you look when you watch your opponent? One of the differences between expert and novice players is where they focus their attention as their opponent hits the ball. Novice players' eyes drift around without focusing on any one particular area. Expert players focus on the racket and lower part of the dominant arm. Focusing on this area allows them to anticipate the type of shot and direction the ball will be hit. Expert players can even predict where the body is going to go when other parts of the body are blocked from view, eliminating cues that could be detected from that part of the body. The key is to focus on the upper body and the swing path of the racket as much as possible.

Second, know the possible shots that can be hit based on the court geometry and your opponent's position. A player drawn out wide and hitting on the run is likely to hit down the line rather than come across the court. Eliminating possibilities will also allow you to react more quickly to a shot. The more choices you have, the longer it takes you to choose the appropriate response. For example, a player who knows he or she is only going to have to move left or right (two choices) is going to be able to react more quickly than a player who has to choose between moving forward, backward, left, or right (four choices). By knowing the possibilities available to the opponent, you can improve your court position and take control of the point.

Third, know the tendencies of your opponent. Some basic scouting can help you anticipate the shots your opponent will use in specific situations. Maybe your opponent likes to serve down the T on big points. Knowing this information can give you an advantage when facing this situation.

Players can use many drills to improve movement efficiency, but drills also provide an opportunity to train cue identification and anticipation. For example, when performing a drill, it is important to initiate the drill using a tennis-specific cue or action. When performing a movement drill in which the player needs to move to the right or left, rather than shout "Right" or "Left," the coach holds a tennis ball out to one side or the other to indicate which way the player should go. In this way the player reacts to a visual stimulus rather than a verbal stimulus.

POSITIONING

One of the most important things in becoming a good tennis player is to be in the correct position to hit the ball. You must have good footwork so that you can get to the ball, and you must have proper balance once you get there. Players need to be in the correct position to provide a solid platform from which to hit the ball.

Balance

Keeping your body and racket under control while you are moving is often referred to as dynamic balance. Static balance (balance without movement) is more easily learned; a typical balanced position is one in which your feet are shoulder-width apart and your center of gravity is directly over your feet. Although it provides a stable base of support, this position is not always possible while playing a point, especially when you are pulled wide for a shot. The key, however, is to try to control your center of gravity as much as possible while you are playing. Proper posture is critical in this regard. Bending at the knees and not the waist for shots will help you maintain good posture. In addition, having minimal head movement not only allows you to maintain better balance, it helps you see the ball better. To optimize movement efficiency, keep your head up and face forward. Reaching or lunging for shots pulls your body off balance, which keeps you from producing powerful shots and slows your recovery.

When responding to an opposing player's shot, your center of gravity cannot be so far outside of your base of support that you are unstable or overcommitted. In tennis, the preparatory movement before such a change of direction is the split step.

Split Step

Although many players are aware of the importance of a split step when preparing for a return of service, it is equally important to focus on the split step in preparation for each of your opponent's other shots. The purpose of the split step is simply to ready the body to move in any direction by putting the leg muscles "on stretch." Typically, the split step involves a slight hop followed by a lowering of the body into the ready position (figure 6.1). The ready position, with weight on the balls of the feet, knees slightly bent, and feet shoulder-width apart allows a player to initiate the split step instantly. The split step is similar to a skier "unweighting" when making a turn. The unweighting (hop) is immediately followed by a contraction of the lower-leg muscles. The leg muscles are stretched at the landing from the split step and store elastic energy, much like a rubber band does. The energy stored in these muscles allows the player to generate a more powerful and explosive movement to the next ball. The best players actually prepare for their next movement while still in the air by slightly turning the foot closest to the ball in that direction. The foot turn is the result of a whole-leg rotation from the hip. This slight outward rotation at the hip enhances a player's ability for lateral movement.

Figure 6.1 Split step: *(a)* ready position; *(b)* initiation of the split step; *(c)* first step.

First Step

The first step toward the ball is the most important. The split step helps you overcome resting inertia. Certainly, recognition of where the ball is going and subsequently initiating movement in that direction as quickly as possible helps the player get from point A to point B faster. Tennis along the baseline is often a series of glide steps, with some crossover steps involved during different periods (especially during change-of-direction and recovery movements). However, when full speed is needed (for example, when your opponent hits a drop shot), an explosive first step becomes vital to quick movement. You can test your short-distance speed with a 20-yard dash test (see chapter 4). First-step explosiveness requires good lower-body power, which also allows a player to accelerate and decelerate quickly.

AGILITY TRAINING

Agility is the ability to change direction efficiently. In a typical match, players need to make a series of directional changes during nearly every point. Agility not only requires the muscular strength and power to decelerate and then accelerate in a different direction, it also depends on flexibility and balance. Great movers typically have great agility and a diverse athletic background that allows them to develop kinesthetic awareness of how the body can move in balance.

The great thing about movement and agility drills is that they often can be integrated into on-court training time and do not necessarily require separate training time. Several tennis-specific drills are included in this chapter.

As you would do with any drill that draws heavily on strength and power, perform these drills when your muscles are fully rested. Provide appropriate rest between sets, and do these types of exercises at the start of a training session before muscles become fatigued. Quality is more important than quantity.

Maintain peak intensity. If you start to fatigue or you see a drop in intensity, stop the drill or give yourself more rest between efforts. For many people, this may mean performing a drill for only 5 seconds. More advanced players strive to do the exercises outlined in this chapter for 10 to 20 seconds while maintaining technique and explosiveness.

AGILITY DRILLS

Lateral Alley

Focus

Improve movement, agility, and footwork; improve tennis-specific conditioning when done multiple times or with other agility and movement drills.

Procedure

1. Start outside the doubles sideline facing the net (figure 6.2a).
2. Shuffle (sidestep) into the court, getting both feet over the singles sideline (figure 6.2b).
3. Quickly reverse direction, and shuffle (sidestep), getting both feet over the doubles sideline (figure 6.2c).
4. Perform this side-to-side movement pattern for 10 to 20 seconds.

Variation

Perform the drill while holding a racket. Hold the racket in the dominant hand as if you were playing a point.

Figure 6.2 Lateral alley drill: (*a*) stand outside doubles sideline, facing the net; (*b*) shuffle both feet over the singles sideline; (*c*) shuffle both feet over doubles sideline.

Forward and Backward Alley

Focus

Improve forward and backward movement, agility, and footwork.

Procedure

1. Start outside the doubles sideline, facing into the court (figure 6.3a).

2. Run into the court, getting both feet over the singles sideline (figure 6.3b).

3. Quickly reverse direction and backpedal, getting both feet over the doubles sideline (figure 6.3c).

4. Maintain good body position (head up, upper body straight, and knees slightly bent). Do not run with your weight on your heels when moving backward.

5. Perform this drill for 10 to 20 seconds.

Figure 6.3 Forward and backward alley drill: (a) stand outside doubles sideline, facing court; (b) run both feet over the singles sideline; (c) backpedal both feet over the doubles sideline.

Lateral Cone Slalom

Focus

Improve lateral movement, agility, and footwork.

Procedure

1. Line up 10 to 12 cones along the baseline about a yard (0.9 m) apart.

2. Start at one end of the cones, facing the net.

3. Slalom (weave) through the cones using small adjustment steps, moving slightly diagonally forward and backward until you reach the end of the cones (figure 6.4).

4. Facing the net, shuffle (side-step) back to the starting position, and repeat.

5. Repeat from the other side of the line.

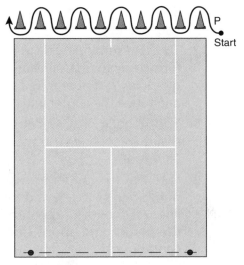

Figure 6.4　Lateral cone slalom.

Forward and Backward Cone Slalom

Focus

Improve forward and backward movement, agility, and footwork.

Procedure

1. Line up 10 to 12 cones along the baseline about a yard (0.9 m) apart.

2. Start at one end of the cones, facing the cones (across the width of the court).

3. Weave through the cones using small sideways adjustment steps, moving forward slightly diagonally until you reach the end of the cones.

4. Backpedal through the cones to the starting position, and repeat.

Spider Run

Focus

Improve movement, agility, and footwork.

Procedure

1. Start at the center mark on the baseline, facing the net.

2. Turn and sprint directly to the corner formed by the baseline and the singles sideline (figure 6.5). Decelerate, and touch the corner with your foot.

3. Sprint back to the center mark, maintain control, and touch it with your foot.

4. Sprint to the corner formed by the right singles sideline and the service line. After regaining control, touch the corner and sprint back to the center mark.

Figure 6.5   Spider run.

5. Next, sprint to the T and back to the center mark.

6. Then sprint to the corner formed by the left singles sideline and the service line.

7. Finally, sprint to the corner formed by the left singles sideline and the baseline.

8. Rest for 30 seconds, and repeat in the other direction.

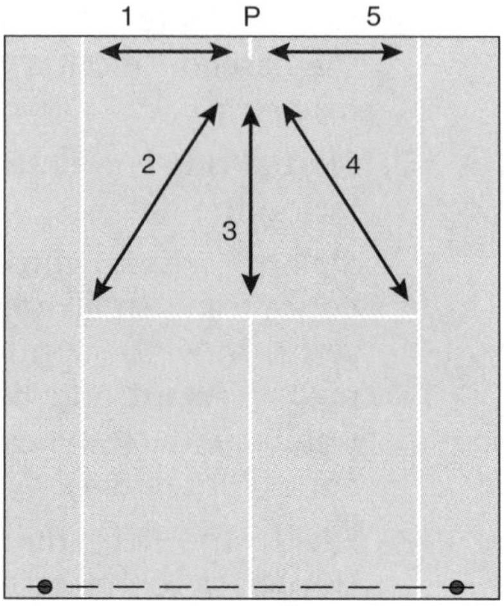

Variations

- Pick up a tennis ball at each station and return it to the center mark on the baseline.
- Simulate a shot at each station. Simulate all forehands, all backhands, or a combination, for example, forehand when moving right, backhand when moving left.

Cross Cones

Focus

Improve movement, agility, and footwork.

Procedure

1. Place cones A and B about 5 yards (4.5 m) apart on the service line so that the center service line (T) is in the middle of cones A and B (figure 6.6).

2. Place cone C about 4 yards (3.6 m) from the T on the center service line.

3. Place cone D 6 to 7 yards (5.5-6.4 m) from the T closer to the baseline.

4. Start at the T, facing the net.

5. Shuffle (sidestep) between cones A and B three to five times, then sprint to cone C on a command from the coach.

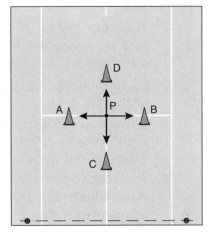

Figure 6.6   Cross cones.

6. At cone C, maintain control, then turn and sprint to cone D.

7. After decelerating and regaining control, turn and sprint to the T.

8. Resume shuffling between cones A and B.

9. Continue the action for 10 to 20 seconds.

Variation

Perform the drill with a racket in your hand. Hold the racket in the dominant hand as if you were playing a point.

Figure 8

Focus

Improve lateral, forward, and backward movement; agility; and footwork.

Procedure

1. Place two cones about 4 1/2 feet (1.4 m) apart; this is the width of the doubles alley (figure 6.7).

2. Start behind one of the cones, facing the net.

3. Move around the cones laterally and slightly diagonally, tracing a figure 8 around the two cones.

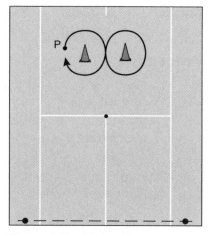

Figure 6.7 Figure 8.

4. The footwork involves small sideways adjustment steps with some small backward and forward adjustment steps.

5. Continue the drill for 10 to 20 seconds.

6. Repeat the drill, starting in front of a cone and facing the net. Move in a forward and backward figure-8 pattern around the cones.

Variation

Perform the drill with a racket in your hand. Hold the racket in the dominant hand as if you were playing a point.

Four-Cone Square

Focus

Improve movement, agility, and footwork.

Procedure

1. On a court, place four cones about 6 yards (5.5 m) apart to create a square (figure 6.8).

2. Starting at cone A and facing the net, sprint to cone B.

3. After regaining control, make small adjustment steps to completely circle cone B.

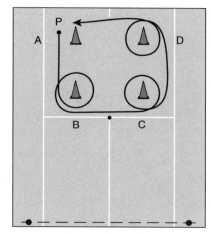

Figure 6.8 Four-cone square.

4. Shuffle (sidestep) from cone B to cone C.

5. After decelerating at cone C, go around C, again making small adjustment steps, and backpedal to cone D.

6. Go around cone D, making adjustment steps, and shuffle to cone A.

7. Repeat the action, starting at cone D and progressing to C, B, and finally A.

8. Perform this drill two or three times in each direction, resting 20 to 30 seconds between efforts.

Variation

Perform the drill without adjustment steps by sprinting from cone A to B, shuffling to C, backpedaling to D, and shuffling laterally back to A.

Service-Box Crossover

Focus

Improve lateral movement, agility, and footwork; improve crossover technique, acceleration, and deceleration.

Procedure

1. Start with one foot in the doubles alley and the other foot in the singles court, facing the net.

2. Using the foot in the doubles alley, cross over in front and move across the court sideways, using crossover steps, until the inside foot gets to the center of the court.

3. Decelerate and change directions, repeating the crossover movement with the other leg.

4. Return to the starting position. Continue the movement for 10 to 20 seconds.

5. Repeat two or three times with 15 to 30 seconds of rest between each repetition.

Variation

Cross half the court six times, then sprint through the other doubles sideline.

Forward and Backward

Focus

Improve forward and backward movement; improve transitions, agility, and footwork.

Procedure

1. Place one cone 5 to 6 feet (1.5-1.8 m) in front of the baseline and a second cone 5 to 6 feet (1.5-1.8 m) behind the court.
2. Start on the baseline, facing the net.
3. In each variation of the drill, move forward and backward, taking a stroke at each cone.
4. Visualize the ball's path over each cone, and see yourself hitting a perfect shot.
5. For the forehand/forehand short–deep combination, start on the left side of the cones (if right-handed; right if left-handed) and alternately stroke a forehand over each cone.
6. For the backhand/backhand short/deep combination, start on the right side of the cones (if right handed; left if left handed) and alternately stroke a backhand over each cone.
7. Perform each drill for 10 to 20 seconds with at least 30 seconds of rest between repetitions.
8. Perform each variation of the exercise two or three times.

Variation

Also perform the drill with the forehand/backhand short/deep combination and the backhand/forehand short/deep combination. During these combinations, you must use a little more dynamic balance and agility because you must cross between the cones and turn your body to perform the strokes properly.

Court Widths (17s)

Focus

Improve movement, agility, footwork, acceleration, and deceleration.

Procedure

1. This drill is timed; set a timer, or have a partner time you.
2. Start at the doubles sideline, facing across the court.
3. Accelerate, and run across the court to the opposite doubles sideline.

4. Reaching the opposite doubles sideline counts as one court width (one repetition).
5. After decelerating and regaining control, accelerate back to the starting sideline, completing the second repetition.
6. Repeat until you complete 17 court widths.
7. Record your time. A good time for boys is less than 50 seconds, for girls less than 55 seconds, and for ages 12 and under less than 60 seconds. You can also use this drill as a fitness test.

Horizontal Repeater

Focus

Improve movement, agility, and footwork.

Procedure

1. Start at the doubles sideline, facing the net.
2. Shuffle (sidestep) to the center service line.
3. Sprint back to the starting position.
4. Turn and sprint across the court to the opposite doubles sideline.
5. Shuffle back to the centerline.
6. Sprint back to the doubles sideline.
7. Turn and sprint back through the starting position; you should start and finish at the same spot.
8. Perform two or three repetitions with 30 seconds of rest between each repetition.

Hollow-Half Horizontal Repeater Variation

After performing steps 1 through 4, instead of immediately performing steps 5 through 8, stop and walk back to the starting position and repeat the sequence.

Variation

Perform the drill with a racket in your hand. Hold the racket in the dominant hand as if you were playing a point.

Vertical Repeater

Focus

Improve forward and backward movement, agility, footwork, acceleration, and deceleration.

Procedure

1. Start at the baseline, facing the net.
2. Sprint to the net.
3. Backpedal to the service line.
4. Sprint to the net again.
5. Turn and sprint back to the baseline.
6. Perform this exercise two or three times with 30 seconds of rest between repetitions.

Variation

Perform the drill with a racket in your hand. Hold the racket in the dominant hand as if you were playing a point.

Diagonal Repeater

Focus

Improve all-around movement, agility, and footwork.

Procedure

1. Start at a corner formed by the baseline and a singles sideline, facing the net.
2. Shuffle (sidestep) along the baseline to the center mark on the baseline.
3. Shuffle back along the baseline to the starting corner.
4. Sprint diagonally to the net where it meets the opposite singles sideline.
5. Backpedal along the singles sideline to the baseline.
6. Repeat the movements in steps 2 through 5 from this back corner.
7. Perform two or three repetitions with 30 seconds of rest between repetitions.

Hollow-Half Diagonal Repeater Variation

After step 5, stop and walk back to the starting position, getting ready to immediately start the next repetition.

Variation

Perform the drill with a racket in your hand. Hold the racket in the dominant hand as if you were playing a point.

Volley Drill

Focus

Improve movement, agility, footwork, and volley technique.

Procedure

1. Place two cones, equidistant from the center service line, about 6 inches (15 cm) in front of the service line. They should be 8 to 10 feet (2.4-3 m) apart from each other.
2. Start the drill just above the service line toward the baseline, facing the net.
3. Alternately move in front of each of the cones, and perform a volley stroke.
4. Recover to the starting position after each volley, and perform a split step.
5. Visualize hitting the perfect volley each time with perfect footwork.
6. Do this drill for 10 to 20 seconds or for a set number of shots. Perform the drill two or three times with 30 seconds of rest between repetitions.

Variations

- Perform a low volley in front of each cone. Be sure to get down well with the legs instead of bending forward at the waist.
- React to a hand signal from your coach or partner whether to hit a forehand or backhand volley or a forehand or backhand low volley.

▶ # Forehand and Backhand Agility

Focus

Improve movement, agility, and footwork.

Procedure

1. Start at the center mark on the baseline, facing the net.
2. Turn and sprint to the forehand side, and perform a stroke even with the singles sideline. Visualize hitting the shot and use proper technique.
3. Recover with a crossover step and a shuffle (sidestep), back toward the center mark.
4. From the center mark, turn and sprint to the backhand side to perform a stroke even with the singles sideline.
5. Again recover with a crossover step and a shuffle, back toward the center mark.
6. Repeat this movement pattern for 10 to 20 seconds or for a specified number of strokes.
7. Perform the entire drill two or three times with 30 seconds of rest between repetitions.

Variations

- For an added challenge, try the next condensed deuce court drill, described next.
- React to a hand signal from the coach whether to hit a forehand or backhand.

▶ # Condensed Deuce Court

This drill is similar to the forehand and backhand agility drill, but it requires quicker footwork because you move only between the sideline and the center mark.

Focus

Improve movement, agility, and footwork.

Procedure

1. Start the drill along the baseline at the middle of the deuce court (for a right-handed player) or the middle of the ad-court (for a left-handed player).
2. Turn, sprint to the forehand side, and perform a wide forehand.

3. Recover with a crossover step and a shuffle (side step), back toward the center mark.

4. After recovering back toward the center of the deuce court, turn and perform a backhand stroke at the center mark.

5. Again recover with a crossover step and a shuffle, back toward the starting position.

6. Repeat this movement pattern for 10 to 20 seconds or for a specified number of strokes. Perform the entire drill two or three times with 30 seconds of rest between repetitions.

Variation

Perform the drill on the ad-side (for a right-handed player) or the deuce side (left-handed player), hitting only forehands. Visualize hitting inside out or inside in from the wide backhand side.

Mini Tennis Z-Ball

Focus

Improve movement, agility, footwork, and reaction time.

Procedure

1. This game is played with two or more players. Players use only the service boxes.

2. Play and score the game like a tiebreaker. Instead of a racket and tennis ball, use a Z-ball (reaction ball). Catch and toss the ball underhand.

3. Using underhand throws, play tennis with your partner by tossing the Z-ball into your opponent's service box.

4. The ball must bounce once in the service box before it is caught. The ball must be caught before it bounces a second time.

5. Play until one player wins a tiebreak game to 7.

Note

If more than two players are involved, play the game using table tennis rules; players alternate in one at a time.

Variation

To make the drill easier, instead of a Z-ball use a tennis ball.

▶ **Medicine-Ball Tennis**

Focus

Improve movement, agility, footwork, core strength, and leg strength.

Procedure

1. Two or more players can play this game. Use only the service boxes. Play and score the game like a tiebreaker.

2. Instead of a racket and tennis ball, use a medicine ball. Catch the ball and toss it from the same side of the body, mimicking a forehand or backhand groundstroke.

3. Be sure to load your outside leg (the leg closest to the ball) behind the ball when you catch it to store energy in the muscles. This will allow you to use the entire kinetic chain to generate force when tossing the ball back.

4. Let the ball bounce once in the service box before catching it.

5. Play until one player wins a tiebreak game to 7.

Note

If more than two players are involved, play the game with table tennis rules; players alternate in one at a time.

ACCELERATION AND DECELERATION

Acceleration is the ability to increase speed rapidly; in other words, it is how well a player can go from a dead stop to full speed. Many players think speed and acceleration are genetically determined; to some extent, they are. However, everyone, regardless of genetics, can improve acceleration by learning some basic drills that teach proper running technique. These drills are outlined later in the chapter.

Deceleration is the ability to slow rapidly. Although a player can attain up to 75 percent of his or her top sprinting speed within 30 feet (9 m), many people expect to decelerate the body from a dead run to a complete stop in one or two strides. This can place a great amount of stress on the muscles and structures that support the knees, hips, and ankles, because muscles contract eccentrically to absorb large amounts of energy. Many strength coaches believe that the ability to decelerate safely and efficiently should be developed before players work on acceleration.

Exercises that develop strength and explosive power, such as plyometrics and variations of Olympic lifts, are essential for laying the groundwork for acceleration and deceleration. Focus on training the body first for deceleration, then for acceleration. Also, work to perform explosive exercises on one leg at a time. In tennis it is seldom that both feet are on the ground at the same time. Players need to be able to maintain balance while generating force when only one foot is on the ground.

Figures 6.9, 6.10, and 6.11 show a simple lower-body plyometric progression that emphasizes deceleration, acceleration, then single-leg power with cue recognition.

Jump from a midsized plyometric box, and absorb the force of the landing (figure 6.9). Land in an athletic position with proper posture. The athletic position is similar to the ready position described earlier; weight is on the balls of the feet, knees are slightly bent, and feet are shoulder-width apart.

Figure 6.9 Phase 1: Deceleration.

Figure 6.10 Phase 2: Deceleration followed by acceleration.

Jump down from a midsized plyometric box, then jump straight up (figure 6.10).

Jump down from a midsized plyometric box, and explode into a run to the right or left depending on a cue from your coach or partner (figure 6.11). A coach or partner may use tennis balls to cue the player.

Figure 6.11   Phase 3: Deceleration followed by acceleration with reaction to a cue.

RUNNING MECHANICS AND FORM

Basic running-form drills are described in this section. Follow these pointers to enhance running technique:

• *Keep the head in line with the body.* Don't lift the chin up or tuck it down toward the chest. You should be able to draw a straight line from the ankle through the knee, hip, shoulder, and ear as the support leg pushes off the ground.

• *Take advantage of gravity.* Gravity is your friend. In most normal instances you want the body to be in balance with the center of mass directly over the base of support. However, when accelerating or decelerating, moving the center of mass outside the base of support and deliberately throwing the body out of balance can help get the body moving. When done appropriately, gravity will pull the body in the direction you want to move.

• *Use the legs appropriately.* When raising the knee, dorsiflex the ankle (pull the toes toward the shin) and land on the balls of the feet. Drive the feet into the ground with the foot making contact just under or slightly behind the body's center of mass.

• *Minimize foot contact time.* Hit the ground and move. The feet should feel like they are popping off the ground. The more time spent in the air, the faster you will be. The more time spent on the ground, the slower you will be.

• *Use the arms.* The arms contribute significantly to running efficiency. Pump the arms in synch with the legs to get more speed. Use a racket to make drills as specific to tennis as possible.

- *Work on various court surfaces if you can.* Movement on hard courts is dramatically different than movement on clay. Practice on various surfaces to get the feel for what it takes to accelerate, decelerate, and change direction while maintaining your balance.

- *Understand ground reaction forces.* When talking about running mechanics, it is wise to remember Newton's third law (for every action exists an equal and opposite reaction). When the foot hits the ground, the ground pushes back. Many players tend to overstride (reach with the foot) in an attempt to get more speed. However, when the foot is in front of the body, the reaction force is directed back toward the body, causing the player to slow down.

RUNNING-FORM DRILLS

High-Knee March, No Arms

Focus

Improve running and movement technique.

Procedure

1. Stand on the doubles sideline, with the body relaxed and little or no weight on your heels. Relax your upper body, and do not use your arms.

2. Lift your left knee high while bringing your heel toward your butt (figure 6.12).

3. Keep your toes up. Imagine you are pulling your toes toward your shin. Do not twist at the hips or shoulders.

4. Drive the leg back down toward the ground, taking a small step forward.

5. Repeat with the other leg. Continue this movement as you march across the court twice.

Note

Keeping the knee up, heel up, and toe up decreases the distance from the hip to the foot, allowing for faster turnover (stride frequency).

Figure 6.12   High-knee march, no arms.

High-Knee March, With Arms

Focus

Improve running and movement technique.

Procedure

1. This drill is done like the high-knee march, no arms, but adds the arm swing.
2. When the arm is next to your side, the elbow should be bent at a right angle.
3. Swing the right arm forward as you bring the left knee up and vice versa for the left arm and right knee (figure 6.13).
4. Raise the hand to about shoulder or mouth level. As the arm swings forward from the shoulder, the angle of the arm may decrease slightly.
5. As the arm swings back, the hand should pass the hip. As the arm continues back, the angle of the arm may increase slightly. This movement, in which the elbow goes back and up and the hand passes the hip serves as your accelerator and is often called "throwing down the hammer."

Figure 6.13   High-knee march, with arms.

6. Continue this movement pattern as you march across the court two times.

Note

The arms are important during sprinting. Many tennis players run with their arms out wide, twisting their bodies, or without using their arms at all.

 ## Skip

Focus

Improve running and movement technique.

Procedure

1. Stand at the doubles sideline, looking into the court.
2. With your arms at your sides, bend your elbows to 90 degrees.

3. Swing the right arm forward as you bring the left knee up and vice versa for the left arm and right knee (much like the motion made in high-knee march, with arms).

4. Perform a skip or slight hop with each step forward as you raise the opposite knee. Lean forward slightly as you skip.

5. Bring the foot down so that it contacts the ground under the body.

6. Continue the movement pattern across the court two times.

Note

In track and field this movement has been termed an "A-skip."

Skip With Leg Extension

Focus

Improve running and movement technique.

Procedure

1. Stand at the doubles sideline, looking into the court.

2. Lift one knee as performed in high-knee march, no arms.

3. As you lift the knee, perform a skip or slight bounce off the ground (figure 6.14).

4. When the knee reaches its highest point, extend the foreleg forward.

5. Just after extending the leg, paw the ground with the foot so that the ball of the foot hits the ground directly under the body.

6. Keep the upper body relaxed, and do not use the arms.

7. Repeat with the other leg while slowly moving forward. Continue across the court two times.

Figure 6.14 Skip with leg extension.

Note

Think *knee up, foreleg reach, paw the ground* as you do this drill. In track and field, it has been termed "B-skip."

▶ Butt Kick

Focus

Improve running and movement technique.

Procedure

1. Stand at the doubles sideline, and rise onto the balls of your feet.
2. Place your hands on your butt, palms facing out.
3. Alternately raise the heels to the buttocks, trying to kick your hands, while running slowly forward.
4. Keep the upper body relaxed, and do not use your arms.
5. Stay off the heels. Do not twist at the hips or shoulders. Keep the knees pointed down.
6. Perform this drill across the width of the court two times, from doubles sideline to doubles sideline.

▶ High-Knee Run, No Arms

Focus

Improve running and movement technique.

Procedure

1. Stand at the doubles sideline, and rise onto the balls of your feet.
2. Alternate lifting the left and right knee up high while slowly moving forward.
3. Put the foot down under the body. To avoid braking or putting the foot down too far forward, remember to keep your nose over your toes.
4. Lean forward slightly. Do not twist at the hips or shoulders or use the arms. Keep the upper body relaxed.
5. Perform the drill across the width of the court two times, from doubles sideline to doubles sideline.

Note

This drill differs from high-knee march, no arms in that the motion is closer to running than just marching and is similar to a football player running through tires.

High-Knee Run, With Arms

Focus

Improve running and movement technique.

Procedure

1. This drill is performed like high-knee run, no arms, but uses the arms.

2. When the arm is next to your side, the elbow should be bent at a right angle.

3. Swing the right arm forward as you bring the left knee up and vice versa for the left arm and right knee (figure 6.15).

4. Raise the hand to about shoulder or mouth level. The angle of the arm may decrease slightly.

5. As the arm swings back, the hand should pass the hip. The angle of the arm may increase slightly. This movement serves as your accelerator and is often called "throwing down the hammer."

6. Continue with this movement pattern as you run across the court two times.

Figure 6.15   High-knee run, with arms.

Note

This drill differs from the high-knee march, with arms in that the motion is closer to running than just marching and is similar to a football player running through the tires.

Variation

Pump the arms as quickly as possible. The legs move as fast as the arms pump. The faster the arms pump, the faster the legs move.

SUMMARY

When you watch the top players in the world, it is apparent that the best players are usually the best movers as well. Proper footwork and agility are critical to success on the court. If you can't get to the ball, it doesn't matter how good your strokes are. In addition, tennis involves nearly every movement imaginable, including changing direction frequently. Players need to learn to go from shuffle steps to sprints, to glides to backpedaling in a matter of a few seconds. The drills in this chapter give you ways to improve your speed, agility, and quickness. This in turn will help tremendously improve your on-court tennis footwork. You'll be amazed at your progress if you perform these drills regularly.

Chapter 7 teaches you the best ways to develop core strength, which will help you have better control and stability and power transfer once you get to the ball. It will also help with energy transfer during all your tennis movements.

Chapter 7

Core Stability Training

Currently one of the most important areas of concentration for training all athletes is the core. Training for tennis is no exception. Core training forms a key part of the resistance training program for tennis players at virtually all levels. In fact, nearly all high-level players use core training as a staple of their training programs for both injury prevention and performance enhancement; so should you.

In a broad sense, you can think of the core as the central third of the human body. More descriptively, the core encompasses the spine, hips, pelvis, thighs, and abdomen. The actual core musculature consists of the abdominal muscles (rectus abdominis, transversus abdominis, and internal and external obliques), low-back muscles (erector spinae, latissimus dorsi, multifidus), and some of the hip and pelvic muscles (gluteals, quadratus lumborum, hip flexors). The key functions of these muscles are to maintain both stability of the region and also, perhaps most importantly for sport, transfer energy generated by the lower body to the upper body through the kinetic chain. In order for the legs and limbs in general to move and function properly, the body must have proper stability in the core. The term *core stability* refers to the ability of the core musculature to control the position and movement of the trunk over the lower limbs. The ultimate end result of proper core stability is the optimum production and transfer of force and motion to the upper body to enhance human performance.

When most people think of the core, they immediately think of abdominal muscles. While the abdominal muscles are a major part of the core, they are just one part of the muscles that comprise this important area. The main, central abdominal muscle is called the rectus abdominis, which runs from the rib cage to the pelvis (figure 7.1).

In addition to the rectus abdominis, several other stabilizers of the trunk comprise the abdominal complex. These muscles include the transversus abdominis (TA), as well as the muscles on the sides, the internal and external obliques. The oblique muscles are mainly responsible for rotating (twisting) the body, which is an essential movement in tennis. These muscles form the main muscles in the front and sides of the core, and they are complemented in the lower back by several important muscles that complete the cylindrical core of muscles that stabilize the trunk. Core back muscles include the erector spinae, latissimus dorsi, and gluteal muscles. Other muscles that contribute to core stability include a group of small muscles on the floor of the pelvis as well as the groups of muscles that move and stabilize the hip joints.

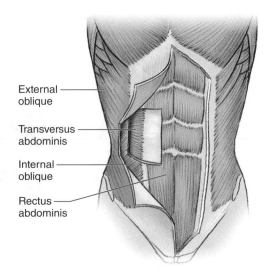

External oblique
Transversus abdominis
Internal oblique
Rectus abdominis

Figure 7.1 Abdominal muscles.

UNDERSTANDING CORE CONCEPTS

To best demonstrate the ways in which the muscles of the core are used during tennis, this text reviews the pertinent mechanics and muscles used during the tennis service motion (see figure 2.5 on page 19).

During the service motion, the abdominal muscles eccentrically contract (lengthen) to stabilize the spine as it extends back, allowing the upper body to position the hand and arm in the required cocked position. The back extensors concentrically contract (shorten) during this movement, while the internal and external oblique muscles assist with the rotation of the torso. In addition, the abdominal muscles and back extensors on the left side of the body are both shortening to perform the side bending of the trunk, while the same muscle pairing on the right side of the body is lengthening, allowing this motion to occur with control. As you can see, a complex interplay exists between concentric and eccentric muscle activity among the core muscles to enable just one part of the service motion to occur. This complex series of muscular work is called co-contraction, which means many core muscles activate to stabilize the pelvis, hips, and spine during tennis strokes and tennis-specific movements. To make matters even more difficult on the body, this interaction is required for thou-

CONDITIONING TIP

Elite-level tennis players show greater abdominal strength compared to their low-back strength. Specific exercises are required in order to balance the muscles of the trunk for preventing injury and enhancing performance.

sands of serves, tennis strokes, and movement patterns as a player trains or competes in a tennis tournament. Tennis players need core strength, power, and muscular endurance. Exercises chosen to train the core should involve co-contraction of many of the core muscles in a stabilizing fashion to closely mimic the function required during tennis.

Strong rationale exists for the emphasis on core stabilization training for tennis players. On virtually all tennis shots, the abdominal muscles contract at very high levels (near their maximum capability) to stabilize the trunk. Therefore, tennis players rely on these important muscles during tennis performance.

The high level of abdominal strength and relative weakness in the lower back among tennis players compared with the rest of the population highlights the importance for balanced training of the core. Sports medicine and fitness professionals must not strengthen the abdominal muscles only (as was done for many years using sit-ups), they must also to focus on the low-back muscles. This idea makes sense when you think of the trunk as a cylinder to be trained all the way around from the front to the back.

An estimated 75 percent of all strokes in the modern game of tennis involve forehands and serves (which, for a right-handed player, requires forceful trunk rotation to the left). Given this fact, trainers may wonder whether tennis players have greater strength during side-to-side rotation in one direction versus another.

In fact, most tennis players have rather equal rotational strength to both the forehand and backhand sides. Therefore, training the core in tennis players must involve rotational training to both the forehand and backhand sides. Whether training both sides equally, or if rotational strength to one side is weaker, emphasis should be placed on balancing a player's rotational strength through a well-designed strength and conditioning program.

TRAINING THE CORE

Now that you have a clear definition of the core and core stability as well some of the characteristics and demands playing tennis places on this area of the body, you can better understand why you need a tennis-specific

---

CONDITIONING TIP

Research shows that elite-level tennis players have similar strength when rotating from one side to the other. Therefore, be sure to include training exercises that encourage balanced strength rotating to both the left and right in your training program.

---

training program for the core. When creating such a program, keep in mind these key components:

- Use methods and exercises that include strengthening the entire abdominal complex, including the lower back.
- Use movement patterns that include trunk rotation whenever possible.
- Include multiple sets of exercises to encourage muscular endurance.
- Think of the core as a cylinder. Include the muscles in the front, back, and sides in your program.
- To promote balanced strength, use rotation in both directions.

This book has emphasized the importance of testing and identifying where each individual player's needs are. Core training is no different. Using the tests for core stability and power in chapter 4 can help you to identify the need for specific areas of training and also gauge progress in those areas when re-testing occurs.

ABDOMINAL EXERCISES

Drawing In

One of the first strategies you can apply when performing exercises for developing the core involves the drawing-in maneuver. Initially you can apply this maneuver by itself to learn the concept and the exercise, and later it you can use it more functionally during a simple exercise such as an abdominal crunch or a complex exercise such as a lunge with rotation. Performing the drawing-in maneuver has been shown to increase the intensity of muscle involvement in the transversus abdominis and other stabilizing core muscles to increase the effectiveness of any core exercise.

Focus

Improve the strength of the transversus abdominis and the stabilizing core muscles.

Procedure

1. Lie on your back on a stable surface or exercise ball, or stand upright.
2. Draw in (suck in) your abdomen (figure 7.2). This action is similar to the action you would do if trying to get into a pair of pants that are just a little too tight.
3. Another way to think of this maneuver is to visualize pulling the belly button back toward the spine.

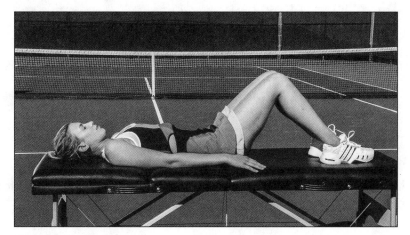

Figure 7.2   Drawing in.

Note

Two excellent examples of core exercises for the abdominal muscles during which you can simultaneously perform the drawing-in maneuver are the traditional abdominal curl (crunch) on an exercise ball and the dead bug exercise.

Abdominal Curl on an Exercise Ball

Use of an exercise ball for virtually any exercise increases the activity of the trunk muscles by forcing the player to stabilize and balance during the exercise movement. The abdominal curl exercise uses only a small range of motion, because flexing the spine more than 45 degrees serves mainly to strengthen the hip flexor muscles and therefore detracts from the primary goal of the exercise—strengthening the abdominals.

Focus

Strengthen the trunk muscles and improve balance.

Procedure

1. Lie with your back on an exercise ball with your feet flat on the ground and hands across your chest.

2. Drawing in your abdominal muscles, lift your shoulders and upper body (figure 7.3).

3. Do not lift your torso past 45 degrees and hold at the top of the movement for one to two seconds.

4. Lower the shoulders and upper body to the starting position, and repeat for 15-30 repetitions.

Figure 7.3 Abdominal curl on an exercise ball.

Advanced Variations

• Use a medicine ball and partner to provide overload and explosiveness during the exercise (figure 7.4a).

Figure 7.4 Advanced variations of the abdominal curl on an exercise ball: (a) with medicine ball and partner.

- Couple the upward (flexing) motion of the trunk with rotation to engage the oblique muscles (figure 7.4*b*).

Figure 7.4 *(continued)* Advanced variations of the abdominal curl on an exercise ball: (*b*) with trunk rotation.

Dead Bug

The practicality of the dead bug exercise is that it activates the trunk muscles and stabilizes the spine while the arms and legs are moving, similar to what tennis players have to do while moving on the court and during the execution of virtually any tennis motion.

Focus

Strengthen the trunk muscles and spinal stabilizers.

Procedure

1. Lie on your back with your hips and knees bent 90 degrees; arms are flexed to 90 degrees and point straight up in the air (figure 7.5*a*).

2. Draw in your abdominal muscles (see Drawing In, discussed earlier). While keeping your back stable, alternately lower your right arm and left leg, keeping your other arm and leg stationary (figure 7.5*b*).

3. As you lower your left leg and right arm, focus on keeping your back and torso braced, working the abdominal and low-back muscles. Hold this position for about 1 second, and return to the starting position.

4. Lower the left arm and right leg while keeping the other arm and leg stationary.

5. Continue this sequence, alternating arm and leg pairs until you fatigue and cannot maintain the stable trunk position.

Figure 7.5   Dead bug: (a) starting position; (b) right arm and left leg lowered.

Note

If this exercise is too difficult and you find yourself unable to stabilize your trunk as you lower the arm and leg, try lowering only one leg, keeping the arms stationary. Once this becomes easy, progress to using the alternate arm and leg pairs.

TRUNK ROTATION

In addition to traditional abdominal exercises, important exercises for the tennis player involve trunk rotation.

Seated Ball Rotation

The seated ball rotation uses an exercise ball to challenge the stability of the player and engages multiple muscle groups and a medicine ball for overload and explosiveness. This exercise simulates the actual stroke patterns of forehands and backhands and can be varied by changing the weight of the ball, direction of the tosses (down-the-line or crosscourt throws) as well as the distance between the partner who is tossing and the exercising player.

Focus

Improve trunk rotation, working all the core muscles.

Procedure

1. Sit on an exercise ball with your feet on the ground approximately shoulder-width apart.
2. Holding a 4- to 6-pound (1.8- to 2.7-kg) medicine ball, simulate a forehand groundstroke, throwing the medicine ball to a partner who is 5 to 10 feet (1.5 to 3 m) away.
3. Repeat multiple times (e.g., sets of 30 seconds) in crosscourt and down-the-line patterns.
4. Perform similar patterns using the backhand groundstroke pattern.

Sit-Up With Medicine Ball Rotation

This exercise combines a sit-up with rotational movements in an endurance format to improve strength and muscular endurance.

Focus

Improve core muscles with rotation.

Procedure

1. Lie on your back with a 4- to 6-pound (1.8- to 2.7-kg) medicine ball in your hands.
2. Sit up approximately 30 to 45 degrees, holding the medicine ball in front of you.

3. While maintaining this position, rotate the medicine ball in both hands from side to side, gently touching the ground with the ball just beside your legs (figure 7.6). Alternate left and right rotations.

4. Repeat for 15 to 20 touches per side, maintaining the sit-up position before returning back to the ground.

5. Repeat for multiple sets to promote muscular endurance (3-5 sets).

Figure 7.6   Sit-up with medicine ball rotation.

▶ Sit-Up With Medicine Ball Rotation Catch

This exercise includes a plyometric medicine ball catch and release to provide additional training stimuli to the core muscles. It emphasizes sustained contractions of the core to foster local muscular endurance.

Focus

Improve core muscles during rotation, improve deceleration.

Procedure

1. Lie on your back with a 4- to 6-pound (1.8- to 2.7-kilogram) medicine ball in your hands.

2. Sit up approximately 30 to 45 degrees, holding the medicine ball in front of you.

3. A partner stands several feet (1-1.5 m) to one side. Maintaining your sit-up position, toss the ball in an underhand fashion, simulating a two-handed groundstroke to your partner.

4. The partner catches the ball and throws it back to you. Catch the ball, and rapidly throw it back to your partner again.

5. Repeat for 15 to 20 repetitions before returning to the starting position.

6. Remember to do the throws to both sides to work trunk rotation in both directions. You can perform these throws alternating or completing a series to one side and then repeated on the opposing side. Do multiple sets of the exercise to improve endurance of these important muscles.

Russian Twist

The Russian twist is another core stabilization exercise that involves tennis-specific rotation while requiring high levels of muscular stabilization to maintain posture and balance. The exercise ball compromises the stability of the player, while the weight of the medicine ball complements the rotational movement inherent in this exercise. One important component of this exercise is the maintenance of the hip and knee position throughout the exercise, which is accomplished by the core stabilizers.

Focus

Improve trunk rotation, stabilization, and balance.

Procedure

1. Lie faceup with an exercise ball under your shoulder blades. Your feet should be shoulder-width apart on the ground and your knees bent 90 degrees. Ensure that your hips are in neutral extension (i.e., don't let your butt sag!).

2. Holding a medicine ball or weight, flex your shoulders close to 90 degrees (hands pointing upward; figure 7.7a).

3. From this position, keeping the abdominal muscles drawn in and buttocks squeezed together, rotate alternately to the left and right slowly and with control (figure 7.7b).

4. Keep the pelvis and torso aligned properly and the elbows extended (arms straight). This exercise also challenges your overall balance as you rotate from side to side. Perform between 10-20 repetitions on each side.

Advanced Variation

To add challenge to this exercise, place a loop of elastic tubing around the thighs to further engage and activate the hip stabilizers.

Figure 7.7   Russian twist: (*a*) starting position; (*b*) rotation.

Lunge With Rotation

Focus

Improve strength of the core stabilizers and quadriceps.

Procedure

1. Standing, hold a weight or medicine ball at shoulder level with the arms extended outward and elbows straight.
2. Take alternating steps forward into a lunge position. Bend the front knee no more than 90 degrees, making sure your knee stays pointed directly over your second toe and does not extend past you toes.
3. When you reach the decent phase of each lunge, rotate the upper body and trunk to the left (figure 7.8*a*), pause a second, return to

Figure 7.8 Lunge with rotation: (a) rotating to the left; (b) returning to center; (c) rotating to the right.

the center (figure 7.8b), pause a second, and then turn to the right (figure 7.8c), pausing a second.

4. Return the ball to the forward position, and lunge forward with the other leg.

5. Repeat this exercise for several sets of 15 to 20 repetitions. Maintain proper posture during the lunge. Avoid bending forward at the waist, and keep the eyes looking forward.

CO-CONTRACTION EXERCISES

Although not truly rotational exercises, two additional exercises are appropriate for this section because they involve muscular co-contraction of many of the core muscles. As stated earlier in the text, co-contraction is the simultaneous activation of multiple muscles or groups of muscles during an exercise or activity. Exercises that promote this type of muscular work are often preferred for improving the stability of a joint or series of joints in the human body. The prone and side plank are two excellent co-contraction exercises for improving core stability.

Prone Plank

The prone plank involves maintaining a properly aligned trunk and hip position for several sets that last a predetermined time. Also important is maintaining proper neck and upper-back alignment. Several sets of 30 seconds in this position is an excellent initial goal; as strength and ability improve, you can increase the length of each set. Rest approximately 20-30 seconds between each set (similar to the rest periods between tennis points).

Focus

Improve core stability.

Procedure

1. Assume a prone (facedown) position on your elbows and toes (figure 7.9).

2. Maintain straight alignment from the head to the heels; don't let your bottom sag or stick up in the air. Minimize wavering or other movement compensation during the period of static hold.

3. Keep the neck aligned so that the eyes are focused down toward the floor at a point approximately 12 inches (about 30 cm) in front of your hands.

4. Maintain this position for several sets of 30 to 60 seconds.

Variations

• If maintaining proper positioning is too difficult for you, try assuming a similar position on the elbows and knees. Lift the feet off the ground, and bend the knees slightly (about 30 degrees). This position is easier due to less loading and muscle recruitment.

• To make the full exercise more challenging, while in the prone position on your elbows and toes, alternately raise each leg approximately 4 to 6 inches (about 10-15 cm) off the ground while maintaining proper balance and positioning. Alternate left and right legs throughout the exercise.

• For a more challenging exercise, increase the hold time and number of repetitions.

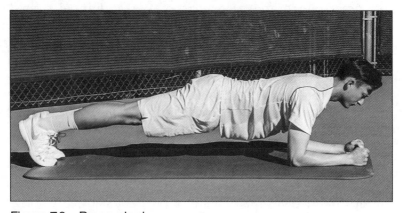

Figure 7.9   Prone plank.

Side Plank

The side plank is particularly important for the oblique abdominals and other muscles on the sides of the body, such as the quadratus lumborum and gluteus medius. Proper alignment is imperative for this exercise, and multiple sets are recommended on both sides. Several sets of 30-second holds can serve as an initial goal; a long-term goal should be to reach 60 seconds with good technique. In order to achieve muscle balance and stay healthy, exercise both sides of the body.

Focus

Emphasize oblique abdominal muscles, quadratus lumborum, and gluteus medius while activating major and minor muscles of the core.

Procedure

1. Lie on one side, positioning yourself on your elbow and the outside edge of the bottom foot (figure 7.10).
2. Maintain straight body alignment, looking directly ahead. Avoid letting the bottom hip sag toward the ground; use your core muscles to lift it upward.
3. Hold this position for several sets of 30 seconds.

Figure 7.10   Side plank.

Variations

- Secure a piece of elastic tubing several feet in front of you. With your non-weight-bearing hand (top hand), perform several sets of 15 repetitions of a rowing exercise while remaining stable in the plank (figure 7.11*a*).
- While maintaining the side plank position, separate the legs, raising the top leg approximately 1 to 2 feet (about 30-60 cm; figure 7.11*b*). Slowly lower the leg back to the starting position. This action further challenges the hip and core muscles. Work up to several sets of 15 repetitions or more as your strength and stability increase.

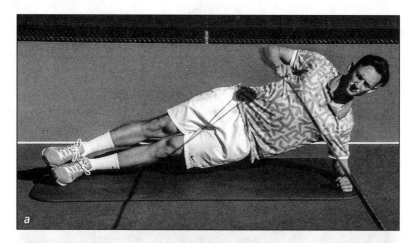

Figure 7.11 Side plank variations: (*a*) with elastic tubing; (*b*) with leg lift.

LOW-BACK EXERCISES

Tennis players need to work on the muscles of the low back to properly balance the muscles of the core.

Superman

This exercise is the simplest one to perform for the low-back muscles (also called the erector spinae, extensor muscles).

Focus

Strengthen the low-back muscles.

Procedure

1. Lie prone (facedown) on the ground with a blanket or pillow under your pelvis if needed for comfort.
2. Reach your arms straight over your head with the palms facing the ground, and extend your legs.
3. Simultaneously lift your feet and hands off the ground; you are now in Superman position (figure 7.12).
4. Hold this position for 1 or 2 seconds before slowly returning to the starting position.
5. During the exercise, draw in the abdominal muscles and tense the gluteal muscles to further challenge the core muscles.

Figure 7.12 Superman.

Variation

Alternate raising only the left arm and right leg together and right arm and left leg together.

Arm and Leg Extension (Kneeling Superman or Quadruped)

Focus

Strengthen low-back muscles.

Procedure

1. Stand on your hands and knees in an all-fours (quadruped) position.
2. Draw in your abdominal muscles, and contract your gluteal muscles.
3. Extend your left arm and right leg. Hold this position for 1 or 2 seconds, trying to maintain stability. Return to the starting position.
4. Extend your right arm and left leg (figure 7.13). Hold this position for 1 or 2 seconds, then return to the starting position.
5. Repeat for the desired number of repetitions (10-15 repetitions each side).

Figure 7.13   Arm and leg extension.

Advanced Variations

- Use hand weights to provide greater resistance, or hook an elastic resistance band around an opposite arm and leg to provide resistance to the movement. Be sure to repeat with the band around the other arm and leg to ensure balanced training.
- Lie on an exercise ball to increase the challenge.

Cobra

This exercise uses trunk extension and also activates muscles in the scapular (shoulder blade) region. Perform multiple sets of this exercise, making sure to engage the gluteal muscles and squeeze the shoulder blades together at the top of the extension.

Focus

Strengthen the low-back muscles.

Procedure

1. Lie prone (facedown) on an exercise ball, with your abdomen on the ball. Place your arms down along your sides.
2. Extend your hips and chest and trunk upward (like a cobra raising its head), rolling slightly forward on the ball (figure 7.14).
3. Hold that position for 1 or 2 seconds, and return to the starting position.

Figure 7.14   Cobra, with arms to the sides.

Advanced Variation

To make this exercise more difficult, move the arms to an overhead position (figure 7.15).

Figure 7.15   Cobra, advanced variation with arms overhead.

Bridge

The bridge is an excellent, no-equipment-required exercise for recruiting the low-back and gluteal muscles to balance the core for tennis players. In its basic form, it is a challenging exercise, but it also can be made more difficult through variations.

Focus

Strengthen the muscles in the core region.

Procedure

1. Lie supine (on your back) with your feet approximately 8 to 12 inches (about 20-25 cm) apart and knees bent approximately 90 degrees. Cross your arms over your chest (figure 7.16a); leaving your arms on the ground will provide artificial stabilization and make the exercise less challenging.

2. Raise your buttocks off the ground by extending your hips (figure 7.16b). Maintain a straight alignment; knees, hips, and shoulders should be in one diagonal line. Hold this position for several seconds (2 seconds for a beginner and up to 10 seconds for an advanced athlete). Return to the starting position.

3. Repeat for multiple sets of 15 repetitions.

Figure 7.16 Bridge: (*a*) starting position; (*b*) bridge position.

Variations

- While holding the bridge position, alternately raise and lower the feet in a marching motion (figure 7.17*a*), lifting them about an inch or two (a few centimeters) off the ground. Repeat until you fatigue to the point you can no longer hold the proper bridge alignment. Return to the staring position to rest and recover. Repeat for multiple sets.

Figure 7.17 Bridge variations: (*a*) marching the feet.

- While in the bridge position, alternate lifting each foot and straightening the leg, holding the pelvis level and taking care not to move (figure 7.17*b*); the lower leg lifts, pivoting at the knee joint while the rest of the body remains stable. Maintain a stable bridge position. Hold the straight-leg position for 1 or 2 seconds before switching legs. Alternate legs for 5 to 10 repetitions, and then return to the starting position. Perform multiple sets to improve endurance. This is an excellent exercise for the gluteal muscles and back extensors (erector spinae and multifidus).

Figure 7.17 *(continued)* Bridge variations: (*b*) straightening one leg.

ADVANCED CORE EXERCISES

For the advanced phase of core training, several exercises ultimately challenge the player's ability to co-contract muscles, maintain proper posture, and perform controlled movements over an exercise ball. Knees to chest, knees to chest with rotation, and diagonal leg tuck all require high levels of core stabilization and body control to ultimately train the core musculature.

Knees to Chest

⊙

Focus

Improve posture and muscle control through co-contraction.

Procedure

1. In a prone (facedown) position, place your hands shoulder-width apart on the ground with an exercise ball supporting your legs just between your knees and ankles; you are supporting yourself on your arms and the ball.
2. While maintaining proper alignment with the abdominal muscles drawn in and the gluteal muscles engaged, bring both knees toward your chest.
3. After a brief pause, extend your knees slowly, returning to the starting position.
4. Repeat the movement for multiple sets of 15 repetitions to improve both strength and endurance.

Knees to Chest With Rotation

⊙

Adding rotation to the knees-to-chest exercise increases the difficulty and the tennis application.

Focus

Improve posture, muscle control, and rotation through co-contraction.

Procedure

1. In a prone (facedown) position, place your hands shoulder-width apart on the ground with an exercise ball supporting your legs just between your knees and ankles; you are supporting yourself on your arms and the ball.
2. While maintaining proper alignment with the abdominal muscles drawn in and the gluteal muscles engaged, rotate your trunk and hips, then bring both knees along a diagonal path toward your chest.
3. After a brief pause, extend your knees slowly, returning to the starting position.
4. Repeat the movement, rotating to the other side.
5. Perform multiple sets of 10 to 15 repetitions to improve your core.

▶ # Diagonal Leg Tuck

Focus

Improve posture, muscle control, and rotation through co-contraction.

Procedure

1. In a prone (facedown) position with an exercise ball under your legs between the knees and ankles, place both hands on the ground approximately shoulder-width apart; you are supporting yourself on your arms and the ball.

2. Take your left leg from the ball, and move it diagonally across the front of your body, reaching the left knee toward the right hip.

3. Hold the end position, then slowly return to the starting position.

4. Repeat the movement, taking the right leg and moving it diagonally toward the left hip.

5. Perform multiple sets of 10 to 15 repetitions to improve your core.

SUMMARY

Many types of exercises can improve core stability. The exercises recommended in this chapter were specifically chosen to address the inherent demands placed on the trunk during tennis play. These exercises emphasize both the abdominal and low-back muscles and truly train the entire core. This chapter especially emphasizes core exercises with rotation, which is a tennis-specific movement. Implementing these exercises in a complete conditioning program will help improve core stability, decrease injury risk, and enhance performance in tennis.

Developing the core is one major aspect of an overall strength and conditioning program. Chapter 8 introduces other tennis-specific exercises to develop upper- and lower-body strength.

Strength Training

Players such as Serena Williams, Andy Murray, and Madison Keys have the ability to hit the ball just as hard in the first game of a match as in the final game of the third or fifth set. These professional players have committed themselves to performing strength training exercises that allow effective energy transfer for one stroke and to developing muscular (strength) endurance so that they can perform tennis strokes at a high level for an extended period of time. This chapter defines common strength training terms, outlines critical components of a strength training program, and provides examples of tennis-specific exercises to improve muscular strength and endurance.

Strength training is a type of exercise that requires the muscles to move or attempt to move against some type of opposing force. *Strength* is defined as the maximum amount of force a muscle can produce. From an athletic perspective, absolute strength is the largest amount of force someone can produce, irrespective of the time it takes to move the force. Think about the performance of a squat. Absolute strength would be measured by the amount of weight (pounds or kilograms) that is on the bar. *Power,* on the other hand, is defined as the amount of work performed per unit of time. Therefore, the absolute resistance is only half of the equation. The time it takes to move the resistance is just as important. To be powerful, you must have the required amount of strength and be able to move forces quickly. Power exercises, including plyometric movements, are discussed in more detail in chapter 9.

Tennis players must have high levels of muscular strength and, because of the repetitive nature of the game, must also be able to repeatedly contract their muscles. The ability to repeatedly contract a muscle or group of muscles is referred to as *muscular endurance.* Training your muscles for tennis must address all three areas: strength, power, and endurance.

TYPES OF RESISTANCE TRAINING

Several types of resistance are used in developing muscular strength. *Isometric (static) strength training* refers to a type of training that uses isometric muscle contractions. An isometric contraction of the muscle is one in which no shortening or lengthening of the muscle fiber takes place. No joint movement occurs with this type of training. An example of an isometric exercise is placing the palms of your hands together in front of your chest and pushing them against each other. This isometric exercise elicits a contraction of the pectoral and biceps muscles among others. Generally 6 seconds of contraction is suggested for isometrics to provide the most benefit from this type of strength training. Typically significant tennis training time is not spent on isometrics because of their lack of joint movement. Because tennis is a rapid, dynamic sport that requires powerful, repeated contractions of the muscles during body movement, more dynamic forms of strength training are recommended.

Isotonic resistance is characterized by a constant weight or tension and is a more dynamic form of strength training that is beneficial to tennis players. In this form of strength training, actual shortening and lengthening of the muscle fibers occurs along with joint movement. Body-weight exercises; free-weight (barbell and dumbbell) exercises; and exercises that use cable or pulley machines, tubing, medicine balls, and other weight machines are the most common isotonic exercises. An example of an isotonic exercise is a biceps curl with a 20-pound weight in which the elbow joint moves. The muscle fibers shorten (concentric contraction) as the hand and weight lift toward the shoulder, then lengthen (eccentric contraction) as the hand and weight are lowered away from the shoulder. This shortening and lengthening of the muscle fibers during training is beneficial because tennis requires these types of muscle contractions in every stroke and body movement. Typically, eccentric contractions are used to decelerate and control or stabilize the body, and concentric contractions produce movement and accelerate the body.

Each form of isotonic exercise offers advantages and disadvantages for the tennis player; no single best form exists. For example, an advantage of using body weight is that it always is available; you carry it with you wherever you go. However, you cannot easily change your body weight to provide greater resistance as you get stronger.

Free weights are cost effective, but they require greater control during lifting because they don't offer a guided path or movement track like isotonic resistance machines do. The use of free weights forces you to stabilize the weight in all directions while moving the weight in the primary movement pattern. This works the secondary muscle groups that stabilize the exercising joints, but it also requires greater skill and supervision to compensate for having less control.

One additional benefit of isotonic resistance machines is the ability of the machine to vary the resistance during the range of motion used during exercise. Look at the pulley system on many resistance machines. Instead of being perfectly round, many are kidney shaped. This unique shape of the cam or pulley on the machine changes the resistance during the exercise, usually making the weight heavier in the middle of the motion and lighter at the beginning and end of the motion, where the body's musculoskeletal system is least efficient.

Another type of isotonic resistance uses elastic tubing or elastic cords. This form of resistance is desirable because it is cost effective and easy to carry on trips; and it is versatile because the farther you stretch the cord, the greater the resistance you generate. A color-coded system of increasing resistance allows for progressive overload as an athlete develops greater strength due to training.

Whatever type of isotonic exercise you perform, the important factor is movement. The joints move, and the muscles lengthen and shorten to mimic the types of actions you perform when hitting serves, groundstrokes, and volleys. Most of the exercises in this chapter and throughout this book are isotonic exercises and use free weights, elastic tubing or bands, and weight machines.

Isokinetic resistance uses a constant velocity and changing amounts of resistance. It requires the use of a highly technical and expensive machine, which makes it impractical for most players to include in their training. Isokinetic machines are used extensively in injury rehabilitation and in research and have given sport scientists important information about the strengths and weaknesses of the musculoskeletal system of tennis players.

SINGLE-JOINT AND MULTIJOINT FORMS OF STRENGTH TRAINING

Typically resistance training involves two primary forms of exercise: single-joint and multijoint exercises. In a single-joint exercise, one primary joint and muscle group are worked. For example, the leg extension involves only movement at the knee joint and works primarily the quadriceps muscle. The squat is an example of a multijoint exercise that works the gluteals muscles, quadriceps, hamstrings, calf muscles, and others, with movement occurring at the hip, knee, and ankle. Both types of exercises are beneficial to tennis players, but multijoint exercises work more muscles and joints simultaneously and certainly are more time efficient. Multijoint exercises, such as the squat and lunge, require balance, proper form, and training. However, they are considered to be more functional and require greater stabilization of smaller muscle groups.

Single-joint exercises are especially beneficial when it is necessary to strengthen a particular muscle group to alleviate a muscle imbalance. An example of this will be covered extensively in chapter 12 and involves a tennis player's dominant shoulder. Repetitive tennis training leads to preferential strength development of the muscles in the front of the body (internal rotators of the shoulder) because of the use of those muscles during the acceleration phases of the serve and forehand. This development creates a muscular imbalance in the shoulder because the external rotators, which are crucial for stabilizing the shoulder and decelerating the arm, become underdeveloped (lack necessary strength) and overshadowed by the powerful internal rotators. Tennis players use mainly single-joint exercises to help balance shoulder strength in the dominant arm and to prevent injury and enhance performance. See chapter 12 for greater detail.

ADAPTATIONS TO STRENGTH TRAINING

Adaptations to resistance training can be broken into two primary forms: neural and morphological. *Neural adaptations* involve the nervous system and its response to resistance training. Neural adaptations can occur in as little as 2 weeks after initiating a resistance training program. When you feel stronger after a couple of weeks of lifting weights, it is primarily because the nervous system is becoming more efficient in the way it recruits ("talks to") the muscle. This recruitment in turn makes you feel stronger, even though little change has occurred within the muscle structure itself.

Morphological (structural) adaptations involve the actual structure of the muscle. Some debate still exists among scientists regarding the exact mechanism of this muscular adaptation. One theory, called *hypertrophy,* explains the increase in the overall size of the muscle as an increase in the cross-sectional area of the existing muscle fibers in the muscle—the muscle fibers that you have, get bigger. The second theory, called *hyperplasia,* states that the increase in overall size in the muscle in response to training occurs when the existing muscle fibers split, resulting in a greater number of muscle fibers. Regardless of the mechanism of muscular adaptation, it takes at least 6 weeks for this type of improvement to occur with training. Therefore, when starting a strength training program for tennis, realize that although you may experience immediate improvements in the way you feel, it will take at least 6 weeks for true changes to occur in the muscle itself.

Misconceptions regarding strength training are prevalent among the athletic and general populations. One of the most common myths among tennis players is that lifting weights will make players bulky and muscle bound and have a negative effect on speed and tennis strokes. This misconception is most easily addressed by educating players and having them follow a strength training program specifically for tennis players. A well-structured, tennis-specific strength training program is personalized to each player's needs. Some athletes need more muscle mass to be able to produce greater forces; others need greater muscular endurance and stability. However, all tennis players can benefit from a high-quality strength training program. As with any type of training, a poorly designed program can cause harm. You should seek training by a qualified instructor who has experience working with athletes, specifically tennis players, and understands how to effectively design tennis-specific training programs. Look for a certified strength and conditioning specialist or a certified tennis performance specialist with a strong educational background and practical experience.

Another myth associated with resistance training is that it will cause stiffness and loss of flexibility. Again, a resistance training program specifically geared for tennis players that uses full ranges of motion and is used along with a comprehensive flexibility program (outlined in chapter 5) not only will prevent a loss of flexibility but should improve flexibility, optimize performance, and prevent injury.

DESIGNING A TENNIS-SPECIFIC STRENGTH TRAINING PROGRAM

The first step in designing a strength training program for any athlete is to develop a needs analysis. Figure 8.1 highlights factors to consider during this first step.

- Chronological age
- Training age (number of years the athlete has been seriously training)
- Body type
- Preexisting general and specific fitness levels
- Strengths and weaknesses identified by the coach, physical therapist, athletic trainer, physician, strength and conditioning specialist, sport chiropractor, certified tennis performance specialist (CTPS), or strength and conditioning coach
- Strengths and weaknesses identified by the player
- Strengths and weaknesses identified by sport-specific field testing and appropriate lab testing, if available and relevant
- General health status
- Status of current or previous injuries
- Tournament and competition goals

Figure 8.1   Factors to consider during a needs analysis.

The concept of specificity is of vital importance. Every resistance exercise program must contain exercises that address the demands inherent in the sport or activity the athlete performs. Knowledge of the biomechanical demands of the sport is also important in the design of a program. It is beneficial from a stroke-specific perspective and also from a movement aspect.

Biomechanical analysis also helps sport scientists to design strength training programs specifically for tennis players. For example, consider shoulder exercises. Analysis of the tennis serve has shown that the shoulder is raised only to about a 90-degree angle with the body at ball contact. The reason the racket is so high over a player's head during a serve is that the trunk is bent at an angle that allows the shoulder to remain in this position and still lets the player hit the serve with maximum efficiency. Awareness of this biomechanical information motivates the recommendation for shoulder exercises that do not raise the arms higher than they are during actual tennis play; in this case, the limit would be above shoulder level. The following sections provide guidelines for developing a tennis-specific strength training program.

Sets

A *set* is a group of repetitions. Typically, 2 to 6 sets of an exercise are required to improve strength and muscular endurance. For tennis, usually 2 to 4 sets of an exercise are recommended. Performing multiple sets of an exercise provides greater benefits than performing a single set and the high volume of training and practice required for player development have led to the recommendation that tennis players use multiple sets of resistance training exercises. Assume that the following exercises all require multiple sets. Rest periods may vary for types of exercises and how these exercises are included in daily, weekly, monthly, and yearly programming. More rest is required for power movements and absolute strength. Less rest is required for muscular endurance and hypertrophy.

Repetitions

The number of *repetitions* performed per set not only determines the amount of work done but also regulates the amount of weight lifted and therefore the intensity of the exercise. For developing power and strength, sets of 3 to 6 repetitions are usually enough, because the higher resistance loads bring about fatigue during the small number of repetitions. Athletes performing sets with more repetitions use less weight than they would when performing sets of 3 to 6 repetitions. Sets of 6 to 15 repetitions develop muscular strength and local muscle endurance. Sets with 15 to 25 repetitions are mainly used for low-intensity muscle endurance and are geared more for muscular endurance. Sometimes they are performed in circuit training formats. Very high-repetition sets (more than 25 repetitions) with very light weights are often used during the early phases of injury rehabilitation.

What is the optimal number of repetitions in a set for a tennis player? Most experts recommend sets of 10 to 15 repetitions, because they provide a strength training and muscular endurance stimulus, both of which are required for tennis. The higher number of repetitions also means the athlete will use a lighter weight. At different times of the training year, the athlete will want to use lower or higher repetitions, depending on goals and timing. Therefore, a structured, periodized training program for the year is key to the tennis player's success.

Intensity

Set the *intensity* of an exercise (determining how much weight to use) by using the repetition maximum (RM) system, which is sometimes referred to as a 1-repetition maximum (1RM) system. In this system athletes select an appropriate weight for a set of exercises that will allow them to perform the desired number of repetitions without breaking proper form and will cause them to feel significant fatigue within the muscle during the last 1 or 2 repetitions of the set. For example, for most players, a 2-pound (0.9-kg) weight for 10 repetitions of a biceps curl would probably not provide enough resistance to cause fatigue by the 9th or 10th repetition. Likewise a weight of 60 pounds would be far too heavy for 10 repetitions of a biceps curl unless you were a 250-pound (113-kg) American football player. When beginning a strength training program, properly applying the RM system takes some trial and error.

Rest

One factor closely tied to the specificity of a resistive exercise is rest. In tennis, the average point lasts less than 15 seconds and is followed by 20 to 25 seconds of rest. Therefore, many of the programs for a tennis player should emphasize 20- to 25-second rest periods between sets. This work-to-rest cycle provides a stress to the muscles similar to the one used in actual tennis play and metabolically stresses the systems used to provide energy to the working muscles just like when you're playing tennis. In addition, because the time needed to perform a complete conditioning program for tennis is precious and limited for all players, to optimize time perform a lower-body exercise, such as the lunge, after working a muscle group in the upper body, such as the triceps. This sequencing allows the triceps to recover without taking long periods of inactivity between exercises.

Frequency

Typically, strength training programs include rest between exercise sessions. Depending on what other elements a player is emphasizing in his or her total conditioning program and where in the periodized training program the player is (see chapter 11 for a complete discussion of program design and periodization), the frequency of strength training can range from once per week to four or five times per week. Most general strength training programs recommend three times per week to build strength, with a day of rest between training sessions. Some players may lift weights nearly every day but alternate the muscle groups and body areas they work so that the working muscles get a day of recovery.

Movement Cadence

The speed at which the weight is moved has a tremendous effect on the quality of the workout. Everyone has seen people working at the gym with too much weight, moving the weight rapidly from start to finish just to complete their repetitions. To ensure good technique when working with heavy resistance, emphasize slow, controlled movement. A slower, more

---

ADDITIONAL STRENGTH TRAINING FACTORS

• **Limit resistance training right before you play tennis.** You don't want to be fatigued while you attempt to perform skill-oriented motor tasks such as serves, groundstrokes, and volleys. It is better to perform resistive exercise sessions on days when tennis workouts are lighter and you can lift weights after you have completed the skill-oriented aspects of your on-court tennis workout.

• **Every good program must be updated and changed based on the principle of overload.** If you always use 10-pound weights to do 10 repetitions of a lunge, in time the exercise will become very easy. To avoid training at too low an intensity level, add resistance when you no longer fatigue by the end of the set. Some athletes increase the number of repetitions by 3 to 5 with the same weight, then when that becomes easy, they return to the original number of repetitions per set but use a slightly heavier weight. Many progressions may be appropriate based on the goals and objectives of a complete conditioning program for tennis.

• **Avoid unnecessary compensation.** If you use too much weight, you will use bigger muscle groups and improper movement patterns that could produce injury. Stay within your own limits of resistance, not the level of your friends or opponents! You should have some degree of supervision or feedback during your resistance exercise program. Have a qualified strength and conditioning specialist, certified tennis specialist, physical therapist, or athletic trainer monitor or at least periodically check your strength and conditioning exercises. Performing an exercise improperly is far worse than not performing the exercise at all.

controlled movement ensures that you raise and lower or push and pull the weight, working the muscle in both the shortening (concentric) and lengthening (eccentric) phases, just as you do during tennis play. Certain movements require explosiveness and quick motion. These types of resistance exercises are described in more detail in chapter 9, which focuses on power.

TENNIS-SPECIFIC RESISTIVE PROGRAM

This chapter provides the general information and background for resistive exercise training and key, tennis-specific exercises that use multiple forms of resistance that fit into nearly any player's training situation regardless of the availability of weight machines or sophisticated machinery and equipment. Review chapter 7 for a complete discussion of core training as well as chapter 12 for detailed information on training the shoulder. This chapter also presents specific training programs that can be performed while traveling, and it presents concepts important for integrating a training program during competition or between tournaments.

LOWER-BODY EXERCISES

Research conducted on elite tennis players shows that lower-body strength is the same on both the left and right sides. Therefore, lower-body training for tennis players should focus on both legs to ensure balanced strength unless one leg has been injured or is underdeveloped structurally. That said, for exercises in which both legs perform the exercise movement simultaneously, such as the leg press, also train each leg independently to isolate each leg and ensure an optimal training stimulus.

Leg Press

Focus

Multijoint lower-extremity exercise that improves the strength of the quadriceps, hip extensors, and calves.

Procedure

1. Several types of leg press machines are available, but nearly all use either a seated or supine (lying on your back) position. Position yourself in the device so that your hips and knees are bent approximately 90 degrees.

2. From the starting position, perform the basic leg press motion of extending the hips and knees simultaneously until the knees reach nearly full extension.

3. Slowly return to the starting position.

4. Perform multiple sets of 8 to 15 repetitions.

Variations

- To increase the number of exercising muscles during this exercise, place a medicine ball between your knees and squeeze it throughout the exercise to keep it in place.

- Decrease the weight, and perform multiple sets of the leg press using each leg independently.

Front Squat

Focus

Strengthen the quadriceps and gluteal muscles.

Procedure

1. Stand upright with feet shoulder-width apart, eyes looking straight ahead. You can hold a dumbbell in each hand and rest them on your shoulders with your elbows pointing forward, or hold a medicine ball or kettlebell with both hands in front of your chest with your elbows tucked into your sides.

2. Descend slowly into the squat, maintaining an upright posture. Do not simply bend forward at the waist. As your knees bend, make sure they are not buckling inward and that you maintain proper alignment. Your knees should be aligned over the second toes of your feet (figure 8.2).

3. As you squat, focus on sitting back and pushing your weight through your heels. If you are struggling with your form, place a bench or chair behind you to provide a feeling of security.

4. Perform multiple sets of 8 to 15 repetitions.

Figure 8.2   Front squat.

Variations

- To make the exercise more difficult, perform the squat on only one leg. This variation further challenges your balance, which is important for optimal tennis performance.
- Stand on a foam platform or mat to challenge your balance. Be sure to look forward and not at the ground.

Partial Squat

Focus

Improve the strength of the quadriceps and hips.

Procedure

1. Begin by standing with the feet shoulder-width apart, looking straight ahead. You can hold a dumbbell in each hand or hold a medicine ball in both hands behind your head and neck to provide resistance. Or you can loop a piece of elastic tubing or an athletic band under both feet, then wrap it in each hand or bring it up over the back of the shoulders to provide resistance as you progress through the partial squat.

2. Bend the knees and flex the hips to descend slowly, keeping an upright posture (figure 8.3). Avoid bending forward at the waist. As your knees bend, make sure they do not buckle inward and that each knee is aligned over the second toe of each foot.

3. Bend to 60 to 90 degrees of knee flexion in a controlled fashion, then pause at the low position for 1 to 2 seconds before returning to the start position.

4. Perform multiple sets of 8 to 15 repetitions.

Figure 8.3   Partial squat.

Note

If you have difficulty with your posture in this exercise, stand with your back against a wall and an exercise ball placed in the small of your back. Perform the partial squat exercise leaning against the ball as you descend and ascend.

Variations

- Perform the partial squat on one leg to further challenge your balance system, which is essential for optimal performance in tennis.
- Stand on a foam platform or pad during the exercise to further challenge your balance (figure 8.4). Be sure to look forward and not at the ground as you perform the exercise.

Figure 8.4   Partial squat variation, one leg on a foam pad.

Lunge

Focus

Improve lower-body strength.

Procedure

1. Stand with your feet parallel and shoulder-width apart. Start by performing the lunge using only your body weight. For greater resistance, grasp a dumbbell in each hand or hold a medicine ball behind your head and neck with both hands.

2. Keeping an upright posture, step forward with one foot, absorbing the load of the body and bending the front knee into a lunge position (figure 8.5). To protect your knee, allow the front knee to bend no more than 90 degrees. Ensure that your knee is directly aligned over the second toe of the foot.

Figure 8.5   Lunge.

3. Immediately push off the front foot to return to the starting position.

4. Perform a lunge with the other foot; you have now completed 1 repetition.

5. Complete multiple sets of 8 to 15 repetitions.

Tennis-Specific Lunge

Focus

Improve lower-body strength.

Procedure

1. Stand with your feet parallel and shoulder-width apart. Start by performing the lunge using only your body weight. For greater resistance, grasp a dumbbell in each hand or hold a medicine ball behind your head and neck with both hands.

2. Keeping an upright posture, perform these tennis-specific lunging movements:

   Lunge forward (figure 8.6a), and return to your starting position.

   To perform a 45-degree forward lunge, position your right foot forward and on a 45-degree angle (figure 8.6b), then return to your starting position.

   To perform a 45-degree backward lunge, position your right foot backward and on a 45-degree angle (figure 8.6c), then return to your starting position.

   To closely mimic on-court movement patterns, perform a crossover step for more tennis specificity (figure 8.6d).

3. Performing each of the four movements on both the right and left leg is considered one repetition.

4. Complete multiple sets of 4 to 6 repetitions (4-6 on left and right legs), alternating right- and left-leg sequences.

Figure 8.6   Tennis-specific lunge: (a) forward lunge; (b) 45-degree forward lunge; (c) 45-degree backward lunge; (d) cross-over step.

Variation

Have a partner stand behind you, looping a long piece of elastic tubing or exercise band around your waist. The partner provides resistance as you step forward into your lunge. This variation not only provides resistance but also challenges your balance.

▶ Calf Raise

Focus

Strengthen the calf muscles (gastrocnemius and soleus).

Procedure

1. From a standing position, feet parallel, shoulder-width apart, come up onto your toes, raising your heels off the ground. For added resistance, hold a dumbbell in your hand.
2. Hold the position for 1 or 2 seconds, and slowly return to the starting position.
3. Perform multiple sets of 8 to 15 repetitions.

Variations

- Place a wood block under the toes to force the ankle to move against a larger range of motion during the exercise.
- To work the deeper calf muscle (soleus), sit in a chair with your knees bent 90 degrees. Place a barbell or dumbbell across your thighs to produce resistance. Raise your heels off the ground, hold for 1 to 2 seconds, and return to the starting position. Place a block of wood under the toes to make this exercise more challenging.

Multihip

Focus

Strengthen the core and lower extremities.

Procedure

Many types of multidirectional hip machines exist. The main advantage of this machine-based exercise is that you can easily work the hip in all four directions of movement (in, out, forward, and backward) with minimal setup or change. Some machines require you to perform the exercise from a seated position; others require a standing position. If you perform the standing version, both legs work at the same time—the stance limb (for stabilization) and the moving leg.

Monster Walk

Focus

Strengthen the hips and core.

Procedure

1. Stand with your feet slightly closer than shoulder-width apart in an athletic stance. Loop an elastic band around your ankles. (Note: The band should not be so heavy that it limits your ability to move and take steps. A light band will go a long way in providing resistance as you exercise, and you can always progress to a heavier band if you feel the band is too easy.)

2. Take a lateral step with one foot while keeping tension on the band. Do not stare at the ground; keep your head up, and maintain an upright posture.

3. Bring the other leg toward the one you initially stepped with, planting the foot while maintaining tension in the band. Your goal is to maintain a shoulder-width hip position throughout the steps.

4. Repeat for 10 to 15 steps in one direction and then change directions and perform 10-15 repetitions on the opposite direction. Perform this movement slow and controlled.

Variation

Perform this exercise on court by taking lateral steps from one doubles sideline to the other, working both hips. You can also take steps forward and diagonally; however, the side-to-side movements are helpful for the hips and core.

Elastic Band Kick

Focus

Strengthen the hips and core.

Procedure

1. Stand with your feet about shoulder-width apart, your weight on one leg, and a band looped around both ankles, similar to the starting position of the monster walk.

2. Keeping an upright stance and slight bend in the knee of the supporting leg, quickly move the other leg to the side lifting approximately 12 inches (30 cm) high and back to the starting position.

3. Keeping light tension in the band, continue kicking with the same foot for 30 seconds (figure 8.7a).

4. Rest for 20 seconds, then repeat the exercise, making rapid forward kicking motions lifting approximately 12 inches (30 cm; figure 8.7*b*) high.

5. After another rest period, make rapid kicking motions in a backward direction approximately 12 inches (30 cm) high for another 30 seconds (figure 8.7*c*).

6. Repeat this series to fatigue on the same leg; then switch to the other leg. You will notice that both the standing leg and working leg work hard and that this exercise challenges your balance. It requires great skill to successfully execute the kick in all three directions while maintaining proper balance.

Figure 8.7   Elastic band kick: (*a*) side; (*b*) forward; (*c*) backward.

Variation

Use a foam balance pad or platform to further challenge your balance system (figure 8.8). If you are traveling and do not have a balance platform, you can stand on a pillow.

Figure 8.8   Elastic band kick on foam pad.

Hamstring Curl

Focus

Strengthen the hamstrings.

Procedure

1. Lie facedown on the ground a few feet from a post or fence. Loop a piece of tubing or elastic band around one ankle, and secure the other end to a sturdy object such as a post.

2. After securing the tubing, position yourself far enough away from the attachment point of the tubing to create slight tension in the band when your leg is extended behind you at a small angle less than 25 degrees (figure 8.9a).

3. Beginning with the leg extended, bend your knee 90 degrees in a slow and controlled manner (figure 8.9b).

4. Return the leg to the starting position.

5. Perform 10-15 repetitions on one leg and then alternate to the opposing leg. Perform multiple sets of this exercise.

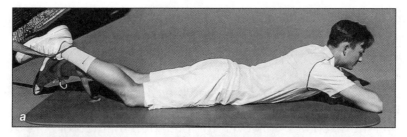

Figure 8.9 Hamstring curl: (a) starting position; (b) curled position.

Note

Be sure to maintain controlled movement during this exercise. A common error is to let the leg rapidly snap back to the starting position rather than using your muscles to decelerate the motion while keeping the knee in a stable consistent position.

▶ Romanian Deadlift (RDL)

Focus

Strengthen the hamstrings.

Procedure

1. Stand with your feet shoulder-width apart and knees slightly bent, similar to an athletic position. Point your toes forward.
2. Hold one dumbbell in each hand in front of the body (a weighted bar can be used as well), and keep your arms straight and down in front of the thighs, resting the weight on the mid-thighs. Keep your chest broad and shoulders back throughout the exercise.
3. Hinging at the hips, slowly lower the weight to the middle of the shins.
4. Hold this position for 1 or 2 seconds.
5. Extend your hips to lift the torso and return to the upright starting position.
6. Perform 6 to 15 repetitions and for desired number of sets.

TRUNK EXERCISES

Review chapter 7, Core Stability Training, for a complete discussion of the specific demands that tennis places on the core and for specific exercises to train this part of the body. You can perform the following exercises using weight machines; however, the preferred method of core training uses body weight, exercise and medicine balls, and other resistance media to foster greater muscular activation and challenge.

In addition to the exercises in this chapter, you should use these exercises (described in chapter 7) as part of a comprehensive core strength program:

Drawing In (page 130)

Abdominal Curl on an Exercise Ball (page 131)

Dead Bug (page 133)

Seated Ball Rotation (page 135)

Russian Twist (page 137)

Lunge With Rotation (page 138)

Prone Plank (page 139)

Side Plank (page 141)

Superman (page 143)

Arm and Leg Extension (Kneeling Superman or Quadruped; page 144)

Cobra (page 145)

Knees to Chest (page 149)

Knees to Chest With Rotation (page 149)

Diagonal Leg Tuck (page 150)

Rotational Chop With Elastic Tubing

Focus

Improve strength and stability of the trunk through rotation.

Procedure

1. Attach a piece of resistance tubing to a fence or pole at least 6 feet (1.8 m) high. Stand tall with a slight bend in your knees with your left side next to the resistance. Grasp the handle of the tubing with both hands together.

2. Using a controlled, rhythmic movement lasting 1 to 2 seconds, with straight arms pull the tubing diagonally across the body high to low (left shoulder to right hip) while bending and rotating at the hips and torso throughout the movement.

3. Slowly return to the starting position.

4. Perform 6 to 15 repetitions, then switch sides. Perform this for multiple sets.

Variations

- An upper-body chop isolates movement in the upper body by keeping the hips and legs anchored to the ground; the hips and legs do not move. The upper body performs the entire movement while the core, hips, and lower body provide stability. This exercise helps develop the muscles for the serve and forehand.

- In the chop with hip rotation, the upper body follows the same movement pattern as in the upper-body chop but in addition the hips rotate at the same time as the upper body. This movement more closely mimics the actual movement of a tennis stroke and allows for a greater range of motion.

Trunk Rotation

Focus

Improve stability in the core.

Procedure

1. This exercise uses a trunk rotation machine. Sit in the machine with the hips and knees bent 90 degrees.

2. Rotate the trunk in one direction then the other, selecting a range of rotational motion with appropriate resistance that is comfortable yet simulates the arc of motion you use during your groundstrokes. Move slowly and with control in both directions of this exercise.

3. Perform 10-15 repetitions per side then rest for 30 seconds and repeat for multiple sets.

UPPER-BODY EXERCISES

Research has identified significantly greater strength in certain muscles in the tennis player's dominant arm. The muscles most developed through tennis play itself include the internal rotators of the shoulder, biceps and triceps, and forearm muscles. Some players question whether the non-dominant arm should be trained at all because it is not used as much, especially by players who use a one-handed backhand. The following exercises are useful for training the nondominant arm and should be performed (if time allows) to provide greater muscle balance between the left and right arms.

Several of the exercises, such as the lat pull-down and seated row, work both arms simultaneously and are excellent for promoting muscle balance of the right and left sides. Even though the amount of time available for strength and conditioning exercises is limited and it is more important to train the rotator cuff and scapular stabilizers on the dominant arm, these exercises could be performed on the nondominant arm when possible, perhaps during the preparation phase of a periodized training program (see chapter 11).

For a good rotator cuff and overall shoulder program, use these exercises described in chapter 12, Solid Shoulder Stability, as part of a comprehensive upper-body strength program:

Sidelying External Rotation (page 222)

Shoulder Extension (page 223)

Prone Horizontal Abduction (page 224)

Prone 90/90 External Rotation (page 224)

Lat Pull-Down

Focus

Strengthen the latissimus dorsi, biceps, and scapular stabilizers (rhomboids and trapezius).

Procedure

1. Sit at a lat pull-down machine or stand in front of a doorway or fence with tubing secured above the door or fence.
2. Grab the handles with your hands slightly wider than shoulder-width apart. Pull the handles or ends of the tubing down, bringing your hands level with your sternum (figure 8.10).
3. Slowly return to the starting position.
4. Perform 6 to 15 repetitions for multiple sets.

Note

Many weightlifters pull down behind the head during this exercise. Pulling behind the head is not recommended for tennis players or because it places undue stress on the shoulder stabilizers and the joint.

Figure 8.10   Lat pull-down.

Seated Row

Focus

Improve the strength of the scapular stabilizers (rhomboids and trapezius).

Procedure

1. Sit on a seated row machine or on an exercise ball with tubing anchored at mid-chest level in front of you. You can also do this exercise from a standing position.

2. With your hands in front of you, grasp both handles of the machine or the tubing. If you are a standing, assume an athletic posture and engage the muscles of the core by drawing in the abdominals and tensing the gluteal muscles.

3. Keeping your torso upright and looking straight ahead, pull the tubing or handles toward you until your hands are near the sides of your body. Squeeze your shoulder blades together as your hands come back toward you.

4. Slowly release the weight or tubing to the starting position.

5. Repeat the movement for 6 to 15 repetitions for multiple sets.

Single-Arm Dumbbell Row

Focus

Improve the strength of the scapular stabilizers (rhomboids and trapezius).

Procedure

1. Using a chair or exercise bench or ball for support, use the nonexercising arm and leg to support your body in a bent-over position.

2. Using a dumbbell or exercise tubing or band, begin with the arm fully extended downward. Raise the hand toward your body in a rowing-type motion until it reaches your side (figure 8.11). Squeeze the shoulder blades together as the hand moves toward your side.

3. Slowly return to the starting position.

4. Repeat for 6 to 15 repetitions for multiple sets.

Figure 8.11   Single-arm dumbbell row.

Core Chest Press

Focus

Improve strength of the upper body.

Procedure

1. Secure one end of tubing or a band at shoulder height. Grab the other end of the tubing, and move away from the attachment point until tension occurs. Stand, holding the tubing in your hand. Face away from the tubing's point of attachment.

2. Begin with your hand directly at your side and elbow bent 90 degrees. Be sure you are standing in a good athletic position. Engage the core muscles by drawing in the abdominal muscles and tensing the gluteal muscles.

3. Push the hand holding the tubing away from the body until it is fully extended at shoulder height. Stretch outward at the end of the exercise to move the shoulder blade forward on the upper back. Don't rotate or use the legs or trunk; they should remain stationary.

4. Slowly return to the starting position.

5. Repeat for 6 to 15 repetitions for multiple sets.

Variation

You can also perform this exercise while holding a dumbbell instead of using the tubing.

Biceps Curl

Focus

Improve strength of the biceps brachii, brachia-lis, and brachioradialis.

Procedure

1. Stand with your feet shoulder-width apart and a piece of tubing secured underneath your feet. Grasp the handles on the tubing with your palms up.

2. Keeping your upper arms at your sides, bend your elbows and lift the handles toward your shoulders (figure 8.12).

3. If you have chosen the correct tension, you should feel resistance but not have to arch your back or lean back during the exercise.

Figure 8.12   Biceps curl.

4. Slowly return to the staring position, making sure you don't hyper-extend or lock your elbows.

Variation

You can also perform this exercise while holding dumbbells instead of using the tubing.

Lying Triceps Extension

Focus

Improve the strength of the triceps.

Procedure

1. Lie on your back holding a dumbbell in your hand with your shoulder and elbow bent 90 degrees. Use your opposite hand to support your upper arm and keep it stationary throughout the exercise (figure 8.13a).

2. Straighten your elbow by raising your hand and weight upward, making sure the elbow does not lock (figure 8.13b).

Figure 8.13   Lying triceps extension: (a) starting position; (b) elbow in extension.

Standing Overhead Triceps Extension

Focus

Strengthen the triceps and elbow joint.

Procedure

1. Standing upright, hold elastic tubing in your right hand. Connect the other end of the tubing to the bottom of a fence or other stable support.
2. Lift your arm so your right biceps is next to your right ear and bend your right elbow to 90 degrees (figure 8.14a).
3. Extend your arm by contracting your triceps (figure 8.14b).
4. Slowly lower your arm to the starting position.
5. Repeat the movement for 6 to 15 repetitions, and switch arms. Perform this for multiple sets.

Figure 8.14 Standing overhead triceps extension: (a) starting position; (b) extension.

FOREARM AND WRIST PROGRAM

 ## Wrist Flexion and Extension Curls

Focus

Strengthen the wrist and finger extensors.

Flexion

1. Sit in a chair with the elbow flexed and forearm resting on a table or over your knee. Hold a light dumbbell in your hand. Let the wrist and hand hang over the edge with the palm facing up.

2. Stabilize the forearm with the opposite hand, and slowly curl your wrist and hand upward. Be sure to move only at your wrist and not at your elbow.

3. Raise your hand slowly, hold for a count, and slowly lower the weight.

4. Perform 10-15 repetitions for multiple sets.

Extension

1. Sit in a chair with the elbow flexed and forearm resting on a table or over your knee. Hold a light dumbbell in your hand. Let the wrist and hand hang over the edge with the palm facing down.

2. Stabilize the forearm with the opposite hand, and slowly curl your wrist and hand upward. Be sure to move only at your wrist and not at your elbow.

3. Raise your hand slowly, hold for a count, and slowly lower the weight.

4. Perform 10-15 repetitions each arm and then switch sides. Perform multiple sets.

Radial and Ulnar Deviation

Focus

Strengthen the muscles that stabilize the wrist during tennis.

Radial

1. Stand with your arms at your sides, and with one hand grasp a dumbbell on only one end (similar to a hammer). The weighted end should be in front of the thumb.

2. With the wrist in a neutral position and the palm toward the thigh, slowly cock the wrist to raise and lower the weighted end through a comfortable range of motion (figure 8.15*a*). All the movement should occur at the wrist with no elbow or shoulder joint movement; the arc of movement will be small.

3. Perform for 10-15 repetitions and switch hands and perform the same movement on the opposing hand. Perform this movement for multiple sets.

Ulnar

1. Stand with your arms at your sides and with one hand grasp a dumbbell on only one end (similar to a hammer). The weighted end should be behind your little finger.

2. With the wrist in a neutral position and palm facing your thigh, slowly cock the wrist to raise and lower the weighted end through a comfortable range of motion (figure 8.15*b*). All the movement should occur at the wrist with no elbow or shoulder joint movement; the arc of movement will be small.

3. Perform for 10-15 repetitions and switch hands and perform the same movement on the opposing hand. Perform this movement for multiple sets.

Figure 8.15   Radial and ulnar deviation: (*a*) radial; (*b*) ulnar.

Pronation and Supination

Focus

Strengthen the forearm pronators and supinators.

Forearm Pronation

1. Sit in a chair with one elbow flexed and the forearm resting on a table or your knee. Let the wrist and hand hang over the edge.
2. Use a dumbbell with a weight at only one end (similar to a hammer). The weight is on the thumb side to start. Begin the exercise with the palm upward so that the handle is horizontal (figure 8.16a). Slowly raise the weighted end by rotating your forearm and wrist until the handle is vertical.
3. Pause for 1 second, then return to the starting position.
4. Perform for 10-15 repetitions and switch hands and perform the same movement on the opposing hand. Perform this movement for multiple sets.

Forearm Supination

1. Sit in a chair with one elbow flexed and the forearm resting on a table or your knee. Let the wrist and hand hang over the edge.
2. Use a dumbbell with a weight at only one end (similar to a hammer). The weight should be on the thumb side to start. Begin the exercise with the palm down (figure 8.16b). Slowly raise the weighted end by rotating your forearm and wrist until the handle is vertical.
3. Pause for 1 second, then return to the starting position.
4. Perform for 10-15 repetitions and switch hands and perform the same movement on the opposing hand. Perform this movement for multiple sets.

Figure 8.16 Starting positions for (a) pronation and (b) supination.

SHOULDER PROGRAM

Shrug

Focus

Strengthen the upper trapezius and scapular stabilizers.

Procedure

1. Stand with your feet shoulder-width apart and your arms at your sides, grasping dumbbells.
2. Keeping your arms at your sides, raise your shoulders upward toward your ears (figure 8.17), then squeeze your shoulder blades together while rolling your shoulders backward.
3. Return to the starting position by slowly lowering your shoulders.
4. Perform 6-15 repetitions with a weight that is appropriate. Start light and progress appropriately. Perform multiple sets of this exercise.

Figure 8.17   Shrug.

Prone Fly

Focus

Strengthen the posterior deltoid, rhomboids, and trapezius.

Procedure

1. Lie prone (facedown) on a narrow bench with your feet off the ground.
2. With dumbbells in hand, extend your arms from your sides at right angles (90 degrees) with elbows also bent 90 degrees.
3. While maintaining a right angle at the shoulders and at the elbow, raise your arms until they are nearly parallel to the ground and hold at the top of the movement for 1-2 seconds.
4. Perform 10-15 repetitions for multiple sets.

▶ **Shoulder Punch**

Focus

Strengthen the serratus anterior, an important scapular stabilizer.

Procedure

1. Lie on your back, and hold a small medicine ball or dumbbell.

2. With your arms straight, hold the medicine ball away from your chest. Push the ball toward the ceiling. Even though your arms are straight, you should be able to push the medicine ball up several inches. This extra motion comes from activation of the serratus anterior (a scapular stabilizer), and the resulting scapular motion it produces.

3. Slowly return to the starting position.

4. Perform 10-15 repetitions for multiple sets.

SUMMARY

The resistive exercises and concepts discussed in this chapter are key to developing a successful tennis-specific strength and conditioning program. Adhering to the guidelines and recommendations in this chapter and integrating them with the material presented in other chapters with area-specific guidelines will enable you to perform safe and effective exercises to enhance performance and prevent injury.

The next chapter focuses on improving power production. Once you've developed a strong base, you can learn to use the strength you've gained through power training, another key factor in a complete conditioning program for tennis.

Chapter 9

Power Training

Generating power is a major factor in becoming a successful tennis player. Developing power in your strokes and movements requires appropriate training on and off the tennis court. Before you are able to achieve the major benefits of power training, you must first develop a base of appropriate strength and stability. Chapter 8 gave you the guidelines and foundational exercises for a tennis-specific strength training program. This chapter explains why power training is so important to tennis, and it provides exercises to help you increase your power production.

The basic equation that defines *power* is

power = (force × distance) / time

Usually strength training aims to alter the first half of the equation (force × distance), increasing the ability to apply a maximum amount of force. However, to develop optimum power output, the time component must also be altered. Therefore, a major aim of power training is to reduce the amount of time it takes to apply a set amount of force. Maximum force production occurs when the speed of movement is very low (e.g., performing a one-repetition maximum lift) or zero (e.g., when performing an isometric exercise). In tennis, having maximum force is not as important as having a very high power output. That is one of the major reasons why training for power is so important. Conversely, as the speed of movement increases, force decreases. At very high speeds, such as when sprinting to a ball or accelerating the racket, force production is low. An optimal point for power development is achieved between the extremes of high force/low speed and low force/high speed movements; that is, maximal power output occurs at intermediate velocities when lifting medium loads as quickly as possible.

Plyometrics are exercises that involve explosive and rapid movements in a special sequence. Plyometric exercises are characterized by an initial eccentric (lengthening) contraction immediately followed by an explosive concentric (shortening) contraction. You can perform many of these exercises using your own body weight; over time you can add external resistance such as bands, medicine balls, dumbbells, weight vests, sandbags, and other implements. Plyometric exercise is one of the best-proven ways to develop power in athletes.

Keep in mind that when the goal is to develop power, you need to attempt to move as quickly as possible and with good technique, whether you use body weight only or apply added resistance.

Box Jump

Focus

Improve strength and power of the muscles in the lower body.

Procedure

1. You will need a 12- to 42-inch (30- to 107-cm) box, depending on your ability.

2. Stand facing the box, approximately 1 to 2 feet (0.3-0.6 m) from the box, with your feet shoulder-width apart and hands relaxed by your sides (figure 9.1a).

3. Jump up onto the box. Focus on touching down as softly as possible on top of the box and sitting back into your hips (figure 9.1b). This focus develops good landing mechanics and reduces the impact on the knee joints.

4. Step off the box, back to your starting position. Focus on absorbing the shock and landing as softly as possible. Keep your chest upright, and maintain a solid posture to absorb the forces produced during the landing.

Figure 9.1   Box jump: (*a*) starting position; (*b*) jump onto box.

5. Perform 3 to 8 repetitions with a short rest between each repetition to allow for explosive movements. The goal is to jump explosively, so resting between repetitions provides a contrast to the powerful movement.

Single-Leg Box Jump Variation

A more advanced version of this exercise is to perform the same movement using one leg. Use a box that is lower in height. Start at a very low height, and progress gradually to taller boxes. Remember, this version is an advanced exercise; you should perform it only after many months of training so that you have developed the appropriate strength and stability base.

Depth Jump

Focus

Improve strength and power of the muscles in the lower body.

Procedure

1. You will need a 12- to 42-inch (30- to 107-cm) box, depending on your ability. Stand on top of the box (figure 9.2a).

2. Step down from the box. Land on both feet (figure 9.2b) and immediately spring up, jumping as high as possible (figure 9.2c). Try to be on the ground as short a time as possible. Land softly from the jump.

3. Turn around, step back up onto the box, and repeat the process for 3 to 8 repetitions. The goal is to jump explosively. After resting, repeat for an appropriate number of sets.

4. Perform between 2-4 sets with extended rest of between sets 90-180 seconds

Figure 9.2   Depth jump: (a) starting position; (b) landing; (c) jump.

Single-Arm Rotational Dumbbell Snatch

Focus

Improve vertical power production of the muscles in the lower body.

Procedure

1. If you are a right-handed player, stand with a dumbbell in your right hand. (A left-handed player holds a dumbbell in the left hand.) Hold your right hand diagonally across your body, slightly outside your left knee (figure 9.3a). Maintain a tight and stable core and a slight bend in your knees with your feet shoulder-width apart.

2. Rapidly move the dumbbell diagonally from the left knee to an overhead position to the right of the head, ending with the arm extended beside the head (figure 9.3b). Keep the elbow straight.

3. Perform the appropriate number of repetitions (usually less than 8), and then repeat with the opposite arm for coordination and muscular balance.

4. Perform between 2-4 sets with extended rest of between sets 90-180 seconds

Figure 9.3   Single-arm rotational dumbbell snatch: (a) starting position; (b) dumbbell lift to overhead position.

Dumbbell Jump Shrug

Focus

Improve power in the muscles of the lower body.

Procedure

1. Stand with your feet shoulder-width apart. Tilt slightly forward at the waist. Keep your shoulders back, core tight and stable, head relaxed, and eyes looking forward.
2. Hold a relatively light dumbbell in each hand in front of your body, letting your arms hanging straight down (figure 9.4a). Hold the dumbbells just above knee level. Flex the knees in an athletic position.
3. Explosively jump up by extending the ankles, knees, and hips. Jump as high as you can while simultaneously shrugging the shoulders (figure 9.4b).
4. Land softly with your feet shoulder-width apart. Slightly bend the knees to avoid excessive loading at the knees, hips, and lower back.
5. Repeat this exercise for the appropriate number of repetitions (less than 8).
6. Perform between 2-4 sets with extended rest of between sets 90-180 seconds

Figure 9.4 Dumbbell jump shrug: (a) starting position; (b) jump and shrug.

Alley Hop

Focus

Improve power in the muscles used in lateral movements.

Procedure

1. The distance needed for this exercise is the doubles alley on a tennis court, which has a width of 4.5 feet (1.4 m) and a length of 39 feet (11.9 m).
2. Start at the corner of the doubles sideline and the baseline. From this starting position, jump with your outside leg to the singles line.
3. From the singles line, jump on the outside leg toward the doubles line.
4. Perform the appropriate number of repetitions; 5 to 10 repetitions is a good starting point.
5. After sufficient rest, repeat the exercise for the appropriate number of sets.

Speed-Focused Variation

Explode as quickly as possible from the doubles sideline to the singles sideline. The goal is to see how many line touches you can do in 20 seconds.

Stabilizing Strength-Focused Variation

Jump as high as possible from the doubles line to the singles line. Stick the landing, and hold the position on one leg for 2 seconds.

Explosive Single-Arm Tennis-Specific Row

Focus

Improve strength and power in the muscles used in rotational movements (e.g., forehands and backhands).

Procedure

1. Attach elastic tubing to a fence at approximately hip height.
2. Grasp the tubing with your dominant hand (right hand for a right-handed tennis player; left for a left-handed player), and position yourself in one of the four tennis-specific stances (open, semi-open, square, or closed stance).
3. While maintaining a stable body position, explosively pull your hand toward your rib cage while rotating at the hip.
4. This pulling motion should be performed in all four tennis-specific stances and should also be performed using the opposing hand as

well. Therefore, 8 repetitions (four stances with the right and four stances with the left) constitute one set. Perform the appropriate number of sets based on your training goals.

▶ Medicine Ball Overhead Granny Toss

Focus

Improve power output in the muscles of the lower body.

Procedure

1. Stand upright, holding a medicine ball in both hands. Choose a medicine ball based on your age, stage of development, height, and strength level; 4 to 30 pounds is a possible range.

2. From the standing position, drop into a powerful low squat, keeping the back straight and the legs fully loaded, storing energy.

3. From this loaded position, explode upward via triple extension of the ankles, knees, and hips. Release the medicine ball with both hands overhead. The objective is to throw the medicine ball with maximum power.

4. Perform this movement for the appropriate number of repetitions (1 to 10), taking appropriate rest between repetitions.

Service Toss

Focus

Improve strength and power in the muscles used in the serve.

Procedure

1. Stand on the baseline as if you were getting ready to serve. Hold the medicine ball with both hands down by your waist (figure 9.5a).

2. Load up the medicine ball into your service stance position as you would during the loading stage of the serve (figure 9.5b).

3. Throw the ball as far as possible, mimicking the service motion (figure 9.5c). Focus on getting as much distance as possible with each throw.

4. Perform 3 to 10 repetitions.

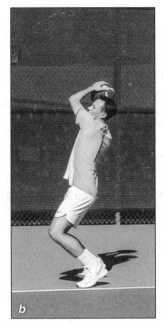

Figure 9.5   Service toss: (*a*) starting position; (*b*) loading the medicine ball; (*c*) throwing the ball.

Forehand Toss

Focus

Improve strength and power in the muscles used in the forehand.

Procedure

1. Stand 8 to 10 feet (2.4-3 m) from a partner. Hold the medicine ball with both hands to your forehand side (right side of the body for a right-handed player; left side for a left-handed player).
2. Step and turn as you would to hit a forehand. Load your body as you would during the backswing of the forehand.
3. Throw the ball to your partner, mimicking a crosscourt ground-stroke.
4. When you receive the ball from your partner, catch and release it back to your partner as quickly and explosively as possible.
5. Perform 3 to 10 repetitions as quickly as possible, then rest. Repeat the exercise for appropriate number of sets.

Variation

Perform this movement using the four major stances for the forehand (open, semi-open, square, and closed).

▶ Backhand Toss

Focus

Improve the strength and power in the muscles used in the backhand.

Procedure

1. Stand 8 to 10 feet (2.4-3m) from a partner. Hold the medicine ball with both hands to your backhand side (i.e., left side of the body for a right-handed player; right side for a left-handed player).
2. Step and turn, just as you would to hit a backhand. Load your body like you would during the backswing of the backhand.
3. Throw the ball to your partner, mimicking a crosscourt ground-stroke.
4. When you receive the ball from your partner, catch and release it back to your partner as quickly and explosively as possible.
5. Perform 3 to 10 repetitions as quickly as possible, then rest.
6. Perform between 2-4 sets with extended rest of between sets 90-180 seconds.

Variation

Perform this movement using the four major stances for the backhand (open, semi-open, square, and closed).

Ball Dribble

Focus

Improve explosive strength of the upper body.

Procedure

1. Holding a small exercise ball or medicine ball, stand 1 to 2 feet (0.3-0.6 m) away from a wall. The distance from the wall depends on the size of the ball. The smaller the ball, the closer to the wall.
2. Hold the ball in an overhead position such that your shoulder is raised to about 90 degrees (figure 9.6).
3. Rapidly dribble the ball against the wall as quickly and explosively as possible for 30 seconds. The ball will travel only 1 or 2 inches (2.5 or 5 cm) away from the wall as you quickly perform the small dribbling motion.

Figure 9.6   Ball dribble.

4. Rest, then repeat for several sets.

Plyometric Chest Pass

Focus

Improve strength of the pectorals, triceps, and scapular stabilizers.

Procedure

1. Stand 8 to 10 feet (2.4-3 m) from a partner. Hold the medicine ball with both hands in front of your chest (figure 9.7a).
2. Pass the ball to your partner explosively (figure 9.7b).
3. When you receive the ball from your partner, catch and release the ball back to your partner as quickly as possible.
4. Perform 3 to 10 repetitions as quickly as possible, and rest. Repeat the exercise for the appropriate number of sets.

Figure 9.7   Plyometric chest pass: (a) starting position; (b) pass.

Variation

This exercise can isolate the upper body even further if you sit on the ground with your legs straight out in front of you and perform the same movement. This variation requires core stability and prevents the legs from contributing to the movement.

SUMMARY

The benefits of improving power production for all tennis strokes and movements are clear. The exercises in this chapter focus on developing tennis-specific power. Power exercises allow the force developed through strength training to be used in the most productive manner on the court. These exercises build on the strength-training exercises provided in chapter 8. You now have the exercises that focus on moving resistance (whether it be body weight or added resistance) as quickly as possible.

Now that you have developed appropriate power specific to the needs of the tennis athlete, you need to develop tennis-specific endurance so that you can produce the power you have developed over 2 or 3 hours during a long match. The next chapter teaches you how to train your endurance in a highly tennis-specific way.

Chapter 10

Tennis Endurance Training

Optimal tennis performance requires a combination of high-intensity, powerful bursts of activity, such as serve-and-volley sequences or running wide to cover a crosscourt groundstroke, and the stamina and endurance to repeatedly perform these activities over a match lasting several hours. Often tennis practice is even more grueling than match play. Structuring your tennis practice to meet the possible demands of matches is an important component of training specifically for tennis. The intense physical demands in the modern game of tennis require tennis players to possess high levels of both aerobic and anaerobic fitness. As mentioned previously, match analyses indicate that 300 to 500 bursts of energy are required over the course of a tennis match that can last for 2 to 3 hours. Designing a program that addresses a tennis-specific endurance requires attention to both aerobic and anaerobic fitness. Therefore, you should understand the general concepts and inherent characteristics of the anaerobic and aerobic energy systems.

TENNIS: AN AEROBIC AND ANAEROBIC SPORT

Tennis play during singles practice and match play usually rates as a prolonged moderate-intensity exercise activity. One indicator that exercise scientists and medical doctors use to measure exercise intensity is heart rate. Activities are rated as a percentage of a person's maximal heart rate. Maximal heart rate can be measured directly by performing a treadmill or bicycle ergometer maximal stress test that incrementally increases the exercise intensity until the athlete cannot continue. The heart rate (in beats per minute, or bpm) at the time of exhaustion from the exercise workload is the maximal heart rate. When scientific testing is not practical, you can use this equation to estimate maximal heart rate:

maximal heart rate = 220 – athlete's age

Using the formula for a 20-year-old tennis player would result in a maximal heart rate of 200 beats per minute. Exercise intensities would then be expressed as a percentage of the maximal heart rate.

Most tennis players have an intensity level ranging between 60 and 90 percent of maximal heart rate during training and matches. So, for the 20-year-old player, heart rate would range from 120 to 180 beats per minute during tennis play. This heart rate intensity classifies tennis as an activity that meets the requirement of the American College of Sports Medicine (ACSM) for improving cardiovascular fitness.

Tennis play consists of repeated high-intensity bouts of exertion while maintaining a moderate overall intensity throughout performance. Therefore, it poses both aerobic and anaerobic demands.

Although a tennis player's average heart rate for a match may be 140 to 160 beats per minute, this range involves peaks and valleys throughout the match (figure 10.1). To match these changes in intensity, you should use similar heart rate peaks and valleys during training for tennis-specific endurance.

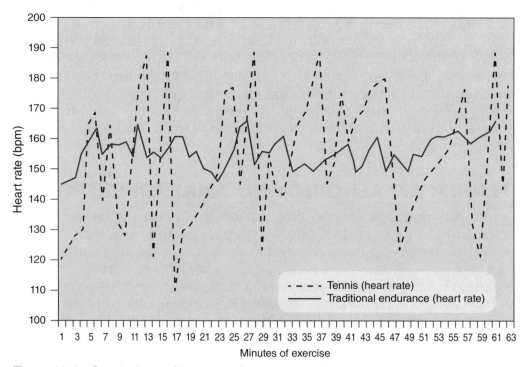

Figure 10.1 Comparison of heart rate between tennis match play and traditional endurance exercise.

TENNIS: A CONTINUUM OF ANAEROBIC AND AEROBIC ENERGY PRODUCTION

Based on the physiological activity patterns of tennis play, a player must develop both aerobic and anaerobic fitness to play at his or her highest level. What exactly does anaerobic and aerobic fitness mean?

Anaerobic means "without oxygen" and refers to two of the energy systems used by the body to produce energy units called adenosine triphosphate (ATP). ATP is required for virtually every activity the body performs, whether breathing, contracting the heart, or engaging muscles to hit a backhand.

Anaerobic energy production, (metabolism), involves two systems. The first and most immediate is the ATP-PC system, which consists of stored energy within the muscles and working tissues. This anaerobic system can produce limited amounts of ATP, only enough to fuel 6 to 10 seconds of maximal-intensity work.

After approximately 10 seconds of intense work, the predominant energy system used by the body is termed *anaerobic glycolytic system*. Glycolysis involves breaking down the carbohydrate taken in by the body from the diet through a complex chemical process and conversion. This process produces ATP. A by-product of anaerobic glycolysis is lactic acid, which is formed during the production of ATP using this system. Eventually with continued high-intensity work by the muscle, lactic acid begins to accumulate in the muscle, and the athlete is forced to stop because of the burning sensation that the lactic acid causes within the muscle.

Anaerobic glycolysis is only an effective energy source for high-intensity exercise lasting 2 to 3 minutes. At that time, exercise activity must either stop or become less intense to allow the next energy system to step in and produce energy for more prolonged activity. This final energy system is the *aerobic energy system*. The aerobic energy system takes in oxygen through the lungs and carries it to the working tissues in the bloodstream. In the presence of adequate amounts of oxygen, the aerobic energy system is a highly efficient producer of ATP and is the primary energy system relied on for long, endurance-oriented sport activities, such as running a 10K or a marathon.

TENNIS AND ENERGY SYSTEMS

Applying the energy system continuum to tennis is easy and helps illustrate the reason that both anaerobic and aerobic conditioning are necessary for enhancing tennis performance. Because tennis ultimately involves repetitive muscular contractions and exertion, the aerobic energy system provides the baseline energy production over the duration of a tennis match or practice session. Aerobic fitness is also important for recovery following a strenuous baseline rally, bursts of movement, and maximal skills such as executing a serve-and-volley sequence or an overhead shot.

Anaerobic energy production is required for maximal activities during points. Testing (in the form of treadmill tests and intermittent endurance runs) on elite tennis players indicates high levels of aerobic fitness. Sprinting and agility tests indicate superior anaerobic power. These results explain a player's ability to maximally sprint from side to side during a baseline rally and then, after 20 to 25 seconds rest, do it again. Athletes with better aerobic fitness levels can clear the accumulated lactic acid from the working muscles more rapidly than players with less aerobic fitness. Likewise, athletes with greater aerobic power can run faster and jump higher because of greater energy stores in the trained muscle. However, tennis requires a balance, and the best tennis players have high levels of both anaerobic and aerobic fitness. Training needs to be structured appropriately to accurately match the demands of the sport of tennis and the player's game style.

TENNIS TRAINING FOR ANAEROBIC POWER

Analysis of tennis matches generally determines that the average point lasts less than 10 seconds; some points can last 20 to 30 seconds. Most players' average rest time is 18 to 20 seconds, with a maximum allowable rest time between points being 20 or 25 seconds, depending on competition rules. The ratio of work time to rest time is termed the *work–rest cycle*. A 1:2 to 1:5 work–rest cycle is most representative of the physiological activity pattern experienced during tennis. This means that for every 1 second of work, you will have 2 to 5 seconds of rest. In practical terms, a 10-second point would result in a 20- to 50-second rest. The reason that some matches involve a work–ratio of 1:5 is that it accounts for the time during change-overs (90 seconds), and some matches have shorter work periods than 10 seconds as well. Therefore, to appropriately cover all environments seen during tennis matches it is appropriate to cycle your tennis-specific training using a 1:2 to 1:5 work–rest ratio. In addition to the work–rest cycle concept, the term *specificity* is often applied. Specificity involves training the athlete in a manner most similar to the actual demands of the sport. It means using movement patterns, distances, and times similar to tennis play. For example, running 5 miles builds aerobic conditioning, but it has very little specificity to tennis play. Performing tennis-specific endurance training involves a number of short-duration, multidirectional movements at high intensity with the work–rest ratios mentioned earlier. This training is more specific to tennis than running at a slow pace for 5 miles.

Anaerobic training techniques in tennis use both concepts of work–rest cycle and specificity. Drills and activities used to improve anaerobic power follow the 1:2 to 1:5 work–rest cycle and include relatively short-duration, multidirectional movement patterns. The characteristics of tennis play that can be incorporated into tennis-specific training include the following:

- A tennis point usually includes four or five directional changes.
- Most tennis points last fewer than 10 seconds.
- Tennis players always carry their rackets during points.
- Players seldom run more than 30 feet (9 m) in one direction during a point.
- Movement patterns contain acceleration and controlled deceleration.

These characteristics can be incorporated into a hitting session with a ball machine or coach (table 10.1). The player takes a 90-second sit-down break between each series. During the 90-second break, the feeder must pick up the balls and prepare for the next series. Heart rate can be recorded at the start and end of each 90-second break between series. The goal would be to reduce heart rate significantly during that time period. Also, you could set up targets to hit within. If so, record the number of balls hit outside the designated target areas. The goal is to keep errors to a minimum during all sequences.

Tennis-specific drills to improve on-court movement and footwork as well as anaerobic power are included in chapters 5 and 6. Any exercise

Table 10.1 Tennis-Specific Endurance Hitting Session

	Series 1		Series 2		Series 3		Series 4		Series 5	
Feed	Balls	Rest (sec)	Balls	Rest (sec)	Balls	Rest (sec)	Balls	Rest (sec)	Balls	Rest (sec)
1	5	15	4	20	10	25	10	20	15	20
2	3	15	20	20	2	25	15	20	10	20
3	6	15	4	20	8	25	20	20	22	20
4	2	15	22	20	18	25	25	20	4	20
5	5	15	10	20	4	25	5	20	20	20
6	3	15	8	20	7	25	10	20	5	20
7	10	15	4	20	22	25	15	20	3	20
8	2	15	25	20	6	25	20	20	16	20
9	15	15	2	20	28	25	5	20	15	20
10	8	15	12	20	5	25	16	20	6	20
11	20	15	22	20	18	25	4	20	18	20
12	5	15	6	20	6	25	10	20	10	20

that includes a relatively short period of maximal-intensity work followed by a period of recovery that is approximately two times longer than the period of work stresses the anaerobic energy system. General anaerobic training drills for tennis include classic on-court movement drills such as cross cones (chapter 6) and line drills such as the sideways shuffle, alley hop, and spider run (chapter 6). To make these general anaerobic training drills more specific to tennis, perform them with a tennis racket in hand as you would do when you play tennis.

Another beneficial training exercise is also sometimes used as a fitness test for tennis. The MK drill (described as a test in chapter 4) is one of the most useful training exercises to develop tennis-specific endurance; it follows ratios of work to rest for tennis and covers distances seen on the tennis court; you sprint 36 feet (10.97 m) in one direction before turning. The MK drill is a good drill that takes 15 to 20 minutes and can be performed on the tennis court once or twice per week as part of a structured periodized training program to help improve tennis-specific endurance.

AEROBIC TRAINING FOR TENNIS

Aerobic means "requiring oxygen." For an exercise activity to stress the aerobic system, you must adhere to several basic concepts. Aerobic exercise training activities typically involve major muscle groups and are repetitive for an extended period of time. Examples of aerobic activities are running, swimming, stair stepping, sliding, and biking. Additional characteristics of aerobic exercise include frequency, duration, and intensity.

Improving and maintaining aerobic fitness levels are important parts of the overall training program for tennis players. Coaches should identify players with low levels of aerobic fitness using the fitness testing guidelines outlined in chapter 4.

Include aerobic exercise depending on the degree of need in the training program. Traditional long, slow, continuous exercise should not be performed frequently, although it is appropriate at certain times throughout the year. The majority of training time should be spent developing aerobic conditioning through tennis-specific endurance activities with work–rest ratios similar to those used in tennis and hundreds of faster bursts with rest periods over an extended period of time. As fatigue sets in, the explosiveness is reduced, although the goal is still to attempt to move as quickly as possible as the exercise continues. Tennis-specific endurance work should be performed after tennis practice, strength training, or other activities in which high-level motor skills are required.

Just as you would with other types of exercise training, start aerobic training gradually, once or twice a week along with other training activities. Progress based on individual needs. In addition, choose an aerobic training activity that best suits you or the player you are coaching. If a player has a history of knee or another lower-extremity injury, adding significant amounts of running to the training program may not be as appropriate as cycling, sliding on a slideboard (or other lateral-movement exercise), or swimming. Use cross-training to prevent boredom, encourage multiple muscle group development, and increase enjoyment. Use testing to measure aerobic fitness levels and gauge improvement. Plan your training sessions wisely. Although aerobic exercise is part of a complete conditioning program for tennis, keep in mind that excessive aerobic training may invite overuse injuries and take precious training time away from anaerobic and skill-oriented tennis training.

SUMMARY

Optimal performance on the tennis court requires high levels of both aerobic and anaerobic fitness, so they must be included in a complete conditioning training program for tennis. Tennis-specific endurance is a combination of anaerobic and aerobic training and is more specific to developing the requirements for the tennis athlete. Testing, re-testing, and tracking changes and improvements in a tennis player's fitness levels can serve as an excellent guide for determining how much training in each of these areas to include during the training cycle (refer to chapter 11). Use varied and creative formats to enhance both aerobic and anaerobic fitness levels, and incorporate the specificity principles outlined in this chapter.

The next chapter outlines the best methods for planning a tennis workout and creating a periodized training program to include tennis-specific endurance training in the most productive manner.

Program Design and Periodization

What is the best way to train the body for tennis? Most people approach training with the philosophy that if some is good, more is better; if a little strength training will improve power, then more will improve power to an even greater extent. Using this philosophy a player may think, *I've seen tremendous improvements in my game while practicing 5 days a week; if I practice every day, I will become even better.* Although these sentiments seem to make sense, they are not necessarily true. Every athlete has a different profile and requires different levels of training and recovery. Physical training is actually a complex science and requires a strong understanding of physiology, biomechanics, and biochemistry to optimize the training to allow for optimum performance at the most important times of year (e.g., major tournaments). Think of the complexity of the human body. If a player wants to optimize performance gains in tennis, it is best to work with these systems and not against them. Structuring your programs to work with your body (and not against it) is the major premise behind sound program design principles.

These two principles govern how the body responds to exercise:

1. **Specific adaptation to imposed demands (SAID principle).** This principle states that the body will respond—and adapt—to the demands that are placed on it. Simply put, if you train by lifting heavier weights or performing more explosive exercises, your body will respond by becoming stronger or more powerful, respectively. This principle may sound as if all you have to do is lift more weight or complete more training, and the body will respond. However, you also need to consider the second principle.

2. **General adaptation syndrome (GAS principle).** The GAS principle states that training effects do not occur overnight; in fact, the body adapts gradually over time, if given adequate time to rest and recover. The body needs time to recover from the stress you put on it. For example, after a stressful day at the office, you are likely to come home agitated, tired, and in need of rest in order to regenerate for the next day. The same is true for physical training; your muscles, hormonal systems, bones, and so on need time to recover following a period of stress, such as a training session.

Considering these two principles together, you can shape the quantity and intensity of training for tennis. More often than not, people miss the recovery portion of the equation, resulting in players who train or compete in a less-than-optimal state. Incorporating this balance between work and rest is the foundation of periodization training.

PERIODIZATION TRAINING

The term *periodization* refers to the systematic process of structuring training and competition into phases to maximize an athlete's chances of achieving peak performances. Periodization typically involves a training plan that includes specified periods devoted to building general fitness and muscular endurance, strength and power, high-intensity training, competition, and rest. When structured appropriately, a periodized training program can optimize a player's performance gains and help a tennis player peak at the most important times of the season. Incorporating appropriate rest, recovery, unloading, and active rest into the periodized training model is crucial in preventing the injury, burnout, and fatigue that can lead to impaired performance.

Think about your own tennis training and what has produced the best results for you in the past. When you do the same thing every day—the same exercises, the same weights, the same intensity—it does not take long before things get boring or stale. If you are like most people, you likely will lose interest pretty quickly. The body likes variation, and the muscles and cardiorespiratory system respond in much the same way as the mind. When things get repetitive, the body tunes out and stops making gains.

Another important aspect of periodized training is specificity, which means matching the training to the demands of the sport and being intentional about what you do. Whether on the court or in the weight room, every training session should have a specific focus and intensity. In addition, every training session should be seen as an opportunity to improve in some way, whether it be a physical or tactical skill for tennis. When you think of what a tennis player needs for top performance, it is easy to assemble a list of attributes that are needed to be successful on the court, such as endurance, strength, flexibility, power, coordination, stability, and many more.

CONDITIONING TIP

Multiple sets of resistance training provide better results than single sets of training.

History of Periodization

Although the concept of periodized training is still not effectively implemented in many tennis players' programs, the ancient Greeks used the concept of alternating periods of intense training and rest with the goal of peaking for important competitions during the early Olympic Games. In the early part of the 20th century, the foundations of modern periodized principles were laid in the former Soviet Union. Although periodized training has been used for some time in other sports, especially Olympic Sports such as weightlifting, track and field, and swimming, it has not yet been fully implemented in many areas of the tennis training environment. Although less research is available on tennis periodization than periodization in other sports, studies have shown that periodized tennis-specific training programs provide better outcomes than non-periodized programs.

Traditional Periodized Training

A well-designed periodized training plan should include a preparation phase, a precompetitive phase, a competitive phase, and an active rest phase.

Preparation Phase

The focus of the preparation phase is on developing a base level of fitness and strength, also called *foundational conditioning and strength*. The training goals of the preparation phase include the following:

- Challenge the aerobic energy system; for example, perform 20 to 40 minutes of aerobic training at 70 to 85 percent of maximal heart rate three or four times per week.
- Establish a strength base; for example, do strength training using a high-repetition (10 to 15 repetitions per set for 2 or 3 sets), low-resistance training program.
- Include technical and tactical training; for example, add on-court training that incorporates changes in stroke mechanics, develops new shots, and other techniques and tactics.

Precompetitive Phase

The precompetitive phase is a period leading up to the competitive season in which the training shifts from general training to training for power and activities more closely related to the demands of the sport. In the precompetitive phase, the intensity level increases, and the goals become more tennis specific. The goals of this phase include the following:

- Challenge the anaerobic energy system; for example, perform on-court training drills and interval training using tennis-specific work-to-rest intervals.
- Improve speed and power; for example, do sprinting and explosive on-court exercises and plyometrics.
- Improve muscular strength; for example, perform 2 to 4 sets with 8 to 10 repetitions, decrease the training volume, and increase the intensity of the resistance exercise.
- Maintain aerobic status; for example, perform aerobic exercise two times per week for 20 to 30 minutes.
- Improve tennis-specific skill; for example, add on-court training focused on tennis-specific drills, practice matches, and simulated points in preparation for competition.

Competitive Phase

During the competitive phase, players should maintain their conditioning and strength over a period of competitions or peak for a specific competition. Training goals are sport specific and include the following:

- Maintain peak performance.
- Keep workout intensity high but overall volume low to limit fatigue. The goal is for the majority of available energy to be used for the competition.
- Participate in tennis competitions or tennis-specific training.

Active Rest Phase

During the active rest phase, the athlete takes a mental and physical break from the sport. It is not a time for the athlete to do nothing, but is a time to cross-train. The goals of the active rest phase include the following:

- Rest from tennis.
- Participate in other activities to maintain fitness levels.
- Emphasize fun, low-intensity workouts.
- Rest for 1 to 4 weeks.

This periodized structure works well for sports with well-defined seasons and off-seasons, but what about tennis? Tennis has no real off-season, and competitions occur almost every weekend throughout the year. Does this training model have a place in tennis? The next section tackles this question.

PERIODIZATION TRAINING FOR TENNIS

The quick answer to the question of whether tennis players can benefit from periodized training is yes. However, several factors make traditional periodized training more difficult in tennis compared to other sports. It is important to recognize these obstacles and acknowledge that they exist before identifying ways to get around them.

Tennis is a year-round sport, which for most players has no well-defined preseason or off-season. Tennis players do not have the luxury of peaking once every 4 years, like athletes in Olympic sports, or even several times per year, like players in many other sports. Tennis players feel the need to be ready to compete at a high level week in and week out. How do you incorporate preseason and off-season training into a training plan if such seasons don't exist in tennis?

A player competing in a tournament does not know when he or she is going to lose. A player can lose in the first round or advance to the finals. This uncertainty makes it difficult to plan a training schedule in advance.

Tennis tends to reward more successful players, allowing them more time to recover between peak performances. Top professional players have the luxury of being able to skip events and still win enough money to make a living or earn ranking points. Similarly, top junior players do not have to chase points across the country or around the world. The players who are trying to make it to the next level feel they have to play more to earn ranking points and consequently have little or no downtime between events. Even in light of these factors, periodization is still important for tennis players. However, training must be approached a bit differently for tennis players than for football players, swimmers, or soccer players.

Obstacles in Tennis

Tennis is a tough sport to train for. It would be great if all a player had to do to optimize fitness, conditioning, and strength was to practice hitting balls and compete. Unfortunately, many players take this approach and never realize that they are selling themselves short and are not reaching their full potential.

A player cannot completely recognize his or her full potential without structured strength and conditioning training. Why bring this point up here, in a chapter on periodization? Because following a periodized training plan means that you may have to sacrifice short-term gains in exchange for greater rewards and improved performance down the road. Periodized training requires that you develop a preseason in which you work on building fitness, strength, power, or whatever attributes are key to your game. It may mean training through some tournaments, during which the priority may be training rather than peaking for competition.

The upside is that when other players are getting injured late in the season or are becoming fatigued, you can draw on the fitness and strength you developed earlier in the year. You are also setting the stage for success years down the road. An 18-year-old player who advances from the junior to the professional ranks without engaging in a strength and conditioning program cannot expect his or her body to transform overnight and be able to compete with adults. Strength training and conditioning must be a part of a developing player's tennis training from early on. This early focus will ease the transition to a higher age group or even the professional ranks. The following section of text outlines the three main obstacles that face tennis players and discusses possible ways to counter them.

Length of the Season

Devoting time within the competitive season (ideally 6 to 8 weeks) to focus on building a base of fitness and strength will serve you well. Keep in mind that although you can still compete during this time, performance may be less than optimal. However, this base will allow for improvement in the areas of fitness or strength and serve as the foundation from which to draw late in the season when other players are faltering. Finding this time somewhere in the competitive season to do high volumes of work—high repetitions—and work hard to build tennis-specific endurance will be beneficial for your long term success.

Not Knowing When the Tournament Will End

This obstacle is a tough one because every week can be different. However, recognize that strength and conditioning training does not necessarily require a weight room or fancy equipment. Players at all levels should travel with equipment. This equipment could include elastic tubing, a stretch strap, a small medicine ball, several cones for movement drills, and a plan for what will happen if they lose in the first round or the second round or make it to the finals so they can start training without missing a beat. Remember that when you aren't maintaining or improving fitness or strength, you are losing it. Therefore, plan for any scenario, and be prepared to train at an event if necessary.

Lack of Rest for Players Chasing Money or Ranking Points

Rest is key for any player, and it is important to incorporate it into your training plan. Players who train or compete day after day with limited or no breaks don't give their bodies a chance to recover, adapt, or grow. The general recommendation is that in a 7-day training week, 1 day be devoted to complete rest with little or no intense physical activity and 1 day involve active rest. *Active rest* means doing something other than playing tennis or training for tennis in the weight room or through on-court conditioning. So, once a week go for a bike ride, play soccer, swim, or do something that still involves activity but relieves the body of the stresses it experiences when training for tennis. Some players may benefit from an extra day of rest, especially after a few weeks of heavy training or extended tournament play.

In addition, players need a period (or periods) during the year away from serious tennis training. Again, it is a time for recovery from the demands of a competitive season and intense training. This rest phase provides not only a physical break but also a mental break, allowing time to recharge. It may seem counterintuitive, especially for a player who feels the need to compete every week to earn every conceivable ranking point. However, think about what happens to the quality of your play when you have no time to recharge or rest. Similarly, recognize that you feel recharged after taking a short break from the sport. Your attitude, intensity, and focus improve after a vacation. The same holds true for your work or study performance, too. Do not shortchange yourself on rest; it pays great dividends down the road. Without these planned rest and recovery periods, the chance of injury, mental and physical burnout, and illness increases. It is much better to reduce the chance of these occurrences rather than trying to reactively deal with them once they occur.

Rest is a vital part of any training plan and is a necessity for any athlete to reach his or her full potential. It is easy for a tennis player to become overtrained (a phenomenon exemplified by sluggishness, tiredness, and feelings of apathy) because of all the training tennis players typically engage in. Although the risk of overtraining is especially high for high-performance players, it is also possible for recreational players to fall into this trap, especially if they are rededicating themselves to fitness or training and making drastic changes to their training plan.

Training Specificity

The term *specificity* refers to how well training matches the physical and physiological demands of the sport. As a general rule, the closer you get to an important competition or a series of competitions for which you hope to peak, the more your training should match the demands of the game. During the time in which you are building a base of strength and fitness, the exercises can be nonspecific. However, the intensity and types of exercises should change as you get closer to your main competitive season. Examples follow.

Strength

When developing a strength and fitness base, perform a high number of repetitions of exercises using weights light enough that you can perform 3 sets of 15 to 20 repetitions. Exercises can include many of the traditional weight room exercises to build strength—squat, lunge, lat pull-down—but limit (or in many instances avoid) overhead lifting. During this period overall general strength is typically the goal.

Once you get closer to the in-season, (competitive) phase, you will increase training specificity and incorporate exercises that involve multiple planes of motion, including rotation. These exercises should engage the entire kinetic chain and incorporate movements similar to those seen in tennis. The number of repetitions will decrease, and the amount of weight will increase (an increase in intensity). In addition, you typically increase the number of sets as your total repetitions are lower. An example is performing 4 sets of 4 repetitions of a partial squat with a medicine ball.

Power

Early in the periodized training cycle, the development of power is usually not the major goal. *Power* means generating force quickly, and you need to build a base level of strength before truly optimizing power output. Engage in low-level plyometrics early on, but as you get closer to the competitive season, shift your emphasis to more exercises that develop explosiveness and power. Power is a major focus of development for nearly all tennis players; structuring your workouts appropriately will aid in this development. Exercises that emphasize power also require increased rest. Take several minutes between sets to ensure high quality.

Tennis-Specific Endurance (Cardiorespiratory Fitness)

As the season progresses, long distance training, which can be used to build a base of cardiorespiratory fitness, should give way to more targeted tennis-specific endurance that incorporates interval training with work–rest ratios similar to what a player experiences in tennis (1:2 to 1:5). For example, perform a movement drill for 10 seconds, and take 20 to 30 seconds of rest.

Sample Periodized Plans for Tennis

A player could structure a season in many ways in terms of the number of tournaments to play and the times at which he or she wants to peak during the year. Keep in mind the guidelines set forth earlier for how much time to dedicate to each phase of training and the ability to peak.

The periodized training program shown in figure 11.1 (page 210) is designed for a player who wants to peak twice in a year. Maybe it is an elite junior player who wants to peak for the International Spring Championships in the spring and the U.S. Open Junior Tennis Championships in late summer. Maybe it is an adult league player who hopes to perform his or her best at the country club spring and summer championships. Although the specific exercises and weights used may differ between these two players, the overall structure of their plans will be similar. Pay attention to the following guidelines:

- In the preparation phase, training volume should be high and intensity should be low to moderate.
- In the precompetition phase, the training shifts to lower volumes but higher intensity.
- During the competition phase, the volume should be very low but intensity should be high. Matches count as high-intensity exercise. Also, players should not be afraid to train during a tournament. Many of the exercises presented in this book can be done on the road.
- During the active rest phase, volume and intensity decrease.

Figure 11.1 shows one possibility for structuring the season; however, it is not the only way. You see that even within a phase, the volume and intensity fluctuate somewhat to provide varied stimuli to the body while also allowing times to recover.

Plan your schedule by first identifying the main tournaments you want to peak for, identifying preparation and precompetition phases, and then varying the volume and intensity of the work within each phase.

Because tennis is a year-round sport and competitions occur very frequently—in some instances three times per month—a traditional

BUILDING YOUR PERIODIZED TRAINING PLAN

1. Start by identifying the most important tournaments on the calendar.
2. Identify a period (or several periods) of 6 to 8 weeks that you are willing to devote to building a strength and conditioning base.
3. Identify a period (or several periods) that you will take off from tennis for an active rest phase.
4. Develop a chart or table, and select an emphasis for each week of the year. For example, during the strength-building phase, the emphasis may be on building tennis-specific endurance. However, 2 weeks before the main competition, the emphasis may be on maximizing power or improving on-court movement.
5. Become even more detailed, and outline exercises, sets, and repetitions for each day. You do not have to lay out every day of the year on January 1, but some foresight should go into your planning, and you should know what you are going to do several weeks or months down the line.

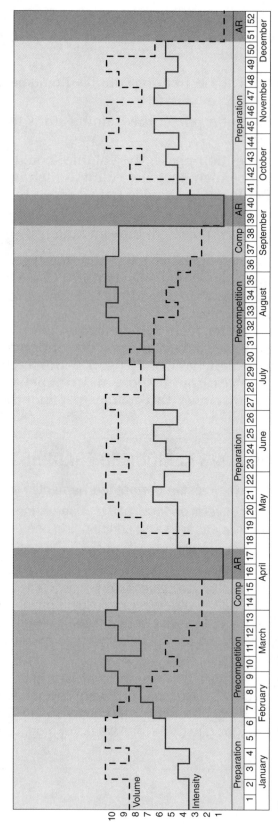

Figure 11.1   Sample periodization training program for a tennis player who wants to peak once in the spring and once in the summer.

Table 11.1 Undulating (Nonlinear) Periodized Weekly Training Schedule

Day	Monday	Tuesday	Wednesday	Thursday	Friday	Saturday
Training component	Speed (<30% 1RM* and very high velocity)	Power (30 to 60% 1RM and highest possible velocity)	Recovery	Strength (75 to 90% 1RM)	Hypertrophy (50 to 75% 1RM)	Muscular endurance (<50% 1RM)

* 1RM = 1-repetition maximum

Adapted, by permission, from International Tennis Performance Association, 2012, *Certified Tennis Performance Specialist (CTPS) workbook and study guide* (Marietta, GA: ITPA).

periodization model as described may be challenging in certain circumstances. Since the early 2000s, an undulating model of periodization has become popular. This model involves performing strength, power, endurance, and hypertrophy (increasing muscle size) all during the same week, with alterations in the intensity and volume based on the goals of the specific week of the program. Table 11.1 highlights how workouts may be structured in a particular week based on this undulating periodized model. This type of programing allows for more flexibility and may be appropriate when daily and weekly structure is altered due to tournament wins and losses, travel schedule, or other interruptions such as weather.

Daily Planning

Once your yearly plan is created with major periods to peak for tournaments, then the process moves into the monthly and weekly planning to structure your programs effectively. From that situation, you move into daily planning which, for most people, is the most interesting. This is when you choose specific exercises, design the flow of the workouts, and decide how on-court and off-court training fit into the overall structure. Significant flexibility exists during these daily workouts as long as the purpose of the day is appropriate and fits within the larger periodized program. The International Tennis Performance Association (iTPA) has provided some good general recommendations to help when structuring daily workouts for tennis (figure 11.2).

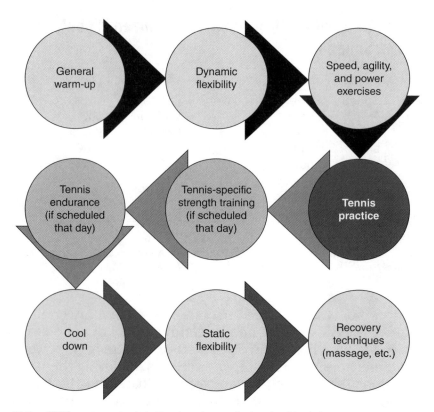

Figure 11.2   iTPA suggested daily structure of physical training.

Reprinted, by permission, from International Tennis Performance Association, 2012, *Certified Tennis Performance Specialist (CTPS) workbook and study guide* (Marietta, GA: ITPA).

TRAINING ON THE ROAD

Changes in strength and conditioning training have made it much easier for tennis players to continue training while on the road. These changes have included a shift away from large machines traditionally housed in gyms and training centers to functional exercises performed on court or virtually anywhere tennis players find themselves. By traveling with several easily portable pieces of equipment, such as elastic tubing and bands, a foam pad, cones, and a medicine ball, players can perform nearly every exercise in this book while away from home.

Another key aspect of strength and conditioning training while on the road is the lack of time available for training while traveling. Therefore, a periodized model is essential for providing an organized and systematically varied program that can be carried out over an extended period. For example, while traveling between tournaments, players typically perform fewer strength and conditioning exercises because of the increased emphasis on tennis-specific, on-court training. However, by using elastic tubing and other portable exercise equipment, players can maintain key strength relationships in the shoulder and upper back or continue working on the hip and core muscles, making the most of their limited time. Targeting the areas of need identified through the testing protocol outlined in chapter 4 is an excellent way to focus on-the-road training in light of the time limitations typically encountered.

SUMMARY

Although tennis is a year-round sport, the concept of periodization training is no less important for tennis players than it is for other athletes. In fact, by properly structuring training and competition into phases, players maximize their chances of peaking at the desired times. A solid program design focuses on the long-term benefits of training, not just immediate results. The previous chapters and video exercises each focused on specific components of a well-designed training program. Planning and organizing these components into a periodized training schedule will allow you to improve your performance at the desired times.

Chapter 12

Solid Shoulder Stability

The shoulder is one of the most frequently injured areas in elite-level tennis players. The stresses on the shoulder are repetitive and can easily lead to overuse injuries if proper technique and strength are not maintained. However, players can prevent many of these injuries by engaging in a strength and conditioning program that targets the muscles of the shoulder and upper back. An understanding of the basic structure and function of the shoulder is important for any tennis player or coach. This chapter provides information about the shoulder and also presents specific exercises that you can use to prevent injury to this critical link in the kinetic chain.

BASIC SHOULDER ANATOMY AND STRUCTURE

The actual shoulder joint, also known as the glenohumeral joint, is best described as a ball-and-socket joint. The head of the humerus (upper arm bone) makes the ball, and it fits into the socket, which is called the glenoid fossa, on the scapula (shoulder blade). This arrangement makes the shoulder one of the most mobile joints in the human body. However, the structure of the shoulder also makes it susceptible to injury. Unlike other joints in the body, the shoulder has few ligaments to provide support; a thin joint capsule provides a small amount of overall stability to the joint. Muscles provide the main stabilizing forces in the shoulder. The most important stabilizers are the four muscles that make up the rotator cuff (figure 12.1)—the supraspinatus, infraspinatus, subscapularis, and teres minor. These muscles help with shoulder movement but also are important for pulling the ball into the socket. Weakness in these muscles, which is common in tennis players, can lead to early fatigue, altered technique, and ultimately injury.

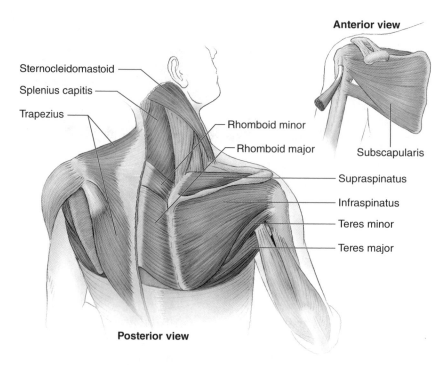

Figure 12.1   View of the shoulder showing the rotator cuff.

In addition to providing stability to the shoulder joint, specific muscles of the rotator cuff contract concentrically to provide powerful internal rotation, the motion a tennis player uses to hit a forehand and accelerate forward to contact the ball on the serve. Other rotator cuff muscles contract eccentrically to provide the critical arm deceleration following ball contact on all strokes. This deceleration of the arm can be stressful to tendons and is one of the main reasons the rotator cuff tendons become overloaded and injured with repetitive tennis play.

CHARACTERISTICS OF THE TENNIS PLAYER'S SHOULDER

It would be natural to think that because of all the balls a player hits, the shoulder muscles in a tennis player's dominant (tennis playing) arm would be much stronger than those in the nondominant arm. In fact, some of the muscles, those that internally rotate the shoulder, are much stronger on a tennis player's dominant side. In the modern game of tennis, forehands and serves make up as much as 75 percent of all shots. These shots involve a great deal of internal rotation and strengthen the internal rotators quite a bit.

However, research has shown that the muscles that externally rotate the shoulder (bring the arm back) can actually be weaker in the tennis-playing arm. This phenomenon is common in tennis players and likely results from the stress placed on these muscles during the follow-through of the service motion, where the muscle works eccentrically (lengthens during contraction). This repetitive stress can overload the muscles and cause tendon breakdown. It then becomes a vicious cycle, because the breakdown contributes to greater weakness, which then places the tennis player's shoulder at an even greater risk for injury. The decreased strength in these important muscles further compromises proper joint function.

The discrepancy between the strong internal rotators and the weak external rotators creates a strength and muscle imbalance in the shoulder. It has been likened to having a sports car in the front of the shoulder (internal rotators) and an old jalopy in the back (external rotators). If left unaddressed, this imbalance can lead to improper tracking, lack of stability, and possibly injury of the shoulder joint.

Many players and coaches ask, "Doesn't playing tennis simply strengthen these muscles? Isn't that all the training I need?" The answer is no. Simply playing tennis does not adequately strengthen the muscles in the back of the shoulder. In an attempt to restore balance to the shoulder, play-ers need to engage in tennis-specific exercises that focus on strengthening the muscles that externally rotate the shoulder as well as the muscles in the upper back that stabilize the shoulder blade. These strengthening exercises need to be done *after* tennis play or on days when limited tennis play occurs. One mistake that players often make is doing shoulder exercises as part of the tennis warm-up immediately prior to tennis play. This mistake can lead to fatigue of the rotator cuff immediately before playing tennis when a strong and nonfatigued rotator cuff is of para-mount importance.

Another adaptation seen in the shoulders of many tennis players is the ability to externally rotate the arm farther than a normal shoulder can (see figure 12.2). This increased flexibility into external rotation, coupled with the fact that the tennis player's shoulder can be unstable, has led therapists to label tennis players

Figure 12.2   External rotation range of motion of the dominant arm in a right-handed tennis player.

as having a "Gumby shoulder" (like the bendable rubber cartoon character). Because of this looseness and increased flexibility in external rotation, players and coaches are cautioned against performing additional stretches of these muscles. Placing the arms behind the body and forcibly stretching the shoulder in external rotation was a common practice among tennis players and baseball pitchers years ago, but based on current research and playing styles it is not recommended today.

Although tennis players frequently show increased flexibility in shoulder external rotation in the dominant arm, research also shows that players tend to have flexibility deficits in the opposite direction (internal rotation) compared to the nondominant arm. This lost internal rotation likely comes from the repetitive overuse of certain shoulder muscles and joint structures, resulting in chronic tightness in the muscles in the back of the shoulder. The loss of internal rotation seems to increase with the amount of tennis a person plays and actually creates harmful movements inside the shoulder that can lead to injury. Tennis players should have a physical therapist or trainer measure their shoulder flexibility several times a year to identify flexibility deficits in internal rotation. These health care professionals can recommend stretches to increase internal rotation range of motion.

SHOULDER INJURIES IN TENNIS

The most common injury site in the shoulder is not the rotator cuff muscles themselves but rather the tendons that attach these muscles to the upper arm. There is not a lot of space inside the shoulder. When muscles fatigue or improper technique is used, it is very easy for one of the rotator cuff tendons that pass through this space to get pinched. When this happens over and over again, it can injure the tendon. The labrum or cartilage in the shoulder socket also can become injured (torn) in overhead athletes, especially those with very loose shoulders and poor rotator cuff strength and shoulder stability. Many of the shoulder injuries seen in tennis can be prevented with a proper stretching and strengthening program.

STRETCHES TO PREVENT SHOULDER INJURIES

The two most important shoulder stretches for tennis players are the cross-arm stretch and the sleeper stretch. Research shows that using these stretches as part of a regular program will improve the range of motion of internal rotation.

PREVENTIVE SHOULDER STRETCHES

As with any stretch, perform them after tennis play and complete 2 or 3 repetitions of each stretch, holding each for 20 to 30 seconds. This will improve or maintain flexibility in the shoulder.

Posterior Shoulder Stretch (Cross-Arm Stretch)

Focus

Improve flexibility of the muscles in the back of the shoulder and back of the shoulder joint capsule.

Procedure

1. Stand next to a doorway or fence. Raise your racket arm to shoulder level. Brace the side of your shoulder and shoulder blade against the wall or fence to keep the shoulder blade from sliding forward when you begin the stretch.

2. Using the other hand, grab the outside of the elbow of your racket hand and pull your arm across your chest (figure 12.3). You should feel the stretch in the back of your shoulder.

3. Hold the position, then switch sides.

Note

If you feel a pinching sensation in the front of your shoulder, discontinue this stretch and use the sleeper stretch to accomplish a similar stretch for this portion of the shoulder.

Figure 12.3   Cross-arm stretch.

Sleeper Stretch

Focus

Improve flexibility of the muscles in the back of the shoulder and back of the shoulder joint capsule.

Procedure

1. Lie on your dominant shoulder in a position you might adopt when sleeping on your side (hence the name).
2. Place your dominant arm directly in front of you at a 90-degree angle, keeping the elbow bent 90 degrees as well.
3. Using your other arm, push your hand down toward your feet, internally rotating your shoulder (figure 12.4).
4. Hold the position for 20 to 30 seconds, then switch sides.

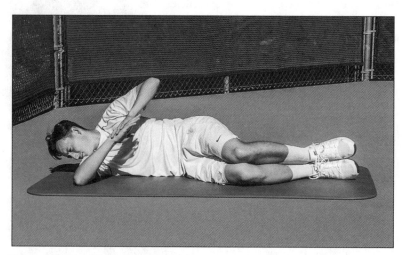

Figure 12.4   Sleeper stretch.

STRENGTHENING EXERCISES TO PREVENT SHOULDER INJURIES

Increasing muscular endurance and building a base level of strength in the rotator cuff and upper back should be the goals of any shoulder-strengthening program. The following exercises can be used to strengthen the back, or posterior part, of the rotator cuff. Perform each of these exercises slowly and with proper form.

Begin by performing these exercises using three sets of 15 to 20 repetitions. However, you must maintain proper technique when performing these exercises, even on the 20th repetition in the third set. Do not hesitate to do fewer repetitions or sets if you cannot maintain proper technique; it is better to do fewer repetitions correctly than more repetitions incorrectly. When done correctly, these exercises should not produce pain, just a feeling of burning around the shoulder. These exercises should be done after tennis play, to prevent fatiguing the shoulder prior to tennis play. The exercises are most important to be done with the dominant (tennis playing) shoulder.

SHOULDER STRENGTHENING EXERCISES WITH WEIGHTS

Most young players need to use only a 1-pound (0.45-kg) weight to start strengthening the shoulder muscles. Remember, these muscles are small, and tennis players do not need to lift a lot of weight to strengthen them appropriately. In fact, if using too much weight, players will substitute and use muscles other than the rotator cuff to perform the exercise.

Older, more experienced players will experience significant muscular fatigue doing these exercises using a 1.5- or 2-pound (0.7- or 0.9-kg) weight if the exercises are done correctly. Control the weight as you lift it (while muscles are shortening) and when you lower it (while muscles are lengthening), because this control prepares the muscle for the specific performance demands encountered during tennis play. As you get stronger, increase the weight in 1/2-pound (0.2-kg) increments, but only after you can do all three sets without significant fatigue and without using other parts of your body to compensate.

Sidelying External Rotation

Focus

Strengthen the external rotator muscles of the shoulder.

Procedure

1. Lie on one side with your working arm (top arm) at your side and a small pillow between your arm and body. Hold a small dumbbell in the hand of your working arm.

2. Keeping the elbow of your working arm bent and fixed to your side, raise your arm into external rotation until it is just short of pointing straight up (figure 12.5).

3. Slowly lower the arm to the starting position.

4. Repeat the exercise on the other side.

Figure 12.5   Sidelying external rotation.

Shoulder Extension

Focus

Strengthen the rotator cuff and scapular muscles.

Procedure

1. Lie prone (facedown) on a table with your working arm hanging straight to the floor (figure 12.6a). Hold a small dumbbell in the hand of your working arm.

2. With your thumb pointed out, raise your working arm straight back into extension toward your hip (figure 12.6b).

3. Slowly lower your arm.

4. Repeat the exercise with the other arm.

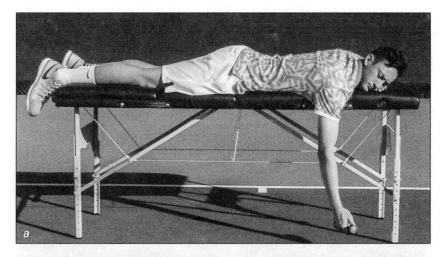

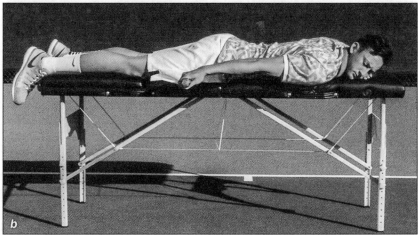

Figure 12.6   Shoulder extension: (a) starting position; (b) arm raised.

Prone Horizontal Abduction

Focus

Strengthen the rotator cuff and scapular muscles.

Procedure

1. Lie prone (facedown) on a table with your working arm hanging straight to the floor. Hold a small dumbbell in the hand of your working arm.

2. With your thumb pointed out, raise your arm straight out to the side until it is parallel to the floor; this movement is called *abduction.* (figure 12.7).

3. Slowly lower your arm.

4. Repeat the exercise with the other arm.

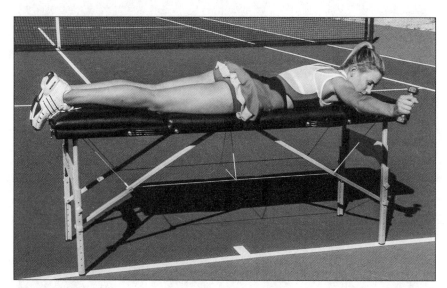

Figure 12.7   Prone horizontal abduction.

Prone 90/90 External Rotation

Focus

Strengthen the rotator cuff and scapular muscles.

Procedure

1. Lie prone (facedown) on a table with your working shoulder abducted to 90 degrees and your arm supported on the table, elbow bent 90 degrees (figure 12.8*a*). Your hand is hanging off

the edge of the table toward the floor. Hold a small dumbbell in the hand of your working arm.

2. Keeping the shoulder and elbow fixed, externally rotate the shoulder to lift the forearm so that it is parallel to the floor (figure 12.8b).

3. Slowly lower the arm to the starting position.

4. Repeat the exercise with the other arm.

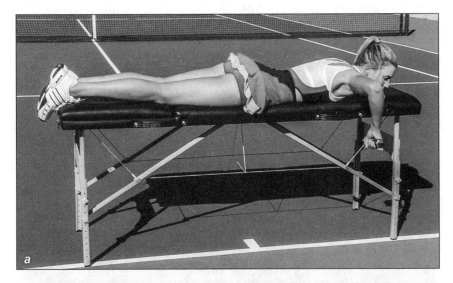

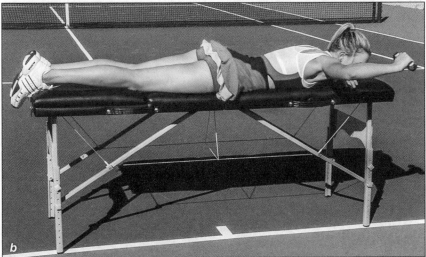

Figure 12.8   Prone 90/90 external rotation: (a) starting position; (b) shoulder externally rotated.

SHOULDER STRENGTHENING EXERCISES WITH BANDS

Other exercises that require elastic tubing or bands can further assist in providing muscle balance to a tennis player's shoulder. The bands or tubing are particularly practical because they can be available while travelling and make for a constantly available exercise source to strength the rotator cuff and shoulder blade muscles. The standing external rotation exercise works the posterior portion of the rotator cuff as does the external rotation at 90 degrees of abduction exercise.

As with the other strength training exercises, perform three sets of 15 to 20 repetitions to build muscular endurance. These exercises are easily performed using elastic tubing; the tubing is inexpensive and fits easily in a tennis bag. Start with a low level of resistance (e.g., if using a Thera-Band, this would be the yellow or red tubing), and progress to greater resistance when you are able to easily perform 3 sets of 20 repetitions with proper technique. Avoid using heavy or thick bands or tubing, because they create loads that are abnormally high for the shoulder, thus encouraging compensation from other muscles.

Recognize that elastic tubing comes in various colors and strengths. A red band made by one company may not offer the same resistance as the red band made by another company. When purchasing bands and tubing, ask questions to make sure you get the resistance level that is right for you. In addition, large quantities of these bands are rather inexpensive, making it possible to buy enough for an entire team to perform these injury prevention exercises.

▶ Standing External Rotation

Focus

Strengthen the external rotators and scapular stabilizers.

Procedure

1. Stand sideways to a door or secure object. Secure one end of the tubing or band to the doorknob or object at approximately waist height, and hold the other end in the hand of your working shoulder. Your exercising shoulder should be farthest away from the attachment point. Place a rolled towel under the exercising shoulder. Hold the exercising shoulder slightly in front of the body.

2. Begin with slight tension in the band with the hand against the abdomen. Slowly rotate the arm out approximately 90 degrees until your arm points directly in front of you (neutral position).

3. Slowly return to the starting position. It is important to work slowly against the resistance of the band in both directions.

4. Repeat the exercise on the other side.

Standing External Rotation at 90 Degrees of Abduction

Focus

Strengthen the external rotators and scapular stabilizers in an elevated position to simulate the service motion.

Procedure

1. Secure one end of a piece of tubing or elastic band just above waist height to a doorknob or stable object. Hold the other end of the band in the hand of your working shoulder. Stand facing the door or attachment point with your exercising shoulder elevated 90 degrees (shoulder level) with your elbow bent 90 degrees.

2. From this position with your arm out to the side, move your upper arm and elbow forward about 30 degrees. This places the shoulder and upper arm in the proper position and closely simulates the position your arm is in when the racket contacts the ball and follows through during the serve.

3. Before beginning the exercise, maintain the position of your upper arm and lower your forearm until it is horizontal. It may help to use your other hand to support your elbow in the exercise position to better isolate the rotation during the exercise.

4. Slowly move your hand and forearm to a vertical position by externally rotating your shoulder.

5. Hold for 1 second in the vertical position, and return to the starting position.

6. Repeat the exercise on the other side.

Variation

Start from the vertical position as described. Rapidly rotate your shoulder inward to the forearm-horizontal position to stretch the muscles in the back of your shoulder. Immediately after hitting the horizontal position, rapidly return your shoulder to the forearm-vertical position. This is a plyometric-type variation of the traditional external rotation exercise and can be used as a progression or variation.

Note

When performing external rotation with the arm raised to 90 degrees, the upper arm should be approximately 30 degrees forward (as opposed to having the upper arm straight out to the side) for greater comfort and to target the appropriate muscles.

PLYOMETRIC EXERCISES FOR THE SHOULDER

After progressing through the initial strengthening exercises, move on to exercises that work the muscles more quickly and more closely to the manner in which they will be used during actual tennis play. Plyometrics use a combination of muscle contractions (eccentric contraction followed by a rapid concentric contraction) to develop power and explosiveness. These are advanced exercises, and you should perform them only after establishing a base level of strength.

Four plyometric exercises for the shoulder are presented in this chapter. In each one, players should use a small 1- or 2-pound (0.45- or 0.9-kg) medicine ball to work the back of the rotator cuff while the arm is at the side (first and second plyometric exercises) or in the serving position (third and fourth plyometric exercises).

PLYOMETRIC SHOULDER EXERCISES

▶ Sidelying Plyometric Ball Drop

Focus

Strengthen the external rotators and scapular stabilizers when the arm is near the side of the body, similar to the position from which groundstrokes are performed.

Procedure

1. Lie on your nondominant side with a towel roll under your dominant side.
2. Hold a small medicine ball in your hand in neutral rotation, forearm parallel to the ground.
3. Rapidly release and catch the ball for 20 to 30 seconds to promote fatigue in the muscles. Do not let the ball hit the ground. Perform 2 or 3 sets.
4. Repeat the exercise on the other side.

Plyometric Sidelying Reverse Toss

Focus

Strengthen the external rotators and scapular stabilizers when the arm is near the side of the body, similar to the position from which groundstrokes are performed.

Procedure

1. Work with a partner. Lie on your non-tennis playing side, with a towel roll under your dominant (tennis playing) side.

2. Rotate your dominant arm back in a position to receive the small medicine ball from your partner.

3. Your partner uses an underhand toss to throw the ball to you. Catch the ball, and decelerate it after catching it while the hand and arm move down during the eccentric part of the exercise toward your abdomen.

4. Using an explosive movement, change direction with the ball in your hand and throw the ball decisively back to your partner. Repeat the exercise for several sets of 15 to 20 repetitions.

5. Repeat the exercise on the other side.

90/90 Prone Plyometric Ball Drop

Focus

Strengthen the external rotators and scapular stabilizers in an elevated position to simulate the position of the service motion.

Procedure

1. Lie prone (facedown) on a table or exercise ball. Hold a small plyometric ball in the hand of your working shoulder.

2. Repeatedly drop and quickly catch the small plyometric ball. Be sure to keep the elbow bent 90 degrees and rapidly drop and catch the ball.

3. Do this movement as fast as possible for 30 seconds, repeating the entire effort two or three times with 15 seconds of rest between sets.

4. Repeat the exercise on the other side.

90/90 Plyometric Reverse Toss

Focus

Strengthen the external rotators and scapular stabilizers in an elevated position to simulate the position of the service motion.

Procedure

1. Kneel with your dominant arm out to the side and your elbow bent 90 degrees so that the fingers point to the sky. A partner with a light medicine ball stands 3 to 6 feet (0.9-1.8 m) behind you. The partner should stand closer as you are learning the exercise and move farther away as you gain explosive strength in the rotator cuff and scapular muscles.
2. Your partner throws a light medicine ball slightly in front of your hand. Catch the ball, decelerate the motion, and immediately throw the ball back forcefully to your partner.
3. Keep your elbow up (approximately 90 degrees) during the exercise.
4. Perform multiple sets of 15 to 20 repetitions.
5. Repeat the exercise on the other side.

Variation

Perform this exercise while sitting on an exercise ball.

ROLE OF THE SCAPULA (SHOULDER BLADE)

Another area of weakness and vulnerability in a tennis player's shoulder is the scapula (shoulder blade). Although the ball-and-socket joint is what most people think of when they consider the shoulder, the shoulder blade, and how it moves, affects shoulder function as well. To demonstrate this point, put your hand on a partner's upper back and ask him or her to raise and lower the arms. You should be able to appreciate how much the shoulder blade moves during normal shoulder motion and why weakness in the muscles that control the shoulder blade can affect shoulder health.

When lifting and lowering the arms, the shoulder blades should remain flush with the torso as they move. Any scapular winging (when the shoulder blade pops off the torso) signifies weakness in the scapular stabilizers. Prominence of the outline of the shoulder blade on the dominant side indicates the need to strengthen several important muscles that stabilize the scapula. Most important are the serratus anterior and trapezius muscles.

Changes in shoulder posture are also common in tennis players (figure 12.9). The dominant shoulder is usually lower than the nondominant

Figure 12.9 Examples of shoulder posture differences in left-handed and right-handed tennis players. The player on the left is left-handed; the player on the right is right-handed. Note how much lower the dominant arm is.

shoulder. The reason for this difference is not completely understood, but this adaptation is not thought to place the shoulder at any greater risk for injury.

EXERCISES TO STRENGTHEN THE SCAPULAR STABILIZERS

Recommended exercises for increasing the strength of the scapular stabilizers are presented in this section. These include the seated row, external hand rotation, step-up, chest punch, and a variation of the prone plank. Perform all of these exercises in three sets of 15 to 20 repetitions, with no more than 30 seconds of rest between sets. Perform them slowly and under control to build strength and endurance. Similar to the rotator cuff exercises outlined earlier in this chapter, these exercises are best performed after tennis play to avoid fatiguing these important muscles prior to tennis play.

SCAPULAR STABILIZER STRENGTHENING EXERCISES

▶ ## Seated Row

Focus

Strengthen the scapular stabilizers.

Procedure

1. You can perform this exercise using elastic resistance or on various exercise machines. The video shows the exercise being performed with elastic tubing while the player is seated on an exercise ball. Attach the elastic tubing around a stable object at waist height. Sit on an exercise ball facing the object anchoring the tubing. Hold a handle in each hand with your palms down and arms out in front.
2. Pull your hands toward your chest while squeezing your shoulder blades together.
3. Slowly return to the starting position.

Note

The keys to success in this exercise are squeezing the shoulder blades together as you pull your hands toward your chest and then slowly returning to the starting position. This squeezing movement engages the scapular stabilizers to a greater extent. A common question is whether the elbows should be down or out to the sides during the exercise. It does not matter. The different techniques will engage slightly different muscles in the back and shoulders, but when performed properly, both will help strengthen the scapular stabilizers.

External Rotation With Shoulder Retraction

Focus

Improve the strength of the rotator cuff and scapular stabilizers.

Procedure

1. From a standing position, grasp a piece of elastic band or tubing in your hands (figure 12.10a).
2. Rotate your hands out 3 to 6 inches (about 8-16 cm), then pinch your shoulder blades together (figure 12.10b). Hold this position for 1 or 2 seconds.
3. It helps to activate the appropriate muscles if you stick out your chest while squeezing the shoulder blades together.
4. Return to the starting position.

Figure 12.10 External rotation with shoulder retraction: (a) starting position; (b) rotating hands out and pinching shoulder blades together.

Step-Up

Focus

Strengthen the serratus anterior, one of the scapular stabilizers.

Procedure

1. Kneel with both hands on the ground in front of a 6- to 8-inch (about 15- to 20-centimeter) step.

2. One at a time, move your hands up onto the step, making sure to press your upper body away from the floor at the top of the movement. Round your back like a cat in the up position.

3. One at a time, return the hands to the starting position.

Variations

- As you develop greater strength and core stability, perform the exercise on your toes instead of your knees, as in the push-up starting position.

- Loop a piece of elastic tubing around your wrists as you perform the exercise. The band provides resistance as your arms move side to side as they do during the monster walk exercise for the lower body.

Note

Although the step-up is recommended for the scapular stabilizers, and it does resemble a push-up, push-ups are not recommended for tennis players. A push-up performed so that the chest touches the floor is not appropriate, because it places a great deal of stress on the front of the shoulder. In addition, exercises that stress the shoulders by positioning the hands behind the body and exercises that load the shoulders in an overhead position (e.g., behind-the-neck lat pull-down or military press) are not recommended. The exercises in this book specifically address the imbalances and needs of tennis players and other overhead athletes.

Chest Punch

Focus

Strengthen the serratus anterior, one of the scapular stabilizers.

Procedure

1. Lie supine (on your back) with your shoulders flexed to 90 degrees and elbows straight. Hold a small medicine ball in both hands.
2. Keeping your elbows straight, raise your hands toward the ceiling as far as you can (figure 12.11).
3. Slowly return to the starting position. If you do this correctly, your hands will move only about 6 inches (about 15 cm) up and down.

Figure 12.11   Chest punch.

Variation

Perform this exercise with one arm at a time. Instead of a medicine ball, you can use other weights, such as a bag of flour or a rock.

Serratus Prone Plank

Focus

Elicit high activity in the serratus anterior muscle, which plays a big role in stabilizing the shoulder blade during repetitive tennis-specific movements.

Procedure

1. Assume the traditional prone plank position on your forearms and toes. If you are unable to assume this position with confidence and authority, start on your forearms and knees.

2. Once in a stable prone plank position, round your shoulder blades and upper back (similar to a cat; figure 12.12), causing the shoulder blade to protract (move forward). While this movement occurs, do not move the rest of your body, especially not the buttocks or bottom. The movement is isolated to the scapulae (shoulder blades). It strengthens the serratus with the rest of the core. Hold the rounded position for 1 or 2 seconds, and then lower back to the starting position. Repeat the exercise for multiple sets of 15 repetitions.

Figure 12.12   Serratus prone plank.

SUMMARY

Perform the exercises in this chapter to improve shoulder strength, endurance, and flexibility and to protect the shoulder from the repetitive stresses that ultimately lead to muscle imbalances and range-of-motion loss. All of these exercises can be performed several times per week within a periodized training program. Because these exercises can be completed using elastic bands or tubing and light weights, they are ideal for players who are traveling and competing. However, do not perform these exercises immediately before playing tennis. Because you do not want to try to perform tennis stroke patterns with a fatigued rotator cuff, these exercises are best performed after tennis play or on days when you play little tennis. The exercises and stretches highlighted in this chapter are effective in developing shoulder strength and are necessary; simply playing tennis every day does not ensure balanced development of shoulder strength and optimal shoulder range of motion. Incorporating these exercises into a complete conditioning program will prevent shoulder injury and enhance performance. The following chapter will provide information on injury prevention and rehabilitation for the rest of the body.

Chapter 13

Injury Prevention and Rehabilitation

When asked about a tennis injury, many players will remember the sudden onset of pain during tennis play after one shot or a forceful movement on court. Even though they can remember that one shot or movement, the injury likely resulted not from that one event but rather from the repetitive events that led up to that moment on court when the injury occurred.

Tennis injuries typically fall into the category of overuse injuries, which occur because tennis players constantly exert and produce forces in a repetitive pattern, leading to an accumulation of minor traumas that cause tissue breakdown. For example, overuse injuries can result from the effects on the shoulder of serving thousands of times or the effects on the knees from playing hundreds of points with pivots, twists, and aggressive stops and starts.

Injuries in tennis players fall into two additional categories: acute and chronic. An acute injury is a new injury or complaint from the time it occurs and the relatively short period of time following the start of the injury. A common acute injury in tennis players is an ankle sprain. A chronic injury is an injury that recurs because of continued tennis play or a lack of proper rehabilitation. An example of a chronic tennis injury is tennis elbow that has been present for 1 to 2 years and flares up every time the player enters a long, grueling tournament or attends a tennis camp. Acute tennis injuries are much easier to take care of. If treated correctly and quickly, players can prevent an acute injury from becoming chronic.

One of the unique things about the game of tennis is that it stresses nearly all areas of the body. Although most people immediately think of tennis elbow as the ultimate tennis injury, the elbow is only one area commonly injured in tennis players. Injuries can occur to all parts of the body because of the nature and stresses of tennis; however, areas most frequently injured in elite players include the shoulder, low back, hip, and knee. Data from the U.S. Open Tennis Championships consistently identify the shoulder and back as the leading areas of injury.

In addition, a recent USTA study of elite junior players identified the shoulder and back as the leading areas of overuse injury, confirming that the demand on these two areas is consistent from junior players to the pros. To address these areas of injury, chapter 7 is dedicated to improving core stability and chapter 12 to improving shoulder strength; those chapters include the latest concepts in injury prevention and performance enhancement for those areas. In addition, this chapter provides general injury care and rehabilitation guidelines and specific training recommendations for other areas of the body in order to keep you healthy and reduce the likelihood of injury.

PREVENTING INJURIES

Many factors play a part in preventing injuries in tennis. The best thing you can do to prevent an injury is to condition yourself optimally for tennis and prepare your body for the stresses incurred in the game. Many health professionals and tennis coaches used to say, "Play tennis to get in shape." Although tennis certainly provides inherent fitness benefits to the heart, lungs, muscles, and bones, that philosophy doesn't reflect current thinking. The appropriate advice for preventing injuries and optimizing performance in tennis is clearly, *Get in shape to play tennis.*

In addition to performing strength and flexibility exercises, using proper technique and selecting equipment appropriate for your playing style and body type also play a critical role. Although many elements of tennis equipment deserve mention, the racket's stiffness, weight, grip size, and string tension are important for injury prevention. Racket stiffness refers to the amount of racket deflection during ball impact. Frame material affects deflection, and therefore racket stiffness. In general, moderately stiff rackets are recommended. Rackets that are either too stiff or too flexible may negatively affect your arm. For example, players with insufficiently developed muscles using a very stiff racket and improper technique may endure excessive shock during impact, which over time may increase their risk of injury. Each major racket manufacturer produces a range of rackets with a variety of stiffness ratings. Pick one near the middle unless otherwise directed by your tennis teaching professional.

In addition to stiffness, the weight of your tennis racket is important. Although a superlight racket is easy to maneuver, playing with one may create greater impact stress because less racket weight is present to absorb the stress of impact, consequently more heavily loading the player's arm. On the other hand, a heavy frame may prove difficult to maneuver and lead to technical challenges and the inability to consistently achieve optimal positions at ball contact. This difficulty results in greater muscle use and fatigue. Use a racket that has enough weight to absorb the stress of impact but not enough to make it difficult to maneuver.

The racket's grip size has significant ramifications for injury prevention as well. A grip that is too small forces the forearm muscles to work harder to simply hold the racket. Estimate grip size by gripping the racket and ensuring that enough space exists between the longest finger and the fleshy muscle at the base of the thumb for the little finger of the opposite hand to fit between. If the longest finger touches the fleshy muscle, the grip is much too small. Likewise, if you have more than enough space for the little finger, the grip may be too large.

String tension also plays an important part in injury prevention and in optimizing the performance of the racket. Each racket comes with a recommended range of string tensions that the manufacturer feels will cover most of the players who play with that particular frame. Although individual preferences exist, the general rule is that for any given string and racket type, a tighter string tension will produce a more controlled response from the racket, and a looser string tension produces more power from the racket. This is contrary to what many players think. Playing with a racket with a very high string tension may create greater stress on the wrist, elbow, and shoulder and lead to injury.

In addition to string tension, the material and type of string affect performance as well. For injury prevention, strings that are made of many fibers (filaments), called coreless multifilament strings, provide greater resiliency and a generally superior feel. Gut strings are made in this multifilament fashion and are regarded as superior to most other types of nylon strings for playability and resiliency. However, stringing with gut is more costly and often not practical for many young developing players. Recently, polyester strings have become very popular. Polyester strings use the latest powerful racket technology to allow players to swing aggressively at the ball with very high racket head acceleration but control the ball's flight path. However polyester strings can cause greater stress to the racket arm, potentially leading to overuse injuries. Many players have found that a hybrid of polyester and coreless multifilament strings achieves the important goal of excellent control without increasing arm stress. Players should consult their tennis teaching professional or a racket stringer or technician certified by the United States Racquet Stringers Association (USRSA) for high-level advice on string type and tension and optimally matching their equipment (string, racket, grip).

Although this section has summarized several aspects of tennis equipment, you should discuss all equipment issues with your tennis teaching professional and perhaps a sport scientist. Carefully select all aspects of your racket frame and string type and tension. Your equipment is a factor in injury prevention and also a tool in recovery. For example, using gut or coreless multifilament strings, a slightly lower initial string tension (e.g., 3-5 lb, or 1.4-2.3 kg), and frame modification to ensure that proper grip size and weight are present can aid in the final steps of the recovery process, allowing a return to tennis with less chance of reinjury or aggravation.

The most important concepts for injury prevention are also important concepts for performance enhancement—flexibility training, strength training, aerobic and anaerobic training, and proper sport biomechanics. Instead of simply summarizing these terms in a general sense, the following section applies these concepts to some of the most common tennis injuries.

Shoulder Injuries

Overuse injury of the shoulder is common in all tennis players, from elite junior players to senior recreational players. Chapter 12 provides detailed information regarding the structure and function of the shoulder and exercises for injury prevention and performance enhancement. In addition to the information in that chapter, some of the common errors that tennis players make are discussed next.

During training, tennis players and other overhead athletes typically use too much weight when performing exercises for the shoulder. Remember, the rotator cuff and scapular muscles are very small and can most effectively be worked using light weights or small-diameter elastic tubing in a repetitive fashion, similar to what players encounter in a tennis match. In addition, as mentioned in chapter 12, you must perform exercises for strengthening the shoulder, specifically rotator cuff and scapular or shoulder blade exercises, after tennis play and not before. Doing these types of strength exercises before tennis play can create shoulder fatigue. As a result, it is not recommended to then go out on the tennis court for 1 to 3 hours of excessive shoulder work. You can perform these exercises after tennis practice or at a separate time throughout the day.

Another common mistake is lifting weights higher than shoulder level or bringing weights behind the plane of the body. For example, during the final descent phase of the bench press, don't lower the weight too far as the bar approaches the chest. This angle stresses the front of the shoulder, as does the end of the descent phase of the standard fly exercise to work the chest. Typically, both the bench press and standard fly exercise are performed in a supine (on your back) position. Although these exercises are not part of an injury prevention program for tennis players, they are general weight training exercises for the chest and arms that many athletes use. In general, these exercises are not recommended for tennis players. However, if they are included in a tennis-specific training program, you should use a narrow grip and lower the bar only one half to two thirds of the way to the chest for the bench press, and use a limited motion during the fly exercise.

Limiting the range of motion by as much as half the typical range specified in weightlifting manuals and texts is often the best advice for tennis players and athletes in overhead sports. Biomechanical analysis of tennis strokes shows that the shoulder is seldom lifted overhead, even during the serve. It is safer and less risky to train the rotator cuff muscles using the patterns described in this book.

Using proper biomechanical stroke technique is another key ingredient that should not be overlooked. Consult your local tennis professional or coach to determine whether your strokes contain movement flaws that may increase your potential for injury and limit your performance.

Trunk and Low-Back Injuries

Injuries to the trunk and low back also afflict many tennis players. In a survey of 148 male professional tennis players, 38 percent reported missing a tournament because of a low-back injury.

The ability to develop power in tennis is often a function of how well the upper and lower parts of the body are connected. The trunk forms a solid unit capable of producing large amounts of power through segmental rotation. The trunk also transfers the power generated by the lower extremities to the arms. This transfer of forces—starting from the feet pushing against the ground; transferring up the legs through the knees and hips and through the trunk; and funneled through the shoulder to the elbow, wrist, and ultimately the racket head—is termed the *kinetic-link concept.* Training the muscles of the trunk optimizes your ability to apply the kinetic-link concept in the generation of power for your strokes. It also

---

STROKE TECHNIQUE AND INJURY PREVENTION: OPEN-STANCE FOREHAND

Over the past few decades, the open-stance forehand has grown in popularity. However, use of the open-stance forehand can lead to positions in which the player's upper body and lower body are virtually parallel to the baseline at ball contact. Early or premature opening (rotation) of the upper body and trunk can create a lag in which the racket arm trails behind the plane of the body. When this happens during the forehand, it can place excessive stress on the shoulder, particularly the rotator cuff and stabilizing structures, as well as the inside (medial side) of the elbow. Initially it can lead to tendon injury in the shoulder, but it also places the shoulder at further risk for becoming unstable, making it more susceptible to serious injury.

is a major factor in preventing injury. A strong trunk not only prevents injuries in the low back, it also can prevent shoulder and elbow injures by providing a stable platform and force generator, taking stress off the arm.

Changes in the game outlined in chapter 1 have resulted in a greater demand on trunk rotation, particularly in the open-stance forehand (figure 13.1). A powerful open-stance forehand requires a huge transfer of force through the trunk with additional power produced by segmental rotation and derotation of the trunk. The amount of trunk rotation used in an open-stance forehand and in the inside-out forehand (used when stepping or running around a potential backhand) is far greater than in the classic-style forehand.

For proper rotation to safely occur, the abdominal and low-back muscles must support the vertebrae, discs, and ligaments in the low back. Specific information on core training is provided in detail in chapter 7.

Figure 13.1   Open-stance forehand showing how trunk and shoulder rotation generate power and use the entire kinetic chain. Note the amount of trunk rotation.

STROKE TECHNIQUE AND INJURY PREVENTION: SERVE

Aspects of the serve that can lead to injury involve an early opening of the torso and shoulders and inadequate leg drive. As a result of the early opening of the body, players must pull their bodies through the service motion using the abdominal muscles. In addition, having to pull the arm through the hitting zone can place added stress on the abdominal muscles and shoulder as these areas are forced to make up for the break in the kinetic chain that results from a lack of leg drive and improperly timed rotation of the shoulders and torso. The arm lag position created by the premature opening of the body can place additional loading on the front of the dominant shoulder as well as on the inside of the elbow. Rotator cuff tendinopathy and labral tears in the shoulder can result from this excessive loading in the shoulder when in arm lag position during the service motion. Research has shown that a stronger leg drive can reduce the load on the shoulder and elbow during the serve.

Flexibility of the trunk and hips is also an important factor in preventing injury to the low back. Of all the inflexibilities that can develop from playing tennis, tightness in the hamstrings and deep rotators of the hip are particularly harmful for the low back. Hamstring tightness decreases the motion available at the hips and places more stress on the back by forcing it to move more than if the hamstrings were flexible and hips more mobile. In a similar way, a reduction in the range of hip rotation creates greater stress in the low back and also may increase the risk of injury to the hip joints themselves.

LOW-BACK STRETCHES

The stretches listed will ensure that the hamstrings, iliotibial (IT) band, hip flexors, and hip rotators are as flexible as they should be. Using the static stretches included in this chapter as an adjunct to the detailed stretches presented in chapter 5 is especially important for players with a history of low-back and hip injury.

Knees-to-Chest Stretch (page 95)

Hamstring Stretch (page 88)

Figure-4 Stretch (page 92)

Hip Rotator Stretch (page 92)

Seated Spinal Twist (page 96)

Hip Twist (page 91)

Hip Flexor Stretch

Focus

Improve flexibility of the quadriceps and hip flexor muscles.

Procedure

1. Lie on your back so that the edge of a table or supportive surface hits your legs in the middle of the hamstrings. Bring both knees to your chest.

2. While holding one knee tightly toward your chest, slowly lower the other leg toward the table (figure 13.2). Let the leg hang, and flex the knee to 90 degrees. You should feel the stretch in the front of the thigh and hip region.

3. Hold the stretch for 20-30 seconds, then switch sides.

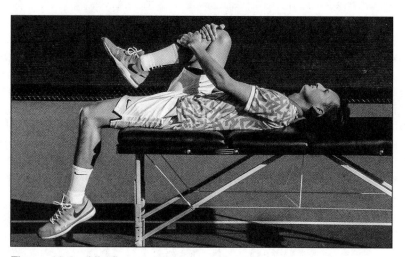

Figure 13.2   Hip flexor stretch.

Note

It may help to have a partner gently press the leg farther down toward the table and floor or bend the knee slightly beyond 90 degrees.

Tennis Elbow

One of the injuries most commonly associated with tennis is tennis elbow. Also known as humeral epicondylitis, the term *tennis elbow* refers to the overuse injury that results from repetitive trauma to the tendons that control movement of the wrist and forearm. The tendons on the outside of the elbow raise the back of the hand toward you (extension) and are the tendons most commonly involved in tennis elbow. This lateral (outside) tennis elbow most commonly results from improper technique during backhands, but it can be caused by any tennis stroke because these muscles and tendons undergo stress during all tennis movements using the arm.

Medial (inside) tennis elbow involves the tendons that bend the wrist down (flexion) or rotate the forearm into a palm-down position (pronation), such as in the serve. This form of tennis tendinitis is more common among highly skilled tennis players, baseball pitchers, and golfers. These muscles and tendons are stressed the most during the forehand and serve. Using technique that does not use the legs, trunk, and arm to produce power but instead uses the elbow, wrist, and hand to produce power, places the player at risk of developing this injury.

The good news about tennis elbow is that in most cases, surgery is not required to alleviate it, and it is preventable. The single biggest factor in preventing tennis elbow is using proper biomechanics during the tennis stroke. Strokes that use the muscles in the forearm and wrist to generate power are particularly stressful to the tendons in the elbow. A leading-elbow backhand is a classic example of an improper stroke technique that can cause lateral tennis elbow. Strokes using a "wristy" technique (overly reliant on the use of the wrist rather than the major muscles of the core/lower body and shoulder) are also particularly bad. To prevent this type of injury, ask your tennis professional to evaluate your strokes.

ELBOW STRENGTHENING AND FLEXIBILITY

Two additional strategies for preventing tennis elbow are strengthening and flexibility exercises. Strengthening exercises involve using a light weight—starting with very little weight, 1 to 2 pounds (0.45-0.9 kg) for young junior players and 3 to 5 pounds (1.4-2.3 kg) for adults and older juniors—and 30 to 45 repetitions of movement patterns that emphasize the wrist and forearm. The forearm and wrist program described in chapter 8 contains the recommended exercises. These exercises not only improve strength, they also increase muscular endurance:

Wrist Flexion and Extension Curls (page 176)

Radial and Ulnar Deviation (page 176)

Pronation and Supination (page 178)

Ball Dribble (page 190)

Isolate the movements at the wrist and hand, and avoid using the rest of the upper body or trunk to cheat. Elastic tubing can be used effectively to strengthen these muscles. Research on treating tennis elbow has consistently shown that the eccentric part of the exercise (when the weight is lowered or tubing is gradually returned to its resting length) can be most helpful and should be emphasized when performing exercises to treat tennis elbow. Adding these exercises to your strengthening program is also an important part of preventing tennis elbow and optimizing your performance.

Flexibility is also an important part of preventing tennis elbow. Researchers measured elbow and wrist motion in elite-level junior and senior tennis players and compared the results of the dominant (racket) side to the nondominant side. Because of the effects of repetitive tennis play, the elbow on the dominant side lost the ability to straighten by approximately 5 degrees. Players with elbow injuries often lack as much as 15 degrees of this range of motion. This finding is also reported in baseball pitchers.

Two stretches directly address the elbow, forearm, and wrist—the forearm flexor stretch and the forearm extensor stretch (described in chapter 5). Tennis players should use these stretches to counteract the loss of flexibility (inability to completely straighten the elbow) in the dominant arm that research has shown to exist in both junior and senior tennis players. Perform these stretches both before and after tennis play. Remember to hold each stretch for 15 to 20 seconds.

Wrist Injuries

It is not often that doing one thing gives you the added bonus of accomplishing another, but in the case of the exercise program for tennis elbow, this appears to be true. The same strengthening and flexibility exercises players use to prevent tennis elbow also prevent injuries to the wrist. Changes in the game such as stiffer rackets, more extreme forehand grips, more powerful strokes, and the prevalence of fast, hard courts, can increase stress to the wrist. In recent years several players have had serious wrist injuries, which resulted in time away from the game. A maintenance program that includes wrist and forearm strength and proper flexibility exercises is the best step to minimize injury risk in frequent players.

Increasing strength and endurance of the muscles that cross the wrist helps to protect the wrist as well as the ligaments that help keep the wrist together. Additional exercises for tennis players that can improve the strength and endurance of the muscles that cross the wrist and elbow include ball dribble and wrist snaps with a medicine ball. The ball dribble can be performed in 30-second sets to improve endurance, with emphasis on dribbling the ball as quickly as possible. Performing 2 or 3 sets of these exercises will help improve local muscle endurance.

STROKE TECHNIQUE AND INJURY PREVENTION: TWO-HANDED BACKHAND

During the preparation phase of the two-handed backhand groundstroke, players often use extreme amounts of ulnar deviation (downward bending) of their dominant-side wrists as the racket is prepared to accelerate toward ball contact. This position is often incorporated as part of the two-handed backhand as players attempt to drop the racket head further below the path of the incoming ball to produce greater topspin. It sometimes occurs in excess when an athlete does not lower the body enough and relies on the wrist to get the racket head below the ball. Wrist injuries can occur on either the radial (thumb) side or the ulnar (little finger) side of the wrist. Repetitive use and the forces experienced at the extreme ends of the wrist's range of motion place greater stress on the tendons that cross this joint. A piece of cartilage on the ulnar side of the wrist, called the triangular fibrocartilage complex (TFCC), is loaded when the wrist is put into a position of extreme extension and ulnar deviation. When repeatedly put in this position, the TFCC can actually tear. When a tear occurs, players may experience a clicking feeling in the wrist and pain as well. This type of injury often requires surgery to correct.

WRIST STRENGTHENING EXERCISES

Ball Dribble

Focus

Strengthen the muscles of the forearm and wrist.

Procedure

1. Stand 1 foot (0.3 m) or so away from a wall or supportive surface.
2. Using a basketball or exercise ball, rapidly bounce the ball back and forth in very small movements against the wall with your dominant arm. The bounce of the ball will only be an inch or two (2.5 to 5 centimeters).
3. Switch sides and repeat this movement with the opposing arm.

Variation

Vary the dribbling pattern so that the ball moves back and forth in front of you like a windshield wiper.

▶ ## Wrist Snaps With a Medicine Ball

Focus

Improve explosive strength of the wrist and forearm musculature.

Procedure

1. In a seated position with your forearm resting on your thigh, hold a medicine ball in your hand with your palm facing the floor. Extend your wrist (bend it upward) to prepare to forcefully propel the medicine ball toward the floor.

2. Be sure to keep your forearm against your thigh throughout the exercise, because using the elbow and rest of the arm during this exercise reduces the focus on the wrist and forearm muscles.

3. After forcefully throwing the ball by snapping the wrist downward, catch the ball as it pops back up into your hand, and repeat the exercise.

4. Switch sides and repeat with other arm

Knee Injuries

Tennis places a great deal of stress on the knee joints because of the bending, quick starts and stops, and explosive accelerations required for top-level play. Because tennis is technically a noncontact sport, the bone-crushing knee injuries people equate with football or skiing are not all that prevalent. Instead, injures to the patellofemoral (knee) joint are probably the most disabling among tennis players. The patella (kneecap) rides in a shallow groove at the end of the femur (thighbone). If a player endures repeated stress to the legs during tennis play in the absence of sufficient strength and endurance of the thigh muscles (especially the quadriceps), the kneecap can become irritated. This irritation is caused by the lack of support from the surrounding muscles as they fatigue; a kneecap without muscular support will not glide properly in the groove in the end of the thighbone. This repeated irritation can wear down the back of the kneecap and produce significant pain. Braces can support the kneecap, but the best support comes from the muscles.

Preventing knee injuries focuses on two main strategies: improving flexibility and improving strength. To strengthen your knees, use the exercises described in chapter 8. When performing exercises for the knees, limit the movement pattern to decrease the stress to the knees. Pressure between the kneecap and the end of the thighbone is greatest when the knee is bent between 45 and 60 degrees during leg extension–type exercises. Because this part of the movement is particularly stressful, players experiencing knee pain or those who have a history of knee injury should avoid it.

Players with achy knees should also avoid deep squat, lunge, and leg press movements in which the knees bend more than 90 degrees. These exercises cause a large amount of stress while the muscles are being strengthened and should be avoided.

In addition, a very common injury in elite tennis players is patellar tendinopathy. This overuse injury causes pain in the tendon that courses from the bottom of the patella (kneecap) to the tibial tubercle (the bump of bone on the top of your lower leg bone). Pain occurs directly over the tendon during aggressive movements common in tennis. This injury is also called jumper's knee and is common in volleyball and basketball players as well. Players who wear a thin band of tape under the kneecap or a thin brace that goes around the top of the lower leg just below the bottom of the kneecap are trying to ease the pain and provide support to treat patellar tendinopathy.

Many of the exercises described in this section (leg press, squat, lunge, leg extension) to treat patellofemoral pain can be used to treat patellar tendinopathy. The most important phase of these exercises is the eccentric phase. If you have patellar tendinopathy, emphasize the slow lowering during the eccentric phase of the exercise. Also use a brace, and make sure you have ample flexibility in the thigh muscles (hip flexors, quadriceps, and hamstrings).

Common strengthening exercises, such as the lunge and squat, deserve further discussion, because these exercises involve a key component for all tennis players—balance. You can make both the lunge and squat more difficult by using foam pads, which provide a less stable exercise surface. This instability forces you to concentrate and challenge more muscle groups in the lower body and trunk while performing the exercise and assists in the development of balance, an important part of any tennis player's game. When performing the lunge and squat exercises, do not bend the knees too far, which puts excessive loads on the kneecap, and maintain proper knee alignment during the exercise movement. The knee should be aligned over the foot during the exercise. Figure 13.3a shows a player doing a squat on a balance platform, maintaining proper knee and hip alignment during the descent phase. Figure 13.3b shows improper alignment, which is characterized

Figure 13.3 One-leg squat on unstable surface or balance pad: (a) correct knee and hip alignment; (b) incorrect knee and hip alignment; note inward angulation of the standing knee.

by an inward movement of the knee, increasing the angle and stress at the knee. Performing exercises with this improper movement is not only potentially harmful, but it may also lead to promoting this movement during on-court movements while playing tennis. Athletes should pay special attention to using proper technique during these exercises. It is imperative for injury prevention and optimizing performance and should be part of every tennis player's exercise program.

KNEE STRENGTHENING EXERCISES

Leg Press (page 159)

Partial Squat (page 161)

Lunge (multidirectional variation) (page 163)

Multihip (page 164)

Leg Extension (partial range if indicated) (page 144)

Hamstring Curl (page 167)

Leg Raise With Cuff Weight

Focus

Strengthen the quadriceps and hip flexors; rehabilitate the knee after surgery or injury.

Procedure

1. Because no actual motion at the knee occurs during this exercise, it is usually well tolerated. Lie on your back with one leg straight out in front of you. Place a cuff weight onto the ankle of that leg. Keeping the foot on the floor, bend the other knee to approximately 90 degrees to decrease the stress on your low back.

2. Tighten your quadriceps, and raise your leg about 6 inches (15 cm) off the ground, keeping your knee straight (figure 13.4).

3. Hold the position for 1 count before slowly returning to the start position. Then switch sides.

4. Repeat the exercise for multiple sets of 10 to 15 repetitions on each leg.

Figure 13.4   Leg raise with cuff weight.

KNEE STRETCHES

Hamstring Stretch (page 88)

Quadriceps Stretch (page 90)

Hip Rotator Stretch (page 92)

Iliotibial (IT) Band Stretch (page 93)

Hip Injuries

Recent increases in hip injuries have led to more discussion among sports medicine experts and recommendations for injury prevention programs related to the hip. The lower-body stresses discussed in the previous section on knee injuries also provide overload to the hip joint in both elite and recreational players. In addition to wear and tear over many years of tennis play, injuries to the cartilage inside the hip joint can decrease player performance.

The best way to prevent hip injuries is to develop a strong core and flexible muscles around the hip joint. A weak core can significantly stress the hips and lower body, so strictly adhering to a strong and regular program of core exercise is a great prevention strategy. A simple test, the one-leg stability test (chapter 4), can be used to see if you have a lack of hip and core strength and are at risk. Surprisingly, even very elite players often have difficulty with this test and need to work on their hip and core musculature. Exercises in chapter 8 such as the monster walk and elastic band kick are excellent examples of specific resistance exercises that should be performed to protect the hip joint.

Notice how players can cover the court, nearly performing the splits to retrieve wide balls with apparent ease? Those positions would not be possible were it not for exquisite hip flexibility. Players such as Novak Djokovic are frequently photographed in amazing positions with their legs spread apart to perform these shots. Players have to focus on lower-body flexibility, with particular emphasis on stretching the hip flexors, adductors (groin), iliotibial (IT) band, hamstrings, quadriceps, and deep rotators of the hip (piriformis) to ensure that they have adequate hip range of motion. Using the dynamic warm-up recommendations in chapter 5, coupled with focused hip stretches following play or practice is not only a great recommendation; in today's modern game it is a requirement for improving on-court movement and preventing hip injury.

PREVENTING HEAT-RELATED ILLNESS

Although not a musculoskeletal injury, heat stress is a common ailment during tennis play. It can include heat cramps, heat exhaustion, and, most seriously, heatstroke. The most widely recommended prevention strategies for heat illness are proper hydration and nutritional intake, discussed in chapter 14.

While playing tennis in the heat, the body's primary cooling mechanism is sweating. Sweat rates in male and female tennis players can range from 16 and 100 ounces (0.5 and 3.0 liters) per hour depending on fitness level, environmental temperature, and hydration status.

In addition to water, electrolytes are lost in sweat. Sodium and chloride are the primary electrolytes lost during sweating, but potassium and magnesium are also lost. Contrary to popular belief, sport scientists now know that sodium loss through heavy sweating can be a contributor to heat cramps along with neuromuscular fatigue.

Thirst is not always an adequate stimulus for hydration; a person can lose 50 ounces (1.5 liters) of water before feeling thirsty. Therefore, proper hydration involves drinking before you are thirsty and properly hydrating before tennis play. Drinking fluids the night before and early in the day before tennis play improves a player's hydration status before a match. For more information, see chapter 14.

SUMMARY

Following a total conditioning program for tennis will help prevent injury and optimize performance. Your knowledge of the information presented in this chapter will aid in the prevention of some of the most common musculoskeletal injuries. Using the testing battery in chapter 4 to identify any specific musculoskeletal deficits coupled with a complete conditioning program for tennis is an excellent way to decrease injury risk and enhance performance.

Chapter 14

Nutrition and Hydration

The discussion on conditioning for tennis would not be complete without also talking about appropriate fueling. So far this book has taught you how to get fit for tennis by highlighting the best methods to train the many physical aspects of the sport. However, without the information and proper strategy to fuel your fitness, you will not be able to reach your full potential.

Tennis nutrition follows many of the same principles from general sport nutrition research (summarized in table 14.1). However, some specific differences apply to tennis. This chapter highlights tennis-specific nutrition suggestions to apply before, during, and after tennis matches and training sessions. Tennis-specific nutrition usually entails focusing on four broad areas: energy balance, long-term health, body composition, and recovery. Energy balance relates to consuming enough calories (energy) to improve and sustain performance for the entire tennis match or practice. Long-term health is important for everyone, and tennis athletes are no different. Appropriate nutrition helps improve performance in tennis and also contributes to general well-being and disease prevention. Body composition is all about having the appropriate percentage of fat in relation to fat-free (lean) body mass. Recovery is important in all aspects of tennis and life, and quality nutrition will speed recovery from the previous training session or match.

The main components of tennis-specific nutrition focus on obtaining the appropriate macronutrients from a variety of sources, predominantly whole-food sources. The needs of tennis players differ from the needs of many other athletes because of the intermittent nature of the sport and the need to play for extended periods, sometime multiple hours at a time. The major areas of focus include water and electrolyte intake (hydration), the consumption of carbohydrate and fat for energy, and protein ingestion for muscle recovery.

Table 14.1 Nutrition Basics

Macronutrients			
Nutrient	Calories per gram	Major dietary sources	Function
Carbohydrate	4	Bread, pasta, potatoes, fruits, vegetables, grains	Provides energy for the brain, nervous system, blood, and muscles.
Fat	9	Animal products, grains, nuts, seeds, fish, vegetables	Provides energy and insulation, cushions organs, and is the medium for fat-soluble vitamins.
Protein	4	Meat, poultry, milk products, eggs, fish, legumes, nuts	Makes up parts of enzymes, bone, blood, muscles, and some hormones and cell membranes; repairs tissue, regulates water and acid–base balance, and aids in cell and muscle growth; can supply energy.
Micronutrients			
Nutrient	Calories per gram	Major dietary sources	Function
Water	0	Vegetables, fruits, fluids	Makes up 50 to 70% of the body's weight; is the medium for chemical reactions; transports chemical reactions and chemicals; regulates temperature; removes waste products.
Vitamins	0	All food, but abundant in fruits, vegetables, some grains	Promotes or acts as a catalyst for chemical reactions within cells.
Minerals	0	Most foods	Aids in general body functions; acts as a catalyst for the release of energy.

Adapted, by permission, from International Tennis Performance Association, 2015, *Certified Tennis Performance Specialist (CTPS) workbook and study guide* (Marietta, GA: ITPA).

BEFORE TENNIS PRACTICE OR MATCHES

Prematch or training nutritional guidelines differ greatly from athlete to athlete based on varied physiological factors, body composition, energy expenditure, and other considerations. The best way to know what works

---

TENNIS PLAYER'S NUTRITIONAL CHECKLIST

The tennis player's goal is to take in enough calories to maximize performance and recovery. Having a personalized checklist is important for all players. Although your specific needs may vary slightly, the following list of general nutrition guidelines can help you achieve the appropriate mix of nutrients and fluids for optimal performance on the tennis court.

1. To ensure consistent energy levels, evenly disperse calories throughout tournament day.
2. Hydrate sufficiently. Consume enough fluids and electrolytes before, during, and after performance.
3. Time consumption appropriately before a match. Consume the calories, fluids, and foods that have the right mixture of carbohydrate, protein, fat, and electrolytes to maximize performance.
4. During competition, hydrate and take in proper amounts of carbohydrate.
5. After a match, replace fluids lost and take in appropriate macronutrients (carbohydrate and protein) within 30 to 45 minutes after each competition.

---

is to practice a nutritional strategy on noncompetition days and adjust based on need. Some general recommendations can aid in appropriate preparation and apply to all tennis players. The goal is to ensure that energy in the form of glycogen has been stored in the muscles and the liver. This stored energy can then be utilized for physical activity during training and matches.

Eat a meal 3 or 4 hours before the training session or match time, then follow up with a smaller snack 1 or 2 hours before the training session or match time. The main meal should include complex carbohydrates such as pasta, rice, or potatoes alongside a high-quality protein source such as fish or chicken. The snack 1 or 2 hours before a match or training session should be 200 to 400 calories; it can be in the form of a liquid, energy bar, or small sandwich. The composition can vary, but carbohydrate is the major fuel source for tennis activity and should be more of a focus. Hydration is also very important at this time, so you should take in enough fluid to help maintain good hydration levels. Some players will need more carbohydrates and electrolytes that water alone cannot provide, so taking in sports drinks is recommended when the weather is hot or humid. Here are some good general suggestions to help prepare for intense sessions:

- About 2 or 3 hours before a workout or competition, drink approximately 2 or 3 cups (16-22 oz.; about 0.5-0.7 L) of fluids.

- About 1 hour before a workout or competition, drink approximately 1 cup (8 oz.; about 0.25 L) of fluid.
- About 15 minutes before the workout or competition, drink approximately 1 cup (8 oz.; about 0.25 L) of fluid.

DURING TENNIS PRACTICE OR MATCHES

During tennis play, metabolic heat is produced through all the running, jumping, stopping, and starting. This heat causes the core body temperature to rise. Consequently, fluid loss through sweating (and slightly through breathing) occurs to dissipate body heat and regulate core temperature.

Sweating rates in tennis players range considerably. A player who is a light sweater may lose only 16 ounces (about 0.5 L) of fluid per hour; very heavy sweaters can lose as much as 100 ounces (about 3 L) of fluid per hour. A customized strategy is recommended to ensure appropriate hydration. Body mass assessments can be used to estimate your sweat loss following a workout. Acute body mass change (e.g., from before to after training) represents approximately 32 ounces (1 L) of water loss per 2.2 pounds (1 kg) of body mass loss.

The wide range in sweating rates among players is a result of differences in genetics, maturation, body size, training or match intensity, environmental conditions, and heat acclimatization status. When fluid intake is less than sweat loss, a body water deficit (dehydration) occurs. As little as 2 percent dehydration can have a negative impact on performance factors such as aerobic performance, balance, cognition, mood, and mental readiness. Also the detrimental effects of reduced hydration levels on aerobic performance are exacerbated when combined with heat stress caused by playing tennis in hot conditions. A low level of hydration also impairs the body's heat dissipating mechanisms (skin blood flow and sweating), leading to increased core temperature and risk of heat illness. Therefore, ensuring appropriate hydration during practice and matches is essential. You should undertake an individualized program for hydration as well as make sure you drink enough based on your thirst.

During training and matches that last more than 60 minutes, it is recommended to consume between 30 and 60 grams of carbohydrate per hour. This energy can come in different forms, but simple carbohydrates (e.g., dextrose, sucrose, fructose) are common sources. Taking this carbohydrate in fluid form is usually the easiest to consume and is digested more quickly than solid food. Forms of simple carbohydrates include carbohydrate-based drinks (such as sports drinks), carbohydrate gels, chews, or simple snacks such as fruit, fruit roll-ups or jelly beans. The objective is to consume 30 to 60 grams of carbohydrate per hour. Taking small amounts of protein during training or competition has not been shown to improve performance. Protein is not a major fuel source, but it may provide some benefits in recovery. The challenge with protein is to ensure that it does not negatively impact your stomach or give you digestive discomfort. If you are going to take small amounts of protein, test it out during practice before adding anything new to your match routine. However, taking protein immediately after physical training is recommended to help with muscle repair and recovery. Fat as a fuel source during tennis is less appropriate due to the fact that it takes longer to breakdown into energy, and much of tennis is anaerobic in nature, requiring carbohydrates as the major fuel source.

Eight ounces (about 0.5 L) of a traditional sports drink provides 50 calories, 14 grams of carbohydrate, and electrolytes (sodium and potassium). As a general rule you should consume approximately 8 ounces (about 0.5 L) of sports drink at changeovers during a match in hot and humid conditions. It would provide close to 60 grams of carbohydrate per hour in most matches. This amount may change slightly based on the environment and the individual, but it is a good starting point when developing a strategy for court nutrition and hydration. This amount of carbohydrate could be taken completely in liquid form, or it could be provided half through liquid and half through solid food in the form of bars, chews, or gels.

AFTER TENNIS PRACTICES OR MATCHES

Following tennis play, the objective is to replace what was lost during the physical activity, plus create an environment within your body to help speed recovery for the next tennis session. This includes replenishing carbohydrate stores, adding protein for muscle recovery and repair, and replacing fluids and electrolytes.

Replacing Fluids and Electrolytes

To achieve complete rehydration athletes should drink 32 to 48 ounces (about 1-1.5 L) of a sodium-containing fluid for each 2.2 pounds (1 kg) of body mass lost. Consuming sodium with a fluid replacement beverage also helps stimulate more complete rehydration and whole-body fluid balance compared to ingestion of plain water alone. The addition of sodium is also important to reduce the risk of hyponatremia, a condition sometimes known as water intoxication. Hyponatremia is very rare in tennis players. It occurs when the electrolytes in the blood are diluted as a result of electrolytes and fluid being sweated away but only the fluids (not electrolytes) being replaced. This condition can result in mild to severe problems. To avoid this situation, taking in appropriate fluid levels with sodium and sodium rich foods during the recovery period is recommended. Also, providing a chilled beverage with the addition of flavor and sweetness may improve beverage taste; the better a beverage tastes, the more you will consume.

Consuming Carbohydrate

Because of the stop-and-go nature of tennis, which involves hundreds of quick bursts of speed during every practice or match, carbohydrate is the primary fuel source. Tennis practices and matches, especially those of longer duration and intensity, decrease glycogen stores. Therefore, carbohydrate intake to replenish liver and muscle glycogen before the next training session or match is an important aspect of recovery for the tennis player. Carbohydrate is an important substrate for contracting skeletal muscle and aiding central nervous system function. Glucose concentrations improve endurance performance.

The recommendations for carbohydrate intake during tennis recovery depend on training and competition demands. The more you play and the more intense your play is, the more carbohydrate you need during recovery. If you have less than 8 hours of recovery between practices or matches, you should ingest 1.0 to 1.2 grams of carbohydrate per kilogram of body weight immediately after the first session, repeated approximately every 4 hours. The timing of carbohydrate intake is especially important if you have two practices or matches in a day.

During short recovery periods, the carbohydrate you consume should come from easily digested carbohydrate sources. Avoid foods that are high in fat, protein, and fiber to reduce the risk of gastrointestinal issues during your next match or practice. Because individual differences exist in tolerance to certain foods and fluids, you should also take into consideration your own preferences and previous experiences when selecting the timing, amount, and source of carbohydrate to consume.

If you have 1 or more days between intense training sessions, the timing for glycogen replenishment is less urgent. It is important to provide sufficient carbohydrate in the diet during the 24 hours after the practice or match. Daily needs for carbohydrate fuel to support recovery and replenish muscle and liver glycogen stores in the 24 hours between tennis play is 5 to 7 grams of carbohydrate per kilogram of body weight per day for moderate training (about 1 hour per day) or 6 to 10 grams of carbohydrate per kilogram of body weight per day for moderate to high-intensity periods of training (1-3 hours/day).

Adding Protein

Another important nutritional aspect is the consumption of protein. Protein has many roles in the body, including building and repairing muscle tissue, aiding in enzyme and hormone function, and providing the building blocks of bone, muscle, cartilage, skin, and blood. The consumption of 20 to 25 grams of protein after exercise is recommended in order to stimulate muscle protein synthesis and possibly lower the rate of muscle protein breakdown. Significantly higher rates of protein intake after exercise have not been shown to provide greater benefits.

The type and timing of protein ingestion are important considerations. A high-quality protein that provides all of the essential amino acids (leucine in particular) is needed for the training adaptation to occur. Consuming your post-training or competition protein as soon as possible after exercise is suggested, particularly if optimum muscle adaptation and performance are a high priority. To meet daily protein requirements (in the 24 hours between sessions) when training at high intensity and duration, consume about 1.6 grams of protein per kilogram of body weight per day. This recommendation is similar to the 1.2 to 1.7 grams of protein per kilogram of body weight per day recommended for endurance and resistance training athletes. Remember that individual differences do exist; adjust needs based on personal differences and sometimes preferences.

PREVENTING MUSCLE CRAMPS

Muscle cramps that occur during or shortly after tennis play in players with no underlying metabolic, neurological, or endocrine conditions are usually called *exercise-associated muscle cramps (EAMC)*. These types of muscle cramps usually occur in single, multijoint muscles (e.g., triceps surae, quadriceps, hamstrings) when contracting whereas generalized EAMC occur in multiple muscle groups (sometimes referred to as whole-body muscle cramping). Some types of exercise-associated muscle cramping may be caused by large sodium losses through sweating. However, muscle cramping has multiple causes and is a complex response to stress, fatigue, and lack of ideal muscle contraction control. Cramping in tennis players is reported to occur in the latter stages of tournament play, likely because of the cumulative loss of sodium through sweat and failure to replace losses between matches. In these instances, cramp-prone tennis players can benefit from sodium intake from sports drinks or added salt supplementation (food and drink) to prevent or offset whole-body exercise-associated muscle cramping. You should always drink enough fluid alongside any increase in sodium consumption. Adding salt to most foods can help significantly for tennis athletes who regularly train and compete in hot and humid conditions. Many cramp related scenarios are in competition and it is important to stay relaxed during matches and tension may induce cramping type symptoms.

SUMMARY

Sport nutrition is a highly complex area with thousands of new research studies published each year. Tennis nutrition is a subset of general sport nutrition. Remember that recommendations for other sports or physical activities may not be appropriate for competitive tennis athletes. A good-quality balanced diet is the first step in the nutrition equation. If the base diet is lacking, the extras (e.g., supplements, pills, potions) are not going to have an impact. In other words, supplements will not make up for a poorly executed nutritional strategy. Tennis has unique physiological requirements, and a tennis player's diet is different than the diet needed for many other sports. Just as the principle of specificity applies to strength training and movement training for tennis, the nutrition of the tennis athlete needs to be equally specific. The information in this chapter provides some basic guidelines to help plan tennis-specific nutrition, but it is highly recommended that you work with a sport-trained dietician or physiologist with a strong understanding of the demands of competitive tennis for a more individualized nutritional program. The next chapter explores how best to recover from tennis practice and competition.

Chapter 15

Recovery

As tennis results in changes and adaptations in physiological systems, the goals of training for tennis must include strategies to induce appropriate fatigue. When combined with appropriate and much-needed recovery after training and competition, this fatigue will result in positive training adaptations. The appropriate types of recovery strategies you select to address specific types of fatigue will depend on your recovery knowledge and experience, along with the availability, practicality, and cost of each strategy. This chapter focuses on applied recovery techniques that are easy to implement and relatively low in cost.

The damage and repair processes of training and competition differ based on the different aspects of the body. The demands of tennis play vary according to the characteristics of match play and the players themselves. Factors include training volume, number of matches, playing surface and racket and string type, competitive game style, environmental conditions, and player characteristics such as age, sex, and skill level. A better understanding of the physiological basis of fatigue, how it occurs in tennis, and how it is affected by the characteristics of match play and the individual athlete will aid in identifying and implementing practices that strengthen the physiological systems involved in recovery. Finally, strategies to minimize fatigue and optimize recovery, including proper conditioning and specific recovery modalities, are discussed in conjunction with recognition of the importance of psychological recovery. Nutrition and hydration aspects of recovery were covered in chapter 14.

DEFINING RECOVERY AND UNDERSTANDING FATIGUE

Recovery is a general term that refers to the short- and long-term adaptive responses occurring as a result of overloading activity (a form of stress) that causes fatigue. Fatigue is directly related to the demands and physical characteristics of the person experiencing stress. In other words, fatigue is unique for each athlete, so monitoring individual training programs to ensure appropriate levels of work and recovery is a must.

Understandably, the multifaceted nature of fatigue necessitates a multifaceted approach to recovery. Fatigue is the consequence of overloading stress placed on physiological systems, which in turn dictates the recovery that is needed. When power, strength, or endurance cannot be maintained, fatigue occurs. All tennis matches possess different demands just as all conditioning sessions vary in their fatigue and recovery profiles. All forms of activity produce stress, some good and some bad. Consequently, if optimal recovery is to occur, fatigue must be addressed relative to the exertion that caused it.

The fatigue resulting from tennis play is largely specific to tennis. Tennis-related fatigue affects general physiological functions (e.g., cardiovascular fitness, thermoregulation, neuromuscular function, endocrine function) and tennis-specific functions (e.g., shoulder rotator cuff strength, side-to-side balance of muscular strength and hypertrophy, serve velocity and accuracy). As a result, different types of recovery strategies are needed to help recover from different fatiguing activities.

A normal process from fatigue to full recovery takes on a rather consistent timeline and pattern. Acute fatigue results in a decrease in function that is followed by a recovery phase back to baseline. The amount of fatigue induced by training can result in disruption or damage that spans a continuum from normal to planned disruption as a training strategy to complete dysfunction as a consequence of serious injury or overtraining. For example, significantly elevated heart rates, high blood lactate concentrations, and localized pH decreases are indicative of intense physical stress. These factors may offer guidance in predicting the extent of workload and fatigue.

The eccentric component of movement (the lengthening of muscle under load) results in greater potential for soreness and possibly injury. More dramatic muscle damage arises from stress with a high eccentric component (e.g., running downhill, performing a new unaccustomed exercise) and is especially common when the stressed tissue has not been exposed to training stress previously. Damage is proportional to the intensity, and it is important to structure appropriate recovery time and techniques when introducing new movement patterns in exercises on and off the court. Soreness is a normal part of the adaptation process, but it can significantly impact the quality of follow-up training sessions if not accounted for correctly or if recovery is not applied correctly.

The pain arising from the damage and repair processes associated with training and competition is termed *delayed-onset muscle soreness (DOMS)*. The duration of DOMS is directly related to the amount of overload and tissue damage and the fitness level of the specific muscles. Although extreme DOMS can last for a week, typically trained tennis players may experience soreness for 24 to 72 hours following unaccustomed or over-loaded eccentric exercise.

Understanding the basics of different types of fatigue induced by training, competition and lifestyle factors can help with determining the best methods of recovery. Table 15.1 provides a quick overview of the major types of fatigue, causes, expressions, and simple tennis-related examples.

Table 15.1   Tennis-Related Fatigue

Type of fatigue	Main causes	Expression	Tennis examples
Metabolic fatigue (energy stores)	• Long training sessions (>60 min.) • Several matches a day (e.g., singles and doubles) • Cumulative fatigue from training or competing over many days	• Player fatigues sooner than is normal. • Player struggles to complete a session or event.	• Lethargic body language • Slower walking than normal • Slower response to chasing balls
Neurological fatigue: peripheral nervous system (PNS; i.e., muscles)	• Short, high-intensity sessions (e.g., weights, plyometrics, complex skill execution) • Long training sessions • Several matches over consecutive days	• Reduced localized force production (e.g., slower responses, reduced power)	• Slow feet • Reduced acceleration • Poor technique and coordination • Abnormal number of technical mistakes • Reduced power in shots and strokes

(continued)

Table 15.1 *(continued)*

Type of fatigue	Main causes	Expression	Tennis examples
Neurological fatigue: central nervous system (CNS; i.e., brain)	• Low blood glucose levels • High-pressure training session, especially involving rapid decision making and reactions • Poor motivation (e.g., monotony of training, emotional factors, injury)	• Lack of drive • Slower at processing visual cues	• Quick loss of concentration • Slower at decision making • Slower anticipation timing (e.g., speed and placement of opponent's serve or return)
Psychological fatigue (emotional, social, cultural)	• Personality conflicts • Competition pressures, event venue, residential conditions, parents, coach, media, etc. • Other lifestyle stresses such as home, school exams, personal relationships	• Player loses self-confidence or self-esteem. • Increased signs of anxiety, negative attitudes, etc.	• Player shows a definite lack of confidence during play and off court • More negative than usual especially in self-talk and body language • Change in player communication
Environmental and travel fatigue	• Weather (e.g., wind, heat, sun) • Disruption of normal routines (e.g., sleeping, waking, meal times) • Sedentary and restricted body movement on long journeys • Adapting to different climates and time zones	• Players are slower to start. • Fatigue sooner than normal. • Visual fatigue results from bright or glaring sunlight.	• Player takes longer than usual to get rhythm on court. • Unforced errors in the first 15 minutes are well above normal. • Tired eyes and eye strain occur. • Player tracks ball poorly.

Data from A. Calder, 2009, Coaching perspective of tennis recovery. In *Tennis recovery: A comprehensive review of the research,* edited by M.S. Kovacs, T.S. Ellenbecker, and W.B. Kibler (Boca Raton, FL: USTA), 1-65, and International Tennis Performance Association, 2012, Fatigue and recovery in tennis. In *Certified Tennis Performance Specialist (CTPS) workbook and study guide* (Marietta, GA: ITPA), 13.4, 13.5.

MUSCLE REPAIR

The human body is a highly advanced system that addresses and rebuilds damaged tissue as well as adds damage-preventing proteins. Repair is initiated by appropriate damage as a result of physical training. The repair process is initially signaled by many of the inflammatory responses occurring after exercise stress. Connective structures such as tendon tissue respond to progressive heavy resistance training with increased thickness and strength. This repair process is important for both normal growth and for muscle hypertrophy resulting from heavy resistance exercise.

In skeletal muscle, repair depends on signaling from stressed muscle tissue, hormonal interactions, and other factors within the body. The repair process operates continually in highly resistance-trained tennis players subjected to lower levels of exercise-induced muscle damage. Managing the design of the training program and optimizing other factors (such as nutrition and hydration) aid in faster recovery. The endocrine system responds to the demands of physical training by secreting hormones that initiate acute and long-term adaptations to stressful physical exertion. Prominent examples of endocrine roles in performance include the processes of mental excitement, maintenance of metabolic function at appropriate levels, and tissue recovery. Having appropriate rest and proper nutrition can greatly enhance the hormonal response to provide positive responses. Poor rest and nutrition can have a negative influence on hormonal response and limit the ideal recovery environment. The demands of a given training session or match will dictate the recovery process. (Review the information covered in chapter 1).

NEUROLOGICAL FATIGUE AND RECOVERY

Neurological fatigue is difficult to measure directly, but it is the result of stressful activities encompassing large amounts of power and force production. Because tennis has major power and force producing components, neurological fatigue is a common result of daily training and competition. Neurological fatigue simply means that the signal from the brain to the muscle is slowed, which impacts power and force production, precision of movement, and coordination. Enough recovery time is needed to allow for full recovery. The timeline for neural recovery is different than metabolic (or cellular) recovery. A simple performance test like the vertical jump (see chapter 4), during which maximal power is generated, is an easy method for determining whether you are experiencing neurological fatigue. If you notice a reduction in jump height from one day to the next, it is a sign of possible neurological fatigue and a greater recovery time may be needed. Table 15.2 highlights a sample week of monitoring vertical jump height daily before practice. It is clear to see on day 3 that the athlete in question showed a decrease in performance; this decrease is likely a sign of neural fatigue, and greater recovery was warranted.

Table 15.2   Weekly Monitoring of Vertical Jump Height

	Vertical jump height (in.)
Day 1	25
Day 2	25
Day 3	23
Day 4	24
Day 5	25
Day 6	24
Day 7	25

ACTIVE RECOVERY

Active recovery is one of the best methods to help tennis players recover from stressful practices and matches. The purpose of active recovery is to stimulate blood flow to damaged muscle tissues but without the fatiguing component that occurs with high-intensity exercise. The recommendation is to perform 20 to 30 minutes of slow, constant movement at below 60 percent of maximum heart rate. A typical active recovery technique is slow jogging or slow cycling. Other forms of exercise are appropriate, but the goal is to hit a rating of perceived exertion (RPE) on a 10-point scale between 4 and 6, which is equivalent to a light to moderate exercise intensity.

A general rule for monitoring intensity during active recovery is to use the talk test; you may breathe heavily, but if you cannot keep up a conversation while performing this type of exercise, the intensity is too high to be considered recovery. If you are monitoring heart rate, the recommendation is less than 65 percent of your maximum heart rate. Most active recovery sessions last less than 60 minutes, because they can be somewhat fatiguing, especially if the intensity level is higher than appropriate.

Other modalities include forms of manual therapies such as massage, which can help improve or maintain blood flow. Another method is electrical stimulation, which can be applied to muscles and provide small nonfatiguing muscle contractions that can help improve blood flow. The benefit of this type of recovery is that it can be done while watching television, sitting on the couch, or even during meals (figure 15.1). Also, these devices are portable and easy to use while traveling, and you can use

Figure 15.1   Electronic muscle recovery.

them for longer time periods than traditional active recovery techniques without resulting in fatigue.

TEMPERATURE-BASED INTERVENTIONS (HYDROTHERAPIES)

People have used temperature-based therapies for thousands of years. Some countries and traditions have emphasized warm or hot water therapies, while other cultures have preferred the use of cold water therapies. Over the past few decades, athletes, coaches and healthcare providers have used a number of strategies to help improve recovery with combinations of various temperature-based interventions. This section describes some of the most common strategies that use water to aid in recovery.

Warm Water

Taking a bath in body-temperature (93-97 °F; 34-36 °C) water results in changes to circulatory, pulmonary, renal and musculoskeletal systems throughout the body. Increases in hydrostatic pressure as a result of being in the water lead to a shift of blood from the lower regions of the body to the trunk during immersion. This shift can result in an increase in blood pumping from the heart and also a decrease in systemic vascular resistance, so increased muscular blood flow occurs without an increase in heart rate. Alternating from cool to warm water immersion can accelerate metabolic activity as indicated by faster clearance of blood lactate through an increase in muscle blood flow. Although many players may feel relaxed or perceive a benefit, few research studies have shown hot water therapies to significantly aid in an athlete's recovery.

Cold Water

Cold water immersion (or ice bath) is a common recovery technique. It is recommended that a range of 50 to 60 degrees Fahrenheit (10-15 °C) is appropriate for cold water immersion as a range for cooling soft tissues. Colder temperatures used for long periods risk damage to soft tissues and are not recommended for sporting contexts. Cold water immersion reduces the sensations of DOMS in trained athletes. A typical session should last 10 to 15 minutes. However, use caution with cold water immersion techniques. Although perceived benefits are found in many athletes, regular and consistent use can result in slower long-term adaptions in strength and other recovery capabilities. Therefore, you should use cold water immersion infrequently, such as only after very hard matches or training sessions.

Showers

Showering within 5 to 10 minutes after a training session or match can accelerate recovery. If pool access is available, performing active and static stretching (5 to 20 minutes) in the pool is also beneficial. Using alternating temperatures during showers is another water-based therapy to constrict (cold) and dilate (hot) blood vessels to help with muscle blood flow and to aid in the recovery process. The benefit of showering as a recovery option is that you can do it anywhere a shower is available. Therefore, the ease of use is a major benefit.

COMPRESSIVE CLOTHING

Compressive clothing use has increased over the past few years, partly because of research showing the benefits of compressive clothing to help recovery after strenuous physical activity. Although different types of athletic clothing exist, most of the products available work on the concept of compression, which may provide benefits from graduated pressures that extend from the limbs to the core. Some athletes may perceive a reduction in fatigue and experience other recovery benefits. Compression clothing is designed to work on nearly every limb of the body. For tennis players, the lower body and dominant arm are two main areas of focus for compression-based recovery. Perform this type of recovery after heavy training and competition days. Compression clothing can be used for minutes to hours per day. A starting point is to use compression for 45 to 90 minutes post training or competition; this time can be extended based on individual need.

PSYCHOLOGICAL FATIGUE AND RECOVERY

Although this book is focused on physical conditioning, psychological fatigue and subsequent psychological recovery are part of the recovering from activity. Physical stress, training, and competition can have a profound influence on psychological well-being, performance, and recovery. While difficult to measure biologically, psychological fatigue is generally accepted as a major performance-altering factor. The psychological stress from activity is addressed with close observation of athletes in conjunction with continuous feedback including surveys, informal communication, training logs, autonomic nervous system (both sympathetic and parasympathetic) measures, and journals that record feelings toward competitive stressors. Assessment of mood states may also provide important insight into training and competition. Psychological markers may include perception of effort, motivation, energy and wakefulness, anxiety levels, and changes in performance without measureable changes in biological markers of stress or fatigue. Therefore, you should monitor training and competition both from the physical and psychological perspective to truly optimize recovery. Some areas of psychological recovery include meditation, structured breathing techniques, muscle relaxation methods, positive affirmations, and process-focused training. Using psychological recovery can create a psychological environment that reduces stress and consequently aids in overall recovery.

HEART RATE MEASUREMENT

As technology has improved, tablets and smartphones have become normal tools in the training and rehabilitation of athletes. Coaches, trainers, and players now have access to the latest technologies, and the use of monitoring devices has also increased. Heart rate tracking is a low-cost and noninvasive measure of how hard an athlete is working at any given time, how well he or she may be sleeping, and also how quickly he or she can recover following any specific drill, training session, or tournament. When heart rate is measured, these two areas are usually evaluated: beats per minute (bpm) and heart rate variability.

Heart rate (in bpm) provides a window into how hard an athlete is working at any given time. This measure can be very helpful when designing drills and exercises and working in appropriate rest and recovery periods. For example, during most tennis play an athlete's heart rate will increase and then drop rapidly between points. This allows for the scheduling of work–rest ratios based on different heart rate markers. For example, a top professional player who is 20 years old may have an average heart rate during points of 175 bpm. The average low heart rate at the end of each rest period between points is around 145 bpm. This information highlights the need to perform in this range during training drills and exercises.

Monitoring of the variability in heart rate measures (typically at rest) is one method to evaluate how well an athlete is adapting to training and potentially recovering from training and competition. This technique involves the regular monitoring of the cardiac autonomic nervous system (ANS) through the measurement of resting or postexercise heart rate variability (HRV). Many techniques exist for using HRV, but the premise is to see how consistent the variability is in the R-to-R interval of each individual heartbeat. This type of monitoring can be done with relatively inexpensive and noninvasive techniques that involve a heart rate monitor strap and connection to an app on a mobile device. You can monitor your own heart rate, or a trainer, coach, or medical professional can do it for you.

Overreaching or possibly negative adaptation to training is thought to be generally associated with reductions in certain indices of HRV, whereas increases in fitness and exercise performance are thought to be more associated with increases in vagal-related indices of HRV. As HRV is currently being used in the field in an applied setting with athletes and studied in research, more information and research is coming out each year. Trainers and players can use this information to better implement training and recovery protocols and better monitor training adaptations to assess readiness for training. They can also use it to figure out how to modify or adjust daily and weekly training volumes and intensities.

SELF-MYOFASCIAL RELEASE

Many treatments fall under the umbrella term of *self-myofascial release*. Typically self-myofascial release refers to an exercise in which the soft tissue is gradually stretched and the person's own feedback guides the stretch direction, force, and duration to address specific soft-tissue restrictions.

One of ways that self-myofascial release may help athletes is through its role with fascia. Fascia is a type of connective tissue divided into three broad layers: the superficial layer, a layer of potential space, and a deep layer. Because the fibers of the fascia run in many directions, it is highly movable and changes with the surrounding tissues. Fascia is believed to be one continuous piece of tissue working throughout the body. Therefore, when fascia in one area is stretched, it can cause tightness, restriction, and pain in another part of the body. This is similar to pulling plastic wrap across a plate; when one side is pulled tight, the opposite side becomes even firmer.

The most common type of recovery self-myofascial release is rolling with foam rollers or other firm and semi-firm objects such as massage sticks and tennis balls. The objective of foam rolling is to slowly move back and forth along different muscle groups and series of muscles to help loosen up the area and limit muscle tightness, aiding in range of motion. The following rolling exercises emphasize key muscles and muscle groups for the tennis athlete.

Hamstring Rolling

Focus

Reduce muscle tightness and focus on trigger points within the hamstring muscles.

Procedure

1. Sit on the ground with your feet extended straight out in front of your body.

2. Position the foam roller underneath the hamstrings of both legs and perpendicular to the direction of your legs (figure 15.2).

3. With your hands on the ground, slowly roll up and down along the roller, focusing on the parts of the hamstrings that are tight or restricted.

4. Repeat this back-and-forth motion for 1 to 5 minutes or until the hamstrings have released and feel relaxed.

Figure 15.2   Hamstring rolling.

Quadriceps and Hip Flexors Rolling

Focus

Reduce muscle tightness and focus on trigger points within the quadriceps and hip flexor muscles.

Procedure

1. Lie prone (facedown) on the ground.
2. Position the foam roller underneath the quadriceps and hip flexors (iliacus and psoas) of both legs and perpendicular to the direction of your legs (figure 15.3).
3. Slowly roll up and down along the roller, focusing on parts of the quadriceps and hip flexors (iliacus and psoas) that are tight or restricted.
4. Repeat this back-and-forth motion for 1 to 5 minutes or until the quadriceps and hip flexors (iliacus and psoas) have released and feel relaxed.

Figure 15.3   Quadriceps and hip flexors rolling.

IT Band Rolling

Focus

Reduce muscle tightness and focus on trigger points in muscles through-out the side of the leg around the iliotibial (IT) band.

Procedure

1. Lie on your side with your feet extended straight out.
2. Position the foam roller underneath your IT band and perpendicular to the direction of your leg (figure 15.4).
3. Slowly roll up and down along the roller, focusing on parts of the IT band area that are tight or restricted.
4. Repeat this back-and-forth motion for 1 to 5 minutes or until the area of the IT band has released and feels relaxed.
5. Repeat the exercise on your other side.

Figure 15.4   IT band rolling.

Calf Rolling

Focus

Reduce muscle tightness and focus on trigger points within the calf muscles (gastrocnemius and soleus).

Procedure

1. Sit on the ground with your feet extended straight out in front of your body.
2. Position the foam roller underneath the calf muscles (gastrocnemius and soleus) of both legs and perpendicular to the direction of your legs (figure 15.5).

Figure 15.5   Calf rolling.

3. With your hands on the ground, slowly roll up and down along the roller, focusing on parts of the calf muscles that are tight or restricted.

4. Repeat this back-and-forth motion for 1 to 5 minutes or until the calf muscles have released and feel relaxed.

Thoracic (Upper-Back) Rolling

Focus

Reduce muscle tightness and focus on trigger points in muscles of the upper back (trapezius, rhomboids, and upper latissimus dorsi).

Procedure

1. Sit on the ground with your feet extended straight out in front of your body. Lie on your back.

2. Position the foam roller underneath your upper back and perpendicular to the direction of your spine (figure 15.6).

Figure 15.6   Thoracic (upper-back) rolling.

3. With your hands behind your head and clasped together, slowly roll up and down along the roller, focusing on parts of the upper back that are tight or restricted.

4. Repeat this back-and-forth motion for 1 to 5 minutes or until the upper back muscles have released and feel relaxed.

Lat Rolling

Focus

Reduce muscle tightness and focus on trigger points in the muscles of the back (latissimus dorsi).

Procedure

1. Lie on the ground on one side with your feet extended straight out in front of your body.

2. Position the foam roller underneath your low back and perpendicular to the direction of your spine (figure 15.7).

3. Slowly roll up and down along the roller, focusing on parts of the lats that are tight or restricted.

4. Repeat this back-and-forth motion for 1 to 5 minutes or until the lats have released and feel relaxed.

Figure 15.7　Lat rolling.

SUMMARY

Recovery is one of the most important aspects of any training program. Trainers and athletes use certain recovery techniques to speed the positive adaptations that are the objectives of most training programs. This chapter defined fatigue and provided helpful information on muscular, neurological, psychological, and other types of recovery techniques. Improving recovery can directly and indirectly improve performance and help to limit the likelihood of injuries. Focusing on improving recovery is just as important as focusing on the training side of conditioning for tennis. This shift in thinking has occurred as a result of better understanding of recovery techniques. Recovery can help speed training adaptations and performance of tennis players at all levels of play.

Chapter 16

Age and Gender Considerations

Tennis is a lifelong sport; tennis players can be as young as 3 years of age or over 90 years of age. As a result, it is important to adjust training programs for injury prevention and for performance. For a younger athlete, certain areas of training should be a focus; as an athlete ages, different areas of focus become a priority. Understanding when and how to adjust training based on age and stage of development is important to ensure a well-designed and appropriate training program.

Gender differences exist in both anatomy and physiology. Although generally minor, these differences can significantly influence the type, intensity, and duration of exercises performed.

This chapter highlights important age and gender considerations to help improve conditioning for tennis.

YOUNG TENNIS ATHLETES

Training young tennis athletes to improve athleticism and performance has become a major industry. It is important to understand that young athletes are not just little adults and should not follow the same training programs as their collegiate, professional, or adult counterparts. Although physical limitations do exist in young athletes, many of the roadblocks to skill acquisition are mental and emotional. Coaches and trainers must understand pedagogical principles in young athletes, the internal and external pressures they face, and how well they learn along with the physical limitations and changes of individual players as they age.

Fundamental movements are very important for all athletes but especially for young athletes. These fundamental movement skills should be introduced in multiple ways, including structured learning and fun games.

These are the general fundamental movements and skills that need to be developed in all young athletes:

- **General movements and skills:** Agility, balance, coordination, speed, jumping, climbing, walking, hopping, swimming, skipping, throwing, dribbling (feet and hands), kicking, hitting, catching, landing
- **Sending skills:** Kicking, punting, rolling (ball), striking and hitting (ball, puck, etc.), throwing
- **Receiving skills:** Catching, stopping, trapping
- **Responding skills (receiving followed by immediately sending):** Striking, catching and throwing at targets, and so on.

These fundamental movement skills are essential for a well-rounded athlete. Tennis is a sport built on a combination of athleticism, tennis technique, and strategy. A successful tennis player will develop a wide range of physical skills that he or she can adapt to the needs on a tennis court. Simply developing tennis playing ability does result in good tennis playing ability, but if overall fundamental movement skills are not well developed at a young age, eventually physical limitations occur.

Specialization

Sport specialization is intense training in one sport while excluding others. Specializing in a single sport before 10 years of age may contribute to the following challenges:

- One-sided dominance and lack of full dexterity
- Lack of agility, balance, coordination, and speed (ABCs) and less development of all the basic movement skills
- Greater risk of overuse injuries
- Potentially early burnout
- Potentially earlier retirement from training and competition

However, the sport alone is not the sole factor. Potential problems are a result of excessive volume and the lack of skill development in other areas. All young athletes should be trained to be good well-rounded athletes and encouraged to play a variety of sports. As they age, athletes can specialize in certain areas if they so desire. Unfortunately, many tennis players do not develop their agility, balance, coordination, and speed (ABCs) skills along with basic movement skills to a high level early in life (under 12 years of age), and much remedial work is needed to correct and improve these areas during later years (12 years and older). During puberty it is more difficult to develop the ABCs, so it is highly recommended to prioritize these skills earlier in a young athlete's development. Also, having to re-teach or overemphasize the basics during puberty results in less time for other more targeted development that would speed progress and provide greater long-term success.

Growth refers to the increase in the size of the body as a whole and of its parts. As young children grow, they become taller and heavier and change body composition. Their various organs increase in size along with other physiological changes.

The term *maturation* refers to the tempo and timing of progress toward a mature biological state. Maturation is specific to each biological system. Timing of maturation is the point along a growth continuum when specific maturational events occur. Tempo is the rate at which maturation progresses—how quickly or slowly a person passes from the initial stages of sexual maturation to the mature state.

The term *development* refers to the acquisition of behavioral competence, learning appropriate behaviors and achievement of certain skills expected by society. All three processes—growth, maturation, and development—interact constantly and occur simultaneously at differing rates and to varying degrees.

Relative Age Effect

Being relatively older both chronologically and maturationally within an age group (e.g., 16 and under) provides significant outcome advantages compared with players who are relatively younger. During adolescence annual age groupings are employed, tennis competition can be intensive, and decisions for tournament seeding, sectional and national selections, sponsorships and other opportunities are heavily determined by results within a 1-year age difference. The stages of puberty especially magnify physical, mental, emotional, and performance differences. Therefore, when developing conditioning for tennis, it is important to take into account the athlete's growth and development aspects when determining progress. It is difficult to compare youth players solely on age. Consider relative age, growth, maturation and development when monitoring progress throughout a young tennis player's career.

Peak Height Velocity (PHV)

Peak height velocity (PHV) is the period when maximum rate of growth occurs (figure 16.1). It describes not just how much someone is growing, but actually the speed of growth. PHV varies with each individual athlete. Generally it occurs around 12 years of age in females and approximately 2 years later in males. However, children the same age between 10 and 16 years old can have as much as a 4- to 5-year difference in development. Therefore, chronological age is a poor guide for grouping children from a physical standpoint. In females, menarche (the onset of menstruation) usually comes rather late in the growth spurt, occurring after PHV is achieved. The sequence of developmental events may normally occur 2 years earlier or later than average.

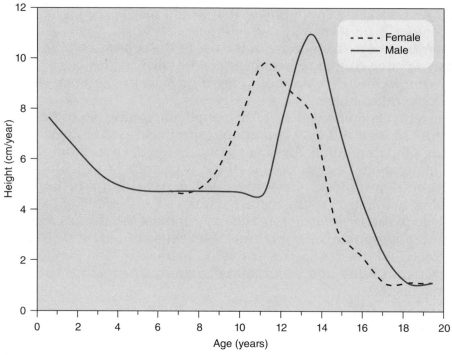

Figure 16.1 Peak height velocity (PHV) chart for males and females.

PHV in boys is more intense than in girls and usually occurs about 2 years after girls. Peak strength velocity (PSV) comes a year or so after PHV. PSV is the time when a young athlete increases strength at the fastest rate, the result of an increase in hormonal factors (growth hormone and testosterone). During this time period it is important to develop overall general and specific strength, hypertrophy, and power. Thus, the male athlete experiences a pronounced late gain in strength characteristics. Early-maturing boys may have as much as a 4-year physiological advantage over their late-maturing peers, which is noteworthy information when structuring training and competition.

Measuring Peak Height Velocity (PHV)

Monitoring PHV is very important for young tennis athletes. It is recommended to standardize the testing of height for consistency. If possible, take measurements in the morning at a consistent time after a rest day.

Once a young athlete turns 6, measure height every 3 months. Record the data using software than has a graphing (charting) capability. Produce a chart with height on the vertical axis and age on the horizontal axis. When a deceleration in growth followed by an acceleration in growth occurs, begin to monitor arm span as well as height. The average age for this period is 10 for girls and 12 for boys, although variability does exist.

Create charts similar to the height charts that display the two measurements (arm span growth and overall height growth). You should notice acceleration in growth at this time. The athlete's training has to be adapted according to these changes and preferred windows of trainability. Once this deceleration and reacceleration of growth occurs, these two measurements should be taken monthly for more accuracy. The next few years are the major time before, during, and after PHV. Remember, PHV is the highest point of growth acceleration. After PHV is attained, a deceleration in growth velocity will happen. The athlete continues to grow, but the velocity of growth is decreased. Continue to monitor growth for 18 months after PHV. The athlete's training has to be adapted according to the windows of trainability. Remember that PSV occurs 6 to 18 months after PHV, so training should be adapted to focus on strength during this important period.

Identifying the Critical Window of Trainability

Although all variables should be trained during a young athlete's career, specific, intense focuses are appropriate during certain periods. Appropriate training stimulus in these different training variables can be timed to achieve optimum adaptation with regard to motor skills, speed, strength, power, flexibility and aerobic capacity.

The optimal window for developing aerobic capacity occurs around the onset of PHV. Aerobic capacity training should occur before athletes reach the milestone to allow for appropriate volume and intensity around PHV.

For girls, the optimal window for strength training occurs immediately after PHV or at the onset of menarche. For boys, it is 6 to 18 months after PHV.

Multiple windows exist for developing speed. For boys, the first window occurs between the ages of 7 and 9, and the second window occurs between the ages of 13 and 16. For girls, the first window occurs between 6 and 8 years and the second window occurs between the ages of 11 and 13 years. During the first speed window, training should focus on developing agility and quickness using movements of very short duration (less than 5 seconds). During the second speed window, training should focus on speed, agility, and quickness movements of less than 15 seconds.

For boys, the optimal window for developing motor skills is between 9 and 12 years; for girls, it's between 8 and 11 years. Fundamental athletic skills should be a high priority, with an appropriate focus on tennis-specific movements. During this time, athletes should develop the ability to "read" the environment and spend time on reacting to and receiving balls and other visual stimulus.

Power development varies based on the growth and development of the athlete. As power development is a combination of strength and speed development, the window of opportunity is rather broad and is a combination of the periods for the development of strength and speed. However, post PHV is a time when the greater power development will be seen.

For both genders, the optimal window for developing flexibility occurs between 6 and 10 years. Focus on flexibility should be increased during PHV and immediately post PHV.

Strength Training in Young Tennis Players

Training for strength is an important component of training young tennis players. However, it must be trained appropriately. All the major medical and strength and conditioning associations have produced position papers and statements supporting the many benefits of strength training in young athletes. These statements suggest that young athletes receive quality and qualified instruction, proper program design, and supervised training in a safe environment with an appropriate gradual and progressive increase in resistance and volume based on the individual athlete's capabilities. When these points are followed, strength training can enhance performance capabilities such as strength, speed and power, and motor skill development, while also providing other benefits such as reducing cardiovascular risk profiles in youth and increasing resistance to sport-related injuries.

GENDER DIFFERENCES

Although the similarities between male and female tennis players far outweigh the differences, significant differences do still exist and must be considered when developing training programs for performance enhancement and injury prevention. Female tennis players usually hit two-handed backhands with a greater reliance on the nondominant hand (e.g., left hand for a right-handed player). Along with poor technique, this reliance on the left hand can result in many more left wrist injuries in the female tennis player than the male tennis player. Female tennis players may experience more left abdominal injuries or left thigh and iliotibial (IT) band issues. The reasons are varied, but many of these injuries are results of poor technique on the serve and a lack of appropriate core strength (see chapter 7) and rotational strength from the lower body up through the entire kinetic chain. (See chapter 2 for more information about the tennis serve and mechanics).

On average, fully mature female athletes have the following characteristics compared to their male counterparts. Female athletes

- are shorter;
- are lighter in total body weight and lighter in fat-free mass, although they are heavier in fat mass and higher in relative body fat;

- are lower in absolute strength but have similar relative strength levels;
- have greater flexibility; and
- have lower lung volumes and lower aerobic capacity.

Female Athlete Triad

Coaches and trainers working with female tennis players must be aware of the concept known as the female athlete triad. The female athlete triad describes three interrelated areas of concern that can influence the health and performance of female athletes, including tennis athletes. The three areas are amenorrhea (the effect of exercise on the menstrual cycle), eating disorders (or disordered eating), and bone mineral disorders.

Amenorrhea

Amenorrhea is the cessation of menstruation in a premenopausal woman. Generally it is defined as less than four menses per year. Although low body fat does contribute to amenorrhea, it is not the only cause. Because amenorrhea is linked closely with high-volume physical training many highly competitive tennis players do train at very high volumes, it is important to understand the effects of excessive training. In addition, preventing potential amenorrhea through appropriate monitoring of volume and intensity of training and competition is key. Exercise alters blood concentrations of numerous hormones, which may disrupt the normal menstrual cycle. Excessive volume of training may result in increased psychological stress. Psychological stress may disrupt the menstrual cycle by increasing blood levels of catecholamine, which plays a role in regulating the reproductive system.

Eating Disorders

Many forms of eating disorders (or disordered eating) exist. Two major types include anorexia nervosa and bulimia. Anorexia nervosa is a form of starvation in which the person becomes emaciated as a result of refusing to eat. In severe cases, the end result can be death. Bulimia is overeating (binge eating) followed by self-induced vomiting (purging). People with bulimia repeatedly ingest large amounts of food and then force themselves to vomit in order to prevent weight gain. An eating disorder can result in severe consequences; tennis players must eat appropriately to meet the energy needs of training and competition. Players who are dealing with an eating disorder must work with qualified experts to heal. Although this section is discussing female athletes, male athletes can also suffer from disordered eating and should work with qualified individuals to assist in treatment as well.

Bone Mineral Disorders

Loss of bone mineral content (osteoporosis) is a concern for female tennis players. Two major causes of bone loss in female tennis players are estrogen deficiency caused by amenorrhea and inadequate calcium intake caused by eating disorders.

If an athlete is suspected of having symptoms related to the female athlete triad, a physician or other qualified health care provider should be contacted. A trained physician or health care provider should direct any care or treatment.

Training Female Tennis Players

This chapter has highlighted a number of differences between male and female tennis players. However, although differences exist, the types of strokes, movement, and match length in tennis competition are similar between men and women. Therefore, the overall general training programs outlined throughout the book are appropriate for both male and female tennis athletes. Adjust programs based on gender differences when necessary. One area of difference may be the match length at the elite level in Grand Slam tournaments (best of 3 set for females at Grand Slams vs best of 5 set for males at Grand Slams). When working with elite players, adjustments in training may be warranted.

Most sport-related knee injuries, specifically anterior cruciate ligament (ACL) injuries, occur more frequently in female athletes, but female tennis athletes do not have a high rate of ACL problems. Even though ACL issues are not a major concern for female tennis players, the same genetic differences that result in higher ACL problems do exist. Therefore, it is wise to add more posterior chain training to the female athlete's program. This includes a greater emphasis on developing hamstring strength and endurance, gluteal muscle strength and endurance, and the ability to stabilize the core and lower body. Through a well-structured, periodized tennis-specific training program, female tennis players can achieve outstanding results and improvements just like their male counterparts.

SUMMARY

At any level, you must consider age and gender when designing and implementing tennis-specific programs. The information covered throughout this book highlights the best methods to train different aspects a successful tennis player. Applying these training exercises and techniques will increase the chances of performance improvements and reduce the risk of injuries. Accounting for age and gender differences will help enhance the overall training program and environment.

Index

Note: Cross references referring to a general topic instead of a specific entry are in all italics.

Note: The italicized *f, t,* and *p* following page numbers refer to figures, tables, and photos respectively.

About the USTA

The **United States Tennis Association (USTA)** is the national governing body for the sport of tennis and the recognized leader in promoting and developing the sport's growth on every level in the United States, from local communities to the crown jewel of the professional game, the U.S. Open.

Established in 1881, the USTA is a progressive and diverse not-for-profit organization whose volunteers, professional staff, and financial resources support the singular mission.

The USTA is the largest tennis organization in the world, with 17 geographical sections, more than 700,000 individual members and more than 7,800 organizational members, thousands of volunteers, and a professional staff dedicated to growing the game.

In addition to the professional side of the sport, the USTA offers sanctioned league-play opportunities to players 18 years of age and older. Camps and other instructional opportunities are also provided to younger players around the country.

About the Authors

Mark Kovacs, PhD, FACSM, CTPS, MTPS, CSCS,*D, USPTA, PTR, is a performance physiologist, researcher, professor, author, speaker, and coach with an extensive background in training and researching elite athletes. He runs a consulting firm focused on optimizing human performance by the practical application of cutting-edge science. He is a consultant to the ATP, WTA, USTA, and NCAA. Dr. Kovacs also is the director of the Life Sport Science Institute and associate professor of sport health science at Life University. He has worked with hundreds of elite athletes and more  than two dozen top professional tennis players, including John Isner, Robby Ginepri, Ryan Harrison, and Sloane Stephens.

He formerly directed the sport science, strength and conditioning, and coaching education departments for the United States Tennis Association and was the director of the Gatorade Sport Science Institute as well as an executive at Pepsico. He is coauthor of the book *Tennis Anatomy* (Human Kinetics, 2011).

Dr. Kovacs currently is the executive director of the International Tennis Performance Association (iTPA), the worldwide association for tennis-specific performance and injury prevention. He is a certified tennis performance specialist and a master tennis performance specialist through the iTPA. He is also a certified strength and conditioning specialist through the National Strength and Conditioning Association (NSCA) and both a USPTA and PTR certified tennis coach. Dr. Kovacs is a fellow of the American College of Sports Medicine. In 2012, he was the youngest-ever recipient of the International Tennis Hall of Fame Educational Merit Award.

Kovacs was a collegiate All-American and NCAA doubles champion in tennis at Auburn University. After playing professionally, he performed tennis-specific research and earned a master's degree in exercise science from Auburn University and a PhD in exercise physiology from the University of Alabama.

E. Paul Roetert, PhD, FACSM, is the chief executive officer of SHAPE America, the largest organization of professionals involved in school-based health, physical education, and physical activity. Founded in 1885, SHAPE America is committed to ensuring all children have the opportunity to lead healthy, physically active lives. He holds a PhD in biomechanics from the University of Connecticut and completed his bachelor's and master's of science degrees in physical education at California State University at Fullerton.

Before joining SHAPE America, Roetert was the managing director of the United States Tennis Association's Player Development Program and tournament director of the U.S. Open Junior Tennis Championships from 2002 to 2009. In that role, he directed the High Performance, Junior, and Collegiate Competition as well as coaching education and sport science departments. He has also served as the executive director of the American Sport Education Program (now known as Human Kinetics Coach Education)

Dr. Roetert has authored four books, including *Tennis Anatomy* (Human Kinetics, 2011). He has written numerous chapters and articles related to the fields of health, fitness, sport science and medicine, and strength and conditioning and has given hundreds of scientific and invited presentations worldwide. He is a fellow of the American College of Sports Medicine and an honorary professional of the Professional Tennis Registry and became a master professional with the United States Professional Tennis Association in 2005. In 2002 he received the Educational Merit Award from the International Tennis Hall of Fame for outstanding service to the game. Roetert received the Editorial Excellence Award in 1999 from the National Strength and Conditioning Association for his work on the *Journal of Strength and Conditioning and Research,* and in 2000 he received the Outstanding Alumni Award from the University of Connecticut.

Todd S. Ellenbecker, MS, DPT, SCS, OCS, CSCS, is a physical therapist and clinic director of Physiotherapy Associates Scottsdale Sports Clinic in Arizona and is the vice president of medical services for the ATP World Tour. He received his bachelor's degree in physical therapy from the University of Wisconsin at LaCrosse in 1985 and a master's degree in exercise physiology from Arizona State University in 1989. He completed his doctor of physical therapy from MGH Institute of Health Professions in 2006. In addition, he is certified as a sport clinical specialist and orthopaedic clinical specialist by the American Physical Therapy Association. He is a certified strength and conditioning specialist by the National Strength and Conditioning Association and was named their Sports Medicine Professional of the Year in 2003. Dr. Ellenbecker is the chair of the International Tennis Performance Association Certification Commission and a certified USPTA tennis teaching professional and was the chairman of the USTA National Sport Science Committee for more than a decade and still serves as a committee member. Todd is also the national director of clinical research for Physiotherapy Associates. In 2007 he received the Ron Peyton Award by the Sports Physical Therapy Section and in 2008 was the recipient of the Samuel Hardy Educational Merit Award from the International Tennis Hall of Fame.

Ellenbecker serves on the editorial boards of the *International Journal of Sports Physical Therapy* and *Sports Health.* He has conducted and published research primarily on upper-extremity athletes as well as shoulder and elbow rehabilitation. He is the author of several books, including *Strength Band Training* (Human Kinetics, 2011) and *Effective Functional Progressions in Sport Rehabilitation* (Human Kinetics, 2009).

Ellenbecker lives in Scottsdale, Arizona, with his wife, Gail.